Lecture Notes in Computer Science   16049

Founding Editors

Gerhard Goos
Juris Hartmanis

The series Lecture Notes in Computer Science (LNCS), including its subseries Lecture Notes in Artificial Intelligence (LNAI) and Lecture Notes in Bioinformatics (LNBI), has established itself as a medium for the publication of new developments in computer science and information technology research, teaching, and education.

LNCS enjoys close cooperation with the computer science R & D community, the series counts many renowned academics among its volume editors and paper authors, and collaborates with prestigious societies. Its mission is to serve this international community by providing an invaluable service, mainly focused on the publication of conference and workshop proceedings and postproceedings. LNCS commenced publication in 1973.

Andrea Kő · Francesco Buccafurri ·
Gabriele Kotsis · A Min Tjoa · Ismail Khalil
Editors

Electronic Government and the Information Systems Perspective

14th International Conference, EGOVIS 2025
Bangkok, Thailand, August 25–27, 2025
Proceedings

 Springer

Editors
Andrea Kő 🆔
Corvinus University of Budapest
Budapest, Hungary

Francesco Buccafurri 🆔
University of Reggio Calabria
Reggio Calabria, Italy

Gabriele Kotsis 🆔
Johannes Kepler University Linz
Linz, Austria

A Min Tjoa 🆔
Vienna University of Technology
Vienna, Austria

Ismail Khalil 🆔
Johannes Kepler University Linz
Linz, Austria

ISSN 0302-9743   ISSN 1611-3349 (electronic)
Lecture Notes in Computer Science
ISBN 978-3-032-02224-0   ISBN 978-3-032-02225-7 (eBook)
https://doi.org/10.1007/978-3-032-02225-7

This Springer imprint is published by the registered company Springer Nature Switzerland AG
The registered company address is: Gewerbestrasse 11, 6330 Cham, Switzerland

If disposing of this product, please recycle the paper.

Preface

In the current era of technological revolution, electronic government has emerged as a powerful force, reshaping our societies. It has revolutionized how governments interact with citizens, businesses, and other stakeholders. The seamless integration of information systems and digitalisation efforts has developed efficient, transparent, and citizen-centric governance models. These models foster collaboration, improve service delivery, and drive societal progress, making electronic government a significant and relevant topic for discussion. Despite remarkable advancements, electronic government still faces challenges such as digital divide, data governance complexities, and the need for ethical AI deployment issues, which many of the papers in this volume critically address.

The 14th International Conference on Electronic Government and the Information Systems Perspective, EGOVIS 2025, took place in Bangkok, Thailand, from August 25–27, 2025. The conference belonged to the 36th DEXA Conference. EGOVIS serves as a platform for experts, scholars, and practitioners to come together and explore the multifaceted landscape of electronic government, delving into the intricate interplay between information systems, digitalisation, innovation, automation, and transformation. Digitalisation, digital transformation, innovation, automation, and information systems are core enablers of e-government. Digital transformation is more than just a technological shift; it requires a fundamental change in processes enabled by the innovative use of digital technologies.

The papers in this volume embody the collective efforts of researchers and professionals at the forefront of shaping the electronic government landscape. These contributions encompass a wide range of topics, including but not limited to the transformative potential of emerging technologies such as artificial intelligence, GenAI, mobile Government and digital inclusion, e-governance frameworks, digital service delivery, data analytics, policy formulation, and legal ontology.

EGOVIS 2025 received 29 paper submissions from 9 countries in Europe, Asia, and the Middle East. Out of these, the Program Committee selected 11 as regular papers, resulting in an acceptance rate of 38%. Additionally, 4 papers were accepted as short papers, aimed at showcasing pioneering research and innovative projects across various disciplines. These short papers highlight early-stage research, novel ideas, and preliminary findings, fostering meaningful discussions and potential collaborations.

Each paper in this compilation has undergone a rigorous single-blind review process with each submission receiving three reviews on average, ensuring the highest quality and relevance to the conference theme. The research's depth and diversity highlight the ongoing efforts to leverage information systems and innovative technologies for effective governance, public service provision, and societal transformation.

We would like to express our deepest gratitude to all the authors who contributed their valuable research and insights to this volume. Their dedication and expertise have enriched the discourse surrounding electronic government, paving the way for novel approaches, best practices, and lessons learned. We also extend our sincere appreciation to the program committee members for their meticulous evaluation and valuable feedback that shaped the selection and refinement of the papers.

Furthermore, we want to thank the conference organisers, keynote speakers, and attendees for their unwavering support and enthusiasm. Through their collective efforts, this conference has become a thriving forum for exchanging knowledge, fostering collaboration, and catalyzing meaningful change in electronic government.

As you delve into the pages of these proceedings, we hope you find inspiration in the insightful research, innovative solutions, and transformative visions shared with-in. Beyond scholarly exchange, EGOVIS continues to inform real-world policy decisions and drive the implementation of evidence-based digital governance strategies.

Whether you are a researcher, a practitioner, a policymaker, or an advocate for citizen-centric governance, we believe that the wealth of knowledge presented here will inspire you to explore new horizons and contribute to the ongoing digital transformation of our governments and societies.

Finally, we want to express our heartfelt appreciation to the conference community. Your dedication, passion, and commitment to advancing electronic government and embracing the information systems perspective have made this event successful.

August 2025

Andrea Kő
Francesco Buccafurri
Gabriele Kotsis
A Min Tjoa
Ismail Khalil

Organization

Program Committee Chairs

Andrea Kő   Corvinus University Budapest, Hungary
Francesco Buccafurri   University of Reggio Calabria, Italy

Steering Committee

Gabriele Kotsis   Johannes Kepler University Linz, Austria
A Min Tjoa   Vienna University of Technology, Austria
Lukas Fischer   Software Competence Center Hagenberg, Austria
Bernhard Moser   Software Competence Center Hagenberg, Austria
Christine Strauss   University of Vienna, Austria
Ismail Khalil   Johannes Kepler University Linz, Austria

Program Committee Members

Alejandra Cechich   Universidad del Comahue, Argentina
Aljosa Pasic   Eviden, Spain
Amira Mouakher   University of Perpignan, France
Bálint Molnár   Eötvös Loránd University, Hungary
Chien-Chih Yu   National Chengchi University, Taiwan
Christos Kalloniatis   University of the Aegean, Greece
Costas Vassilakis   University of the Peloponnese, Greece
Csaba Krasznay   Ludovika University of Public Service, Hungary
Enrico Francesconi   IGSG-CNR, Italy
Erich Schweighofer   University of Vienna, Austria
Fernando Galindo   University of Zaragoza, Spain
Francisco Javier García Marco   Universidad de Zaragoza, Spain
György Drótos   Corvinus University of Budapest, Hungary
Herbert Leitold   A-SIT, Austria
Javier Nogueras Iso   Universidad de Zaragoza, Spain
Jean Vincent Fonou-Dombeu   University of KwaZulu-Natal, South Africa
Luis Alvarez Sabucedo   Universidade de Vigo, Spain
Noppon Choosri   Chiang Mai University, Thailand
Rozha Ahmed   Sulaimani Polytechnic University, Iraq

Sara Lazzaro	Università della Calabria, Italy
Vytautas Čyras	Vilnius University, Lithuania
Wichian Chutimaskul	King Mongkut's University of Technology Thonburi, Thailand

External Reviewers

| Őri Dóra | Corvinus University of Budapest, Hungary |
| Zoltan Szabó | Corvinus University of Budapest, Hungary |

Organizers

Contents

E-Government Cases

Legal Aspects and Semantic Approaches

Mapping EU Legislative Definitions on Sustainable Development Goals Using AI

Muhammad Asif[1,2(✉)] ⓘ and Monica Palmirani[1] ⓘ

[1] CIRSFID, University of Bologna, Bologna, Italy
{muhammad.asif19,monica.palmirani}@unibo.it
[2] Department of Computer Science, University of Luxembourg, Esch-sur-Alzette, Luxembourg

Abstract. This study addresses the challenge of linking European Union (EU) legislative definitions to the Sustainable Development Goals (SDGs) by developing a multilabel classification model. For this purpose, the AI-based multilabel classification model is designed to link EU legislative definitions with the SDGs. Different pre-processing techniques are applied to refine the dataset, including TF/IDF for feature extraction, PCA for dimensionality reduction, and Class Weights to handle imbalanced class problems that optimize the model's performance (i.e., Weighted and Macro F-score). Support Vector Machine (SVM) outperforms with a 70.04% Weighted F-score by taking the text of the first four articles with preambles on the SDGs classification. The result underlines the proposed approach's effectiveness in bridging EU legislative definitions with SDG frameworks. The developed model has been preserved for future policy analysis and sustainable development alignment applications. Finally, definitions of the EU legislation are successfully linked with the SDGs using SVM.

Keywords: Artificial Intelligence · Sustainable Development Goals · Machine Learning · Natural Language Processing · Definition Classification · SDGs Classification · SDGs Actions Linking

1 Introduction

The term 'Sustainable Development' was first sanctioned in 1987 by the Brundtland World Commission, also known as the World Commission on the Environment and Development. It combines the concepts of 'sustainability' and 'development' to emphasize the need for long-term global well-being and growth for future generations. In simplest states, economic growth and development should not come at the cost of wounding the current environmental situation, where the resources are oppressed and exploited beyond the capacity for renewal. Over the years, these indicators of sustainability and development have advanced, leading to the creation of an extended action plan aimed at achieving sustainable development on a global scale. This plan, focused on ensuring the planet's long-term sustainability, was adopted by the United Nations [1].

The United Nations (UN) member states have taken significant steps towards global sustainability [2], leading to the introduction of the Sustainable Development Goals

© The Author(s), under exclusive license to Springer Nature Switzerland AG 2026
A. Kő et al. (Eds.): EGOVIS 2025, LNCS 16049, pp. 3–17, 2026.
https://doi.org/10.1007/978-3-032-02225-7_1

(SDGs) on September 25, 2015 [3]. These Goals are part of the 2030 Agenda for Sustainable Development, aimed at ensuring peace and prosperity for the planet [4]. 193 member states agreed on a set of 17 SDGs [5], with 169 associated Targets [6], designed to create a prosperous future for current and future generations. These Goals are universally applicable to all nations, regardless of geographic location or Gross Domestic Product (GDP). This ambitious agenda for global sustainability serves as the world's roadmap for addressing a wide range of complex challenges [7]. These include poverty, hunger, health & well-being, and the pursuit of peace & justice for all. It also acknowledges critical issues such as combating climate change, providing quality education, protecting biodiversity, promoting economic growth, reducing social inequalities, building sustainable cities & communities, and ensuring responsible production & consumption of goods [8, 9].

One of the key agendas of the SDGs is to achieve 'No Poverty', 'Zero Hunger', and 'Good Health & Well-Being'. The Food and Agriculture Organisation (FAO) has passed resolutions to protect food security and enhance the agricultural sector to address hunger and poverty, thereby contributing to humanity's overall well-being. The European Union is also collaborating with the FAO within the framework of the SDGs, enacting legislation and resolutions to support these Goals [10].

This study introduces a classification system for the mapping of European Legislation (EL) with each SDGs at the Goals and Targets levels. A Machine Learning-based model is employed to quantify the relationship between EU legislative definitions and the SDGs, computing the representation of each of the SDGs: 17 Goals and 169 Targets with legislative definitions [11]. The use of ML algorithms for classification offers several advantages, including the ability to identify trends and patterns within legislative definitions [12].

The classification of SDGs within legislative texts is crucial for monitoring regulatory alignment with global sustainability objectives. This task involves mapping of EU legislative content based on its relevance to specific SDGs, enabling policymakers, researchers, and stakeholders to assess the impact of legal frameworks on SDGs [13]. With the rapid expansion of legislative data, manually identifying relevant SDG-linked provisions becomes increasingly complex. AI-driven classification models address this challenge by leveraging Machine Learning (ML) and Natural Language Processing (NLP) techniques to categorize legislative texts and to classify with the SDGs systematically. Such automated classification not only enhances the accessibility of legal information but also facilitates the linkage of legislative definitions with SDGs, supporting transparency and compliance in policymaking.

2   Literature Review

This section presents previous studies on legislative text and document classification that highlight the role of AI and NLP in this domain. Legal text and legal document classification have been investigated with different ML, Deep Learning (DL), and NLP strategies [14]. In [15] identified argumentative structure, function, and propositions from the European Court of Human Rights (ECHR) and [13] classified an Italian legal text into a relevant domain. The [16] predicted the case where an ECHR legal document was from, what area of law the case was about, and the date the ruling was issued, [17] also focused on the prediction of legal judgments from ECHR cases. Machine Learning was used to predict the ruling of the French Supreme Court and to predict the belonging of cases within the law area [18] and [19] employed models based on Recurrent Neural Network (RNN) to identify necessary parts and realize them in Japanese legal texts. Evidence extraction from Chinese court documents was done using an information extraction task that integrated with the classification of legal articles [20]. Legal text classification also includes the specific tasks in the classification of the law area [13], argumentation mining [15], prediction of court decisions [14] and the identification of rulings of courts [16].

In [21] an open-source online tool (OSDG tool) was proposed by the UNDP SDG AI (Artificial Intelligence) lab to classify the text data into the SDGS using ontology engineering. OSDG tool allows users to tag SDG documents using text, summary, abstract, or the DOI number. In [22] a multilingual tool was proposed for the classification of text data into the Sustainable Development Goals of the United Nations. That tool was supported by 15 different languages. In [23] an SDG-Meter was proposed for the automatic text classification of the Sustainable Development Goals using the BERT model. The limitation is that users can only put up to 512 words. In [24] Knowledge Organization System was proposed by the United Nations Department of Economic and Social Affairs for the United Nations Sustainable Development Goals. It provides an online tool that links text to the SDGs using an ontology-based technique.

3 Methodology

The methodology to classify EU legislative documents into SDGs and to map EU legislative Definitions with SDGs is divided into five phases. The first phase discusses dataset acquisition and preprocessing in detail. The second phase explores model design and experimentation. The results are analyzed and discussed in the third phase. The fourth phase is about identifying the best classification model for mapping EU legislation. The mapping of SDGs is performed on the Definitions in the fifth phase.

3.1 Data Acquisition

The classification of EU legislative documents into the SDGs aims to identify the actions found in them and establish their links to the corresponding SDGs. The data acquisition is performed in two steps: the first is about the extracted Delimiting Definitions from the EU legislative documents (that consists of 11,705 Delimiting Definitions extracted after the annotation in the LEOS dataset that was based on EUR-Lex documents) [25]. The second dataset is scraped from KnowSDGs (Knowledge Base for the Sustainable Development Goals). KnowSDGs platform that provides policy mapping tools to demonstrate how EU policies address the SDGs. The platform offers two different categories of documents: (i) Preparatory documents and (ii) Legal Acts. The legal acts are selected for this study because the LEOS dataset only consists of Legal Acts. These documents belong to two different periods: previous initiatives and current initiatives. The previous initiatives cover the years 2015–2019; these documents are annotated manually, while the current initiatives cover 2019–2024: these are annotated using an AI tool [26]. For this study, the previous initiatives were chosen because these documents are manually annotated, which increases the likelihood of correctness [27]. Therefore, the previous initiatives were selected and scraped using a Python Script.

Pre-processing
The scraped dataset consists of previous initiatives spanning six different legislative types: Directives, Decisions, Regulations, Recommendations, Declarations, and Resolutions. A total of 8,803 records are scraped from the KnowSDGs platform, encompassing six types of documents in EU legislation. The definitions that are extracted from the EU legislation belong to Directives 'L' and Regulations 'R'. For this reason, from the scraped dataset, all the data that belongs to those two classes is separated from the rest. This results in a dataset of 2,784 records, which is used for model development for the classification of SDGs. The remaining dataset is further refined using various data preprocessing techniques. This study incorporated three preprocessing techniques to improve classification results: lowercasing, Removing Stop and Short Words.

Stratified Sampling Train-Test Split
After preprocessing, 2,784 records remained, each containing classified text of legislative files at the Goals and Targets level of the SDGs with an imbalanced class problem. The imbalanced distribution of classes in the training or testing set badly affects the classification results [28]. To overcome this problem, the data is split into 2:1, using a stratified sampling method in the training and testing datasets. Stratified sampling is a method that aims to preserve the proportions of different categories or classes from the original data in both the training and testing datasets [29]. After splitting the dataset, the training dataset consisted of 1,856 records, while the testing dataset contained 928 records. These datasets are used to train and evaluate the classification model.

Oversampling of Training Dataset
As discussed in the above section, the scraped dataset of previous initiatives exhibits a class imbalance issue. Some classes appear only once or twice. While this did not cause problems during training, it led to warnings for unknown classes when these infrequent classes appeared in the test set. To address this issue, the training dataset is oversampled after splitting. During oversampling, the minimal classes are scaled up to have a minimum presence of 20 records per class. After oversampling, the total number of records in the training set increased to 2,497 for the Target-level classification.

4   Model Development

This section provides a detailed discussion of the model design and experimentation aimed at developing a model for SDGs classification. Mainly, the classification is divided into three categories: (i) Binary Classification, (ii) Polynomial Classification, and (iii) Multilabel Classification [30]. In binary classification, the data is categorized into one of two classes. In polynomial classification, an entity is classified into one of multiple possible classes. In a multilabel classification problem, entities can belong to multiple classes simultaneously [31]. This study specifically addresses the multilabel classification problem to classify the SDGs at the Goals and Targets level.

4.1 Model Design

This study utilizes an annotated dataset based on previous initiatives scraped from the KnowSDGs online platform to design the classification model. After preprocessing, the dataset is split 2:1 using the stratifying sampling method. Two-thirds of the dataset is allocated for model training, and one-third is reserved for testing and evaluating the model's performance. Figure 1 illustrates the model design used in this study.

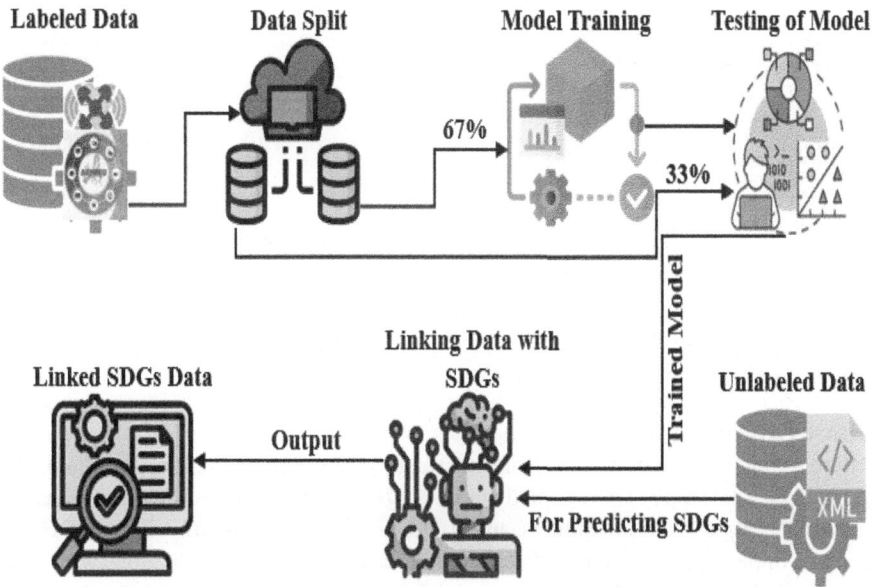

Fig. 1. Model Design

After developing and testing the model, the trained model will be saved and utilized to link the definitions with SDGs. After saving the trained model, the 11,705 definitions are given to the model to link the SDGs at both the Goals and Target levels.

4.2 Model Evaluation

The model's performance is assessed using both the weighted and macro F-scores. The weighted F-score measures the overall performance of the model and calculates the average F-score across all classes. The model is also evaluated with a macro F-score due to the imbalanced class distribution of the dataset. Since the dataset is unbalanced, with some classes having very few samples, the macro F-score provides a more representative evaluation. Unlike the weighted F-score, the macro F-score accounts for class imbalance by treating each class equally when calculating the final score.

4.3 Experimentation Design

For the experimentation design, various Machine Learning and Deep Learning algorithms are implemented to identify the most effective approach for the classification of

SDGs. The classifiers tried in this study are: Naïve Bayes, Random Forest, Text Convolutional Neural Network (Text CNN), RNN, BiLSTM, Logistic Regression, SVM, and KNN. Table 1 shows the results of the tried ML algorithms.

Table 1. Results of Tried Machine Learning Algorithms

	NB	RF	CNN	BiLSTM	LR	KNN	SVM
ACC	30	37.96	38.28	0	0.22	49.81	**56.25**
Precision	98.99	82.19	58.99	1.26	16.6	48.56	**77.48**
Recall	13.51	27.68	33.18	0.09	1.11	55.81	**62.26**
F-score	23.78	41.41	38.43	0.17	1.19	49.62	**67.86**

Based on good results, the SVM is chosen for the final implementation, which is also recommended in previous studies. After the SVM for multi-label classification problems. Feature extraction, dimensionality reduction, and rare event prediction techniques are implemented to improve the model's performance. The remaining details are provided in the following sections.

Feature Extraction

Feature extraction involves converting text data into a structured format suitable for ML models. This study experimented with TF/IDF (Term Frequency-Inverse Document Frequency), Word2Vec embeddings, and N-grams (Uni, Bi, Tri-gram) with TF/IDF. The results of implementing TF/IDF indicate better results than the combinations with other techniques. Therefore, TF/IDF is chosen for final implementation.

Dimensionality Reduction

The dimensionality reduction reduces the number of features while retaining critical information. This study tested Principal Component Analysis (PCA), t-SNE (t-distributed Stochastic Neighbor Embedding), and UMAP (Uniform Manifold Approximation and Projection). Based on superior results, PCA is selected for the final implementation.

Rare Event Prediction

Rare event prediction focuses on identifying and forecasting entities with low frequency with high impact. Class Weights incorporates to handle rare event prediction to improve results. SMOTE (Synthetic Minority Over-sampling Technique) and ADASYN (Adaptive Synthetic Sampling) are also tried, but these techniques are limited to binomial and polynomial classification problems.

Evaluating various techniques, TF/IDF, PCA, and Class Weights are selected based on their enhanced results for the final SVM implementation. For model development, the experiments are designed using four different scenarios (i) First Four Articles' Text, (ii) All the Articles' Text, (iii) First Four Articles' with Preambles Text, and (iv) All the Articles' with Preambles Text, based on the 17 Goals and 169 Targets of the SDGs.

5 Results

The classification is conducted in two stages. First, it is performed on the 17 SDGs Goals using the abovementioned four scenarios; subsequently, it is extended to the 169 SDGs Targets. The detailed results of the SDG classification presented below.

5.1 Classification of SDGs Goals

SVM is applied for the classification of 17 Goals of the SDGs using the abovementioned four consecutive scenarios to get the best classification model that can be used for linking the EU legislative definitions with the Goals and Targets of the SDGs.

The best classification results for SDGs at the Goals level are achieved by applying SVM with the combination of PCA and Class Weights on the text of the first four articles with preambles by achieving a weighted F-score of 70.04% and a macro F-score of 57.94%. SVM with Class Weights also showed notable performance and achieving a weighted F-score of 67.86% and a macro F-score of 54.55%. Similarly, SVM with PCA attained 59.17% with a weighted F-score and a macro F-score of 42.28%. SVM alone performed with 61.15% weighted F-score and a macro F-score of 44.15%. The classification of the 17 Goals of SDGs results by applying SVM by taking the different combinations of text is shown in Table 2.

Table 2. Results of SVM at Goals level Classification of SDGs by utilizing different Scenarios

Scenarios	Evaluation Measures	SVM	SVM + PCA	SVM + Class Weights	SVM + PCA and Class Weights
ARTICLE4	Weighted F-score	0.5534	0.5189	0.6299	0.6435
	Macro F-score	0.3738	0.3331	0.4917	0.5145
ALL ARTICLES	Weighted F-score	0.5600	0.5137	0.6314	0.6378
	Macro F-score	0.3791	0.3310	0.4919	0.5074
ARTICLE4 + PREAMBLES	Weighted F-score	0.6115	0.5917	0.6786	**0.7004**
	Macro F-score	0.4415	0.4228	0.5455	**0.5794**
ALL ARTICLES + PREAMBLES	Weighted F-score	0.5534	0.5189	0.6299	0.6435
	Macro F-score	0.3738	0.3331	0.4917	0.5145

The performance of SVM with PCA and Class Weights is also notable, but it is not as effective in classifying smaller classes when applied to the text of all the articles with preambles. In contrast, SVM with the combination of PCA and Class Weights demonstrated superior overall performance, particularly in classifying smaller classes, when applied to the text of the first four articles and their preambles. By using text from all the articles, including the preambles, the performance of SVM with PCA and Class Weights on the smaller classes achieves a 51.45% macro F-score and a weighted F-score of 64.35%. SVM with Class Weights achieves a weighted F-score of 62.99% and a macro F-score of 49.17%. When considering the text of all the articles, the SVM achieves a weighted F-score of 56.00% and a macro F-score of 37.91%. Meanwhile, the SVM with PCA achieves a weighted F-score of 51.37% and a macro F-score of 33.10%. SVM with Class Weights achieves a weighted F-score of 63.14% and a macro F-score of 49.19%. By combining both PCA and Class Weights, the SVM achieves a weighted F-score of 63.78% and a macro F-score of 50.74% when applied to the text of all the articles. SVM with PCA and Class Weights achieves a weighted F-score of 64.35% and a macro F-score of 51.45% when applied to the text of the first four articles. The visual representation of the results for classifying the 17 Goals of SDGs using different combinations of SVM is shown in Fig. 2.

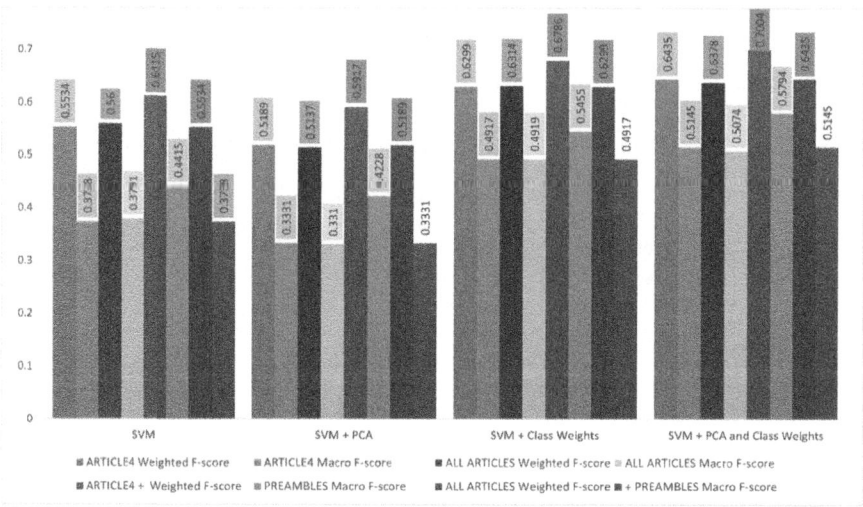

Fig. 2. Representation of Results of SVM on the Classification of 17 Goals of SDGs

5.2   Classification of SDG Targets

As discussed above, the SDGs consist of 17 Goals, each Goal is associated with several Targets designed to achieve specific objectives. In total, there are 169 Targets associated with these 17 Goals of SDGs. In the experimentation on Target level classification of SDGs, the best results are achieved by SVM with Class Weights by taking the text of the first four articles with preambles with 56.92% of weighted F-score and 30.98% of macro F-score. The results of SVM on the Targets level classification of SDGs on the different text combinations are shown in Table 3.

Table 3. Results of SVM at Targets level Classification of SDGs by utilising different Scenarios

Scenarios	Evaluation Measures	SVM	SVM + PCA	SVM + Class Weights	SVM + PCA and Class Weights
ARTICLE4	Weighted F-score	0.4337	0.4337	0.4337	0.4337
	Macro F-score	0.1988	0.1988	0.1988	0.1988
ALL ARTICLES	Weighted F-score	0.4407	0.4032	0.5041	0.5017
	Macro F-score	0.2052	0.1825	0.2589	0.2446
ARTICLE4 + PREAMBLES	Weighted F-score	0.4337	0.4337	0.5692	**0.5640**
	Macro F-score	0.1988	0.1988	0.3098	**0.2944**
ALL ARTICLES + PREAMBLES	Weighted F-score	0.4446	0.4435	0.4442	0.5660
	Macro F-score	0.2080	0.2073	0.2078	0.3061

SVM with PCA and Class Weights achieved a weighted F-score of 56.40% and a macro F-score of 29.77%. SVM with PCA achieved a weighted F-score of 43.37% and a macro F-score of 19.88%. SVM achieved a weighted F-score of 43.37% and a macro F-score of 19.88%. With both the combination of PCA and Class Weights, the SVM performed with 56.60% weighted F-score and a macro F-score of 30.61%. SVM with Class Weights achieved a 50.41% weighted F-score and a macro F-score of 25.89%. The visual representation of the results for classifying the 17 Goals of SDGs using different combinations of SVM is shown in Fig. 3.

6 Saved the Best Model

Experiments are conducted on the 17 Goals of the SDGs and 169 associated Targets, applying SVM. Following detailed experimentation and analysis, SVM with PCA and Class Weights demonstrates superior performance and emerges as the best-performing model for linking the EU's actions at both the Goals and Targets level of the SDGs, particularly by classifying smaller classes effectively by incorporating the text of the first four articles with the preambles. The approach effectively captures the underlying

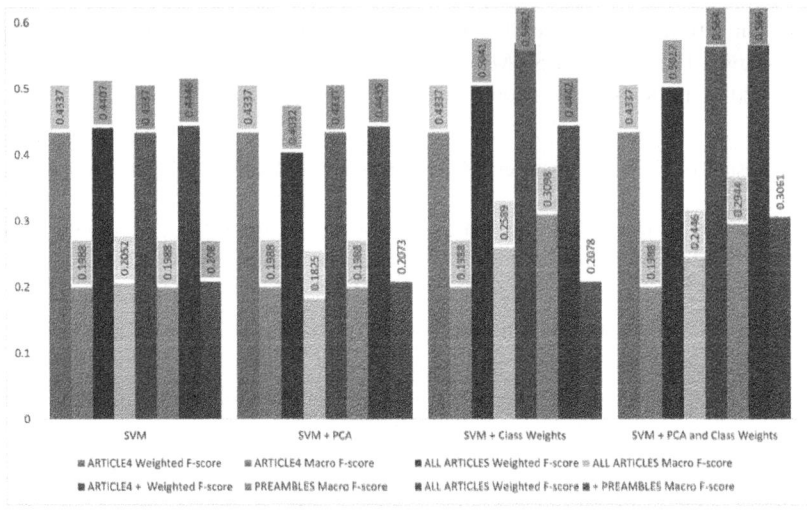

Fig. 3. Representation of Results of SVM on the Classification of Targets of SDGs

patterns within the text, consistently outperforming other methods. It delivers higher F-score metrics across both weighted and macro evaluations. These results highlight the robustness of this methodology in mapping EU legislative actions to SDGs Targets, providing a reliable framework for further analysis and decision-making. This best-performing configuration was selected and saved as the optimal model for linking actions in EU legislation with the SDGS at the Goals and Targets level.

7   Linking Definitions with SDGs

The Delimiting Definitions extracted from EU legislation were provided to the best-performing models to link with the SDGs—at the Goals and Target levels.

7.1   Linking of Definition with Goals of SDGs

Delimiting Definitions are given to the saved SVM model to predict the actions present in each definition and link that specific definition to the appropriate SDGs. The frequency of each SDG goal found in 11705 definitions is illustrated in Fig. 4.

7.2   Linking of Definition with Associated Targets of SDGs

After linking the definitions with SDGs at the Goals level, these 11,705 delimiting definitions are also linked with SDGs Targets. The frequency of each SDGs Targets found in 11705 definitions is shown in Fig. 5.

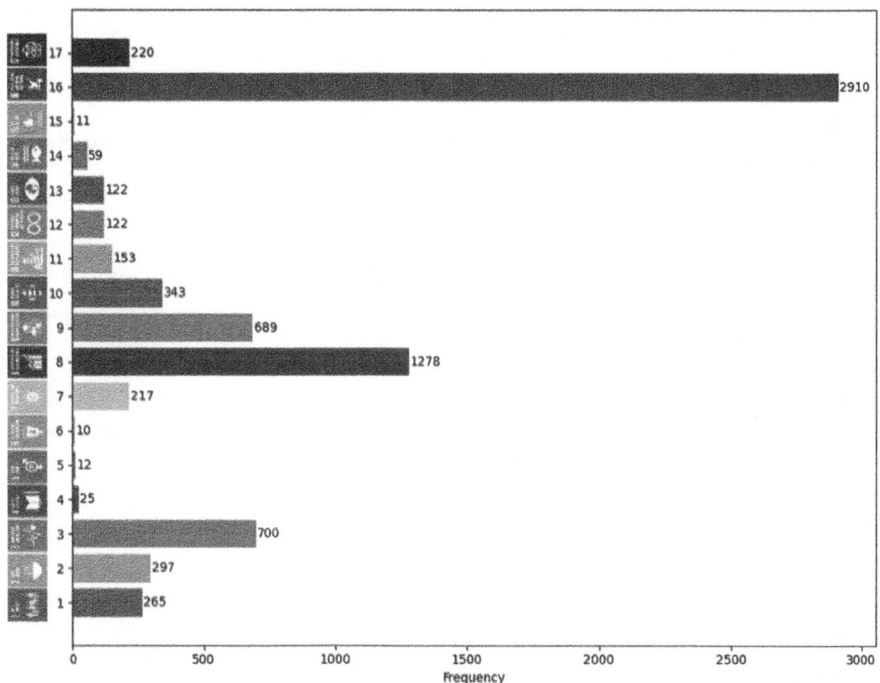

Fig. 4. The frequency of each SDGs Goals found in 11705 Delimiting Definition

8 Discussion

Linking Delimiting Definitions in EU legislation to SDGs at both the Goal and Target levels provides a deeper understanding of how legal Definitions contribute to sustainable policy implementation. At the Goal level, the analysis highlights that SDG 16 (Peace, Justice, and Strong Institutions) has the highest number of linked Definitions (2,910), reinforcing the EU's legislative emphasis on governance, legal integrity, and institutional stability. Similarly, SDG 8 (Decent Work and Economic Growth) and SDG 9 (Industry, Innovation, and Infrastructure) show strong representation with 1,278 and 689 linked Definitions, respectively, reflecting a focus on economic resilience and industrial development. In contrast, SDGs related to environmental sustainability (e.g., SDG 6: Clean Water and Sanitation, SDG 14: Life Below Water, and SDG 15: Life on Land) exhibit significantly lower numbers of linked Definitions, suggesting either a lesser volume of legal Definitions addressing these areas or a broader integration of sustainability concerns with legal frameworks.

At the Target level, the classification model provides more granular insights into how specific legal Definitions map onto SDG Targets. Notably, Target 16.4 (combating illicit financial and arms flows) has the highest number of linked Definitions (999), again emphasising the EU's legislative commitment to institutional transparency and legal enforcement. Other highly linked Targets include 8.1 (sustained economic growth), 7.3 (energy efficiency), and 13.2 (climate policy integration), reflecting the

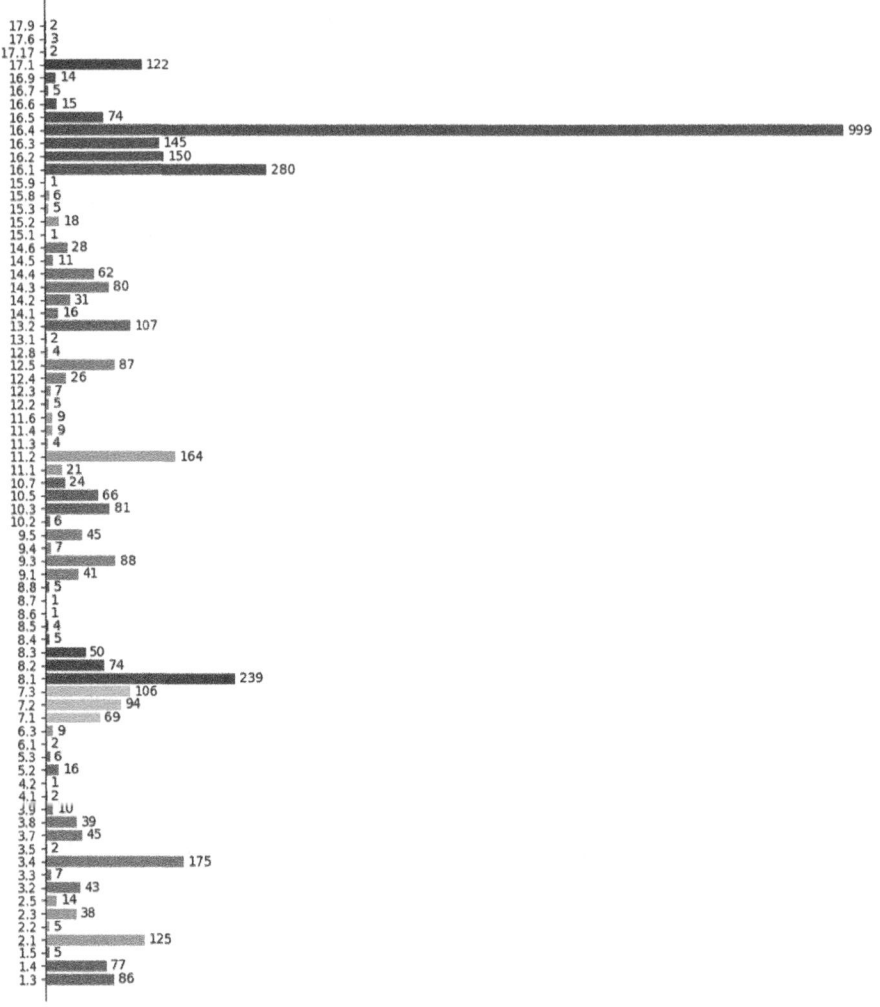

Fig. 5. The frequency of each SDGs Targets found in 11705 Delimiting Definition

EU's broader economic and environmental priorities. However, several Targets (e.g., 4.1: Quality Education, 5.2: Eliminating Violence Against Women, and 6.1: Universal Access to Safe Drinking Water) have significantly fewer linked Definitions, potentially indicating gaps in explicit legal definitions supporting these policy areas. The results demonstrate the effectiveness of machine learning in structuring and analysing legal texts for SDG alignment. The SVM model, enhanced with Principal Component Analysis (PCA) and class weighting, successfully identified patterns in legal Definitions that correspond to sustainable development objectives. However, the observed disparities in linkage frequency across different Goals and Targets suggest potential areas for further legal scrutiny and policy enhancement. Overall, this study underscores the importance of AI-driven methodologies in legislative analysis, offering policymakers data-driven insights to refine legal frameworks for achieving SDGs commitments.

By developing a classification model, this study provides a foundational approach for mapping policy documents to sustainability objectives, enabling policymakers and researchers to better assess legislative alignment with the SDGs, enabling informed decision-making and effective policy formulation.

9 Conclusions

This study presents a multilabel classification approach to link EU legislative texts with Sustainable Development Goals at both the Goal and Target levels. To achieve this, Support Vector Machine is implemented for multinomial classification. Various preprocessing techniques, i.e., lowercasing and stop-word removal for preprocessing, TF/IDF, PCA and Class Weights PCA, demonstrate superior performance. The dataset was split into a 2:1 ratio for training and testing using a stratified method, with the training dataset containing 930 instances and the testing dataset oversampled to ensure a minimum of 20 instances per class. Through a series of experiments, SVM is applied in different scenarios, the first four articles, all articles, and variations incorporating preambles. The best classification performance for SDG Goals is achieved using SVM with PCA and Class Weights applied to the first four articles with preambles, resulting in a weighted score of 70.04% and a macro F-score of 57.94%. At the Target level, SVM with PCA and Class Weights applied to the first four articles with preambles performed with 56.40% weighted F-score and a macro F-score of 29.44%. After evaluation, the best-performing models were saved to facilitate the automated linking of EU legislative texts (EU Legislation in English language only) with SDGs at both the Goal and Target levels. This study provides a foundational approach for mapping policy documents to sustainability objectives, enabling policymakers and researchers to better assess legislative alignment with the SDGs.

Acknowledgments. This study is funded by PON grants of the Italian Government and also the ERC HyperModeLex.

References

1. Żak, A.: Multiple perspectives on sustainable development. In: Organizing Sustainable Development, pp. 77–90. Taylor and Francis (2023). https://doi.org/10.4324/978100337 9409-8
2. Chaaben, N., Elleuch, Z., Hamdi, B., Kahouli, B.: Green economy performance and sustainable development achievement: empirical evidence from Saudi Arabia. Environ. Dev. Sustain. **26**(1), 549–564 (2024). https://doi.org/10.1007/s10668-022-02722-8
3. Liang, B., Cao, J., He, J., Li, S., Zhang, X., Ou, J.: Prioritization decision-making model for sustainable development goals based on multi-factor simulated annealing particle swarm algorithm. SCIREA J. Comput. (2019). https://doi.org/10.54647/computer520400
4. Berbeka, K., Alejziak, W., Berbeka, J.: Sustainable development goals of agenda 2030 in the declarations and aims of international tourism organisations. J. Travel Tour. Mark. **41**(1), 142–153 (2024). https://doi.org/10.1080/10548408.2023.2239862

5. Piadeh, F., et al.: A Critical Review for the Impact of Anaerobic Digestion on the Sustainable Development Goals. Academic Press (2024). https://doi.org/10.1016/j.jenvman.2023.119458
6. Heriyati, P., Yadav, N., Tamara, D.: Accomplishing sustainable development goals through international management system standards and multinational supply chains. Bus Strategy Environ. (2024). https://doi.org/10.1002/bse.3752
7. Alenezi, M., Akour, M.: Digital transformation blueprint in higher education: a case study of PSU. Sustainability (Switzerland) **15**(10) (2023). https://doi.org/10.3390/su15108204
8. Cernev, T., Fenner, R.: The importance of achieving foundational sustainable development goals in reducing global risk. Futures **115** (2020). https://doi.org/10.1016/j.futures.2019.102492
9. Mumtaz, M.: Role of civil society organizations for promoting green and blue infrastructure to adapting climate change: evidence from Islamabad city, Pakistan. J. Clean. Prod. **309** (2021). https://doi.org/10.1016/j.jclepro.2021.127296
10. Sjah, T., Zainuri, Z.: Agricultural Supply Chain and Food Security, pp. 79–88 (2020). https://doi.org/10.1007/978-3-319-95675-6_82
11. Gatto, A.: Quantifying management efficiency of energy recovery from waste for the circular economy transition in Europe. J. Clean. Prod. **414** (2023). https://doi.org/10.1016/j.jclepro.2023.136948
12. Park, S.O., Hassairi, N.: What predicts legislative success of early care and education policies?: Applications of machine learning and natural language processing in a cross-state early childhood policy analysis **16**(2) (2021). https://doi.org/10.1371/journal.pone.0246730
13. Boella, G., Di Caro, L., Humphreys, L.: Using classification to support legal knowledge engineers in the eunomos legal document management system. In: Fifth International Workshop on Juris-Informatics (JURISIN) (2011)
14. Sulea, O.M., Zampieri, M., Malmasi, S., Vela, M., Dinu, L.P., Van Genabith, J.: Exploring the use of text classification in the legal domain. In: CEUR Workshop Proceedings, vol. 2143 (2017)
15. Palau, R.M., Moens, M.F.: Argumentation mining: the detection, classification and structure of arguments in text. In: Proceedings of the International Conference on Artificial Intelligence and Law, pp. 98–107 (2009). https://doi.org/10.1145/1568234.1568246
16. Aletras, N., Tsarapatsanis, D., Preoţiuc-Pietro, D., Lampos, V.: Predicting judicial decisions of the European court of human rights: a natural language processing perspective. PeerJ Comput. Sci. **2016**(10), 1–19 (2016). https://doi.org/10.7717/peerj-cs.93
17. Chalkidis, I., Androutsopoulos, I., Aletras, N.: Neural legal judgment prediction in English. In: ACL 2019 - 57th Annual Meeting of the Association for Computational Linguistics, Proceedings of the Conference, pp. 4317–4323 (2020). https://doi.org/10.18653/v1/p19-1424
18. Şulea, O.M., Zampieri, M., Vela, M., Van Genabith, J.: Predicting the law area and decisions of French supreme court cases. In: International Conference Recent Advances in Natural Language Processing, RANLP, vol. 2017-Septe, no. 2011, pp. 716–722 (2017). https://doi.org/10.26615/978-954-452-049-6_092
19. Nguyen, T.S., Nguyen, L.M., Tojo, S., Satoh, K., Shimazu, A.: Recurrent Neural Network-Based Models for Recognizing Requisite and Effectuation Parts in Legal Texts, vol. 26, no. 2. Springer Netherlands (2018). https://doi.org/10.1007/s10506-018-9225-1
20. Ji, D., Tao, P., Fei, H., Ren, Y.: An end-to-end joint model for evidence information extraction from court record document. Inf. Process. Manag. **57**(6) (2020). https://doi.org/10.1016/j.ipm.2020.102305
21. Pukelis, L., Puig, N.B., Skrynik, M., Stanciauskas, V.: OSDG -- Open-source approach to classify text data by UN sustainable development goals (SDGs) (2020). http://arxiv.org/abs/2005.14569

22. Pukelis, L., Bautista-Puig, N., Statulevičiūtė, G., Stančiauskas, V., Dikmener, G., Akylbekova, D.: OSDG 2.0: a multilingual tool for classifying text data by UN sustainable development goals (SDGs). arXiv preprint arXiv:2211.11252, pp. 0–11 (2022)
23. Guisiano, J.E., Chiky, R., De Mello, J.: SDG-meter: a deep learning based tool for automatic text classification of the sustainable development goals. In: Lecture Notes in Computer Science (including subseries Lecture Notes in Artificial Intelligence and Lecture Notes in Bioinformatics), pp. 259–271 (2022). https://doi.org/10.1007/978-3-031-21743-2_21
24. Joshi, A., et al.: A knowledge organization system for the United Nations sustainable development goals. In: Lecture Notes in Computer Science (including subseries Lecture Notes in Artificial Intelligence and Lecture Notes in Bioinformatics), pp. 548–564. Springer Science and Business Media Deutschland GmbH (2021). https://doi.org/10.1007/978-3-030-77385-4_33
25. Asif, M., Palmirani, M.: Legal definition annotation in EU legislation using symbolic AI. In: Lecture Notes in Computer Science (including subseries Lecture Notes in Artificial Intelligence and Lecture Notes in Bioinformatics), pp. 34–39. Springer Science and Business Media Deutschland GmbH (2024). https://doi.org/10.1007/978-3-031-68211-7_4
26. Mandilara, I., Fotopoulou, E., Androna, C.M., Zafeiropoulos, A., Papavassiliou, S.: Knowledge graph data enrichment based on a software library for text mapping to the sustainable development goals. In: CEUR Workshop Proceedings, vol. 3447, no. May, pp. 51–69 (2023)
27. Han, Q., Snaidauf, D.: Comparison of deep learning technologies in legal document classification. In: Proceedings - 2021 IEEE International Conference on Big Data, Big Data 2021, pp. 2701–2704 (2021), https://doi.org/10.1109/BigData52589.2021.9671486
28. Devi, D., Biswas, S.K., Purkayastha, B.: A review on solution to class imbalance problem: undersampling approaches. In: 2020 International Conference on Computational Performance Evaluation (ComPE), pp. 626–631 (2020)
29. Wu, Z., Wang, Z., Chen, J., You, H., Yan, M., Wang, L.: Stratified random sampling for neural network test input selection. Inf. Softw. Technol. **165**(February 2023), 107331 (2024). https://doi.org/10.1016/j.infsof.2023.107331
30. Qureshi, M.A., et al.: Aspect level songs rating based upon reviews in English. Comput. Mater. Continua **74**(2), 2589–2605 (2023). https://doi.org/10.32604/cmc.2023.032173
31. Qureshi, M.A., et al.: Sentiment analysis of reviews in natural language: Roman Urdu as a case study. IEEE Access **10**(1), 24945–24954 (2022). https://doi.org/10.1109/ACCESS.2022.3150172

Reporting Requirements Ontology for European Legislation

Monica Palmirani[1]([✉])[iD], Andrea Giovanni Nuzzolese[2][iD],
and Generoso Longo[1][iD]

[1] ALMA-AI, University of Bologna, Bologna, Italy
{monica.palmirani,generoso.longo2}@unibo.it
[2] CNR - Institute of Cognitive Sciences and Technologies, Bologna, Italy
andreagiovanni.nuzzolese@cnr.it

Abstract. The reporting requirement (RR) is a particular legislative
provision that commands bodies to execute a task by institutions to other
institutions (e.g., EU Commission to Parliament) (Regulatory reporting
is the periodical provision of structured or unstructured data (qualitative or quantitative) from concerned private and public organisations,
to competent authorities (at EU or national level) as required by the
requirements set in specific legislation. It is a process which entails the
following main stages: the setting of regulatory reporting requirements
in legislation, data collection, data processing, and data use and reuse.
https://interoperable-europe.ec.europa.eu/collection/better-legislation-
smoother-implementation/glossary/term/regulatory-reporting. The reporting requirement is not a legal obligation because there is no violation
and no sanction). However, the reporting requirements are a fundamental
part of the Better Regulation (Review clauses in EU legislation adopted
during the first half of the ninth parliamentary term (2019-2024), EPRS
| European Parliamentary Research Service Author: Nora Hahnkamper,
October 2022) strategy to monitor the simplification of the European
legislation and the correct implementation of EU policies) (European
Commission: Directorate-General for Digital Services and Wavestone,
Case study analysis of regulatory reporting practices across the European
Commission, Publications Office, 2019, https://data.europa.eu/doi/10.
2799/116377). For these reasons, tracking the reporting requirements
permits to evaluate of the policies, their effective implementation and
empowerment, and their evolution over time. This paper presents a legal
ontology to model the reporting requirements, developed with the support of the EU Commission with the scope to monitor the EU policies.

Keywords: Digital-ready policy monitoring · Better Regulation ·
Legal Ontology · reporting requirement · Akoma Ntoso · Knowledge
Graph

1 Introduction and Motivation

Reporting Requirements (or Reporting Requests or Review Clauses - hereafter
RR) are particular legislative provisions that command bodies to execute a task

A. Kő et al. (Eds.): EGOVIS 2025, LNCS 16049, pp. 18–32, 2026.
https://doi.org/10.1007/978-3-032-02225-7_2

by institutions to other institutions (e.g., from the EU Commission to Parliament). The reporting requirement is not a legal obligation from the perspective of the theory of law (Kelsen) because there is no sanction and, consequently, no violation. Often, the RR requires some institutions to prepare a report, plan, budget, opinion, or standard to address other institutions to monitor the quality of the legislation. Such commands are addressed to entities involved in the legislative system process to improve legislation quality, reduce the burden, and implement European policies. Therefore, they are not legal obligations in the classic meaning (addressed to the citizens, with a penalty) but meta-norms for managing and monitoring the law-making process within the legal system. In other words, it is an action addressed to the internal mechanism of the legal system[1]. The European Union (EU) legislation includes extensive reporting requirements involving a diverse range of institutions (e.g., Member States, Departments). Meta-data plays a fundamental role in managing the legal knowledge of reporting requirement[2]. The volume of these reporting requirements has grown substantially because they are effective instruments to monitor the policies and to implement the Better Regulation[3] strategy. On the contrary, the management of the complexity of the evolution over time of their modifications increases the burden of the legal experts of the legislation staff because they should track the changes in the long term, like derogation and exceptions [5]. Failure to manage them means affecting the Better Regulation strategy[4] and also to not have an effective legislative European Agenda[5]. To mitigate these challenges, reporting requirements are continuously monitored and updated by each EU Commission agency manually using SQL Databases and supported by natural language processing tools that scans the EU legislation[6]. For this reason, the European Commission has experimented AI tools combined with legal ontologies to detect and model the RR[7]. The Study on Regulatory Reporting Standards (SORTIS)

---

[1] See the Case study analysis of regulatory reporting practices across the European Commission, https://op.europa.eu/en/publication-detail/-/publication/5a5e5b13-e996-11e9-9c4e-01aa75ed71a1.

[2] See "The Importance of Metadata for Regulatory Reporting", Directorate-General for Informatics, D2 Interoperability, https://interoperable-europe.ec.europa.eu/sites/default/files/document/2021-12/Issue%20-%20The%20Importance%20of%20Metadata.pdf.

[3] https://commission.europa.eu/law/law-making-process/better-regulation_en.

[4] Better Regulation: Joining forces to make better laws, COM(2021) 219, 29 April 2021, European Commission.

[5] See the "Objectives of the Better Regulation agenda" at https://commission.europa.eu/law/law-making-process/planning-and-proposing-law/better-regulation_en.

[6] See, for instance, https://commission.europa.eu/system/files/2023-10/Factsheet_CWP_Burdens_10.pdf.

[7] See the Streamlining regulatory reporting, https://interoperable-europe.ec.europa.eu/collection/better-legislation-smoother-implementation/streamlining-regulatory-reporting.

project[8] has developed a first experiment focused on the extraction and representation of RR[9].

This paper aims to present and evolve the ontology called RRVM[10], which enables the tracking of RRs over time and allows queries. The first version of RRVM has been developed mainly by the authors of this paper, but now a consensus-building group of stakeholders has been involved with the aim to better representing all the user-cases in the EU Commission and from the Member States. A secondary goal is designing to build a legal knowledge graph using the European standards (AKN4EU[11], CELLAR[12], ELI[13], RRVM) to create and ontology of reporting requirements that enables sophisticated queries like:

"Give me all the RRs that the EU Commission shall report, addressed to the European Parliament and Council (contextually), at biannual frequency, but modified during the period 2019–2021 due to COVID".

"Give me all the RRs modified in the last 2 years, and the normative references included in the actions.".

"Give all the RRs that have frequency as TemporalEntity".

To cope with these goals, we want to investigate the following research questions, which revolve around the extent to which we can:

- **RQ1**: How to model the Reporting Requirements in a precise way in all its components (Action, Agent, Role, TemporalEntitySpec), also when different actions are concatenated?
- **RQ2**: How to express the normative references when the legal text delegates the description of some relevant parameters to another legal source?
- **RQ3**: How to model the temporal parameters of the action?
- **RQ4**: How to monitor the evolution over time of the modifications of the RR?
- **RQ5**: How to model the execution of the Reporting Requirements?

Finally, we intend to use CELLAR[14] RDF metadata to connect the information concerning the legislative modifications with the Reporting Requirements. In this manner, we can detect the changes that can affect the Reporting Requirements.

2 Reporting Requirement Anatomy

The RR usually has a pattern composed of basic elements.

---

[8] See the results available at https://interoperable-europe.ec.europa.eu/collection/better-legislation-smoother-implementation/news/streamlining-regulatory-reporting-sortis-project-results,   https://interoperable-europe.ec.europa.eu/collection/better-legislation-smoother-implementation/solution/rrmv.

[9] https://semiceu.github.io/RRMV/releases/0.1.1/.

[10] Available at https://code.europa.eu/regulatory-reporting/rrmv.

[11] See AKN4EU: A Common Structured Format for EU Legislative Documents at https://op.europa.eu/en/web/eu-vocabularies/akn4eu.

[12] See at https://op.europa.eu/en/web/cellar.

[13] See at https://eur-lex.europa.eu/eli-register/about.html.

[14] https://op.europa.eu/en/web/cellar/users.

- **Requirement** is the fragment of the legislative source structure (e.g., article, paragraph) in a given version and language (e.g., version updated at 2025-04-10, in English) that produces at least one **Action** (e.g., present a report) in a given time (e.g., by 1 January 2026), where **Agents** (e.g., Eu Commission) are involved playing specific **Roles** (e.g., addresser).
- **Action** is an event with at least one **Agent** that is a participant in it at a given time.
- **TemporalEntitySpec** is the specification of a temporal entity with non-zero extent or duration.
- Action is **Exectuted** and can change the **Status** of the Action planned (e.g., completed or suspended like during the COVID).
- **Requirement** has also **Topic** classification (e.g., EuroVoc) that qualify semantically the legal context (e.g., Financial).

Here is an example from the Directive 2014/65/EU of the European Parliament and the Council of 15 May 2014 on markets in financial instruments versioned on 2019[15]: "Art. 51 6. omissis... ESMA shall submit those draft regulatory technical standards to the Commission by 3 July 2015". ESMA is the Agent with the Role of addresser that must act as an Action (submit) a Results (draft regulatory technical standards) delivered to another Agent (Commission) in the Role of addressee, at a given time (by 3 July 2015).

More complex is to monitor the RR over time. On 31 December 2019, paragraph number 9 was inserted in article 33, creating a Reporting Requirements:

"Art. 33 omissis... 9. The Commission shall set up an expert stakeholder group by 1 July 2020 to monitor the functioning and success of SME growth markets. By 1 July 2021, the expert stakeholder group shall publish a report on its conclusions".

3   Methodology and Dataset

The methodology used is top-down for the legal theory principles and bottom-up for the analysis of the legal language. We have used the MeLOn methodology developed by Palmirani et al. [6], and used by many scholars [1]. We have used EU Commission's existing databases (e.g., KOEL - Knowledge Online on European Legislation) annotated by legal experts to identify a dataset useful for this work. On this dataset, legal experts have identified the main ontological classes useful for the use case. Additionally, we have detected 529 EU legislative documents from 2000 to 2021 concerning topics linked, usually, with reporting requirements (e.g., finance, food, environment). Then we have transformed all the documents into Akoma Ntoso format to foster the Legal knowledge described in the Legal-DocML XML. A sub-dataset of 86 paragraphs with temporal elements was used to create the statistics presented in this paper in paragraph 8. Another dataset was used for the evaluation.

---

[15] http://data.europa.eu/eli/dir/2014/65/2019-12-31.

4   Competencies Questions

The competencies questions of this ontology are the following:

- When is the next Action forecasted with ActionResult "report" related to Concept "financial instruments"?
- What Action has Status "suspended" related to the Concept "financial instruments"?
- Who is the "addressee" (AgentRole) of the Action with Frequency 2-years in the "next 5 years"?
- Which RRs have been modified?
- Which RRs are connected by other normative references?
- How many RRs have frequency as TemporalEntity?

5   Related Work

In the state of the art of legal informatics, several legislative ontologies exist to model the legal information of rights and obligations, but not this specific goal. We can find a general ontology in ORDL (Open Digital Rights Language)[16] that is capable of modeling the policies, and it describes rights, obligations, and permissions. However, the temporal parameters are insufficient to model complex Reporting Requirements. Secondly, we intend to model also the traceability of the policy in its execution and lifecycle and ORDL has no classes for this purpose. Already Sileno [4] underlines the limits of ORDL in granularity, in precision to model deontic rules, and the evolution of the rules over time. An interesting extension of the ORDL is done by [3], creating the Open Digital Rights Enforcement framework (ODRE), but also in, this new case the temporal aspects are not sufficiently evolved to cover the convoluted cases of the legal language. Notably, the intention in this research is to design an ontology that is interoperable with Akoma Ntoso [8] and with the metadata already designed in the versioning of legal sources [2]. For coping with this, we have considered the following ontologies as relevant to reuse:

- ELI (European Legislation Identifier[17]) is an ontology for creating a persistent URI of legislative resources and connected metadata (e.g., date of publication, enter into force date).
- FRBR[18] is a vocabulary on the Functional Requirements for Bibliographic Records described in the IFLA report. FRBR describes all documents from four different and correlated points of view: Work, Expression, Manifestation and Item; each of which is a FRBR Endeavour.

---

[16] Monegraph, R.I., Villata, S., 2018. ODRL Information Model 2.2. In: W3C Recommendation. https://www.w3.org/TR/odrl-model/.
[17] https://eur-lex.europa.eu/eli-register/about.html?locale=en.
[18] https://vocab.org/frbr/core.html.

- UNDO (United Nations System Document Ontology) aims to provide a framework for the formal description of all entities and the relations that can exist among them in UN Documents, a description that is not provided by Akoma Ntoso itself.[19] [9].
- Web Annotation Data Model specification describes a structured model and format to enable annotations to be shared and reused across different hardware and software platforms[20].

We also take inspiration from the ontology developed for the UN-WHO in order to model the reporting requirements inside the decisions and resolutions with the goal of tracking them over time [7]. In particular, we have taken the part related to the Execution of the reporting requirements capable of checking if the planned actions have been performed or not.

We have also investigated other existing ontologies for the temporal part, like TIME Owl[21] and CCCEV (Core Criterion and Core Evidence Vocabulary) from SEMIC of the European Commission[22]. Time Owl goal is to model real events and not specifications for normative obligation that are strictly connected to internal legislative system mechanisms. CCCEV is closer to our goal, but the convoluted and complex linguistic formula of the temporal parameters included in the legislation make CCCEV inadequate for capturing all the different sophisticated edge cases.

6   Requirement and Action

A Requirement is a fragment of an official legislative source in a given version (linguistic and in time) that includes a reporting requirement. Each Requirement produces at least an Action. In the case of multiple Action, they could be related using rrmv:isRelated (for simple relationships) or rrmv:hasNext (if they are repetitive RR with frequency). A Requirement can be related to other Requirement(s) using eli:releted_To in case of semantic connection (delegated act) or eli:cites in case of explicit citation. In case there is a modification of the provision, we annotate the Requirement with eli:changes property. Sometimes, the RR needs to be integrated with other portions of the legislation to complete the meaning (e.g., some conditions could be expressed in other articles). In this case the end-user can annotate the Action with implicit knowledge or summarise another portion of the legislation. We use oa:Annotation for this purpose and to distinguish subjective interpretation to an authoritative legislative source (Fig. 1).

---

[19] https://unsceb-hlcm.github.io/onto-undo/.
[20] https://www.w3.org/TR/annotation-model/.
[21] https://www.w3.org/TR/owl-time/.
[22] https://semiceu.github.io/CCCEV/releases/2.00/.

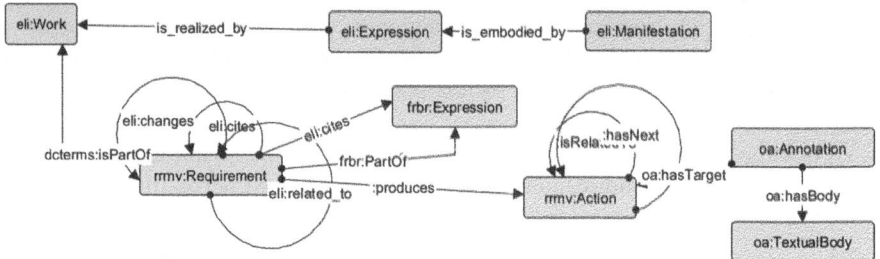

Fig. 1. Requirement and Action Module.

7 Agent and Role

The RR is acted by Agent(s) that play a particular Role (e.g., rapporteur, propo-
nent, delegated) with a particular RoleType related to the action (e.g., addresser,
addressee). Agent could be Person, Organization, Group. The Agent is associated to AgentCategory (e.g., public administration, institutions, SMES, group of
farmers). The AgentRole can change over time for this reason (e.g., ESMA was
funded in 2011, before this agency was nominated CESR Committee of European Securities Regulator CESR in 2001). For this reason, the Agent also has
the temporal parameters (Fig. 2).

8 Temporal Entity Specifications

The RRs have a temporal provision that specifies the deadline for the actions.
The statistic analysis of the sample of European Legislation provides useful
information about the frequency of some temporal linguistic formulae. Most

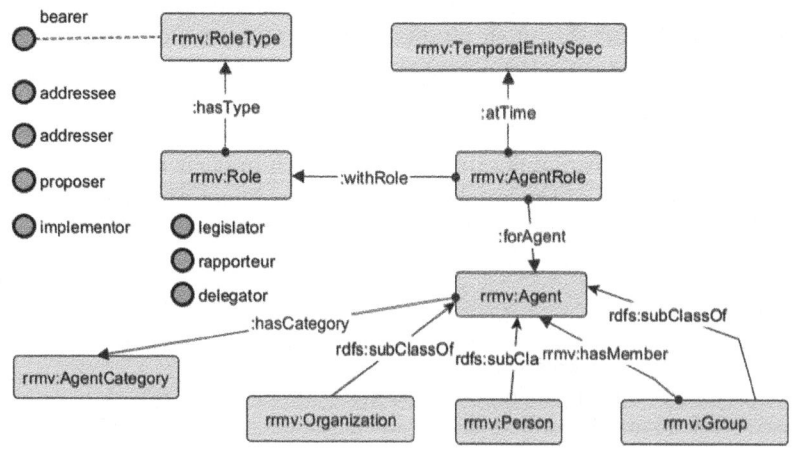

Fig. 2. Agent and Role.

notably, 27% of our sample reports "by date", the 15% "no later than". In the 3 we can see the statistics over 82 temporal linguistic expressions included in 95 RR, in 86 paragraphs in Fig. 3. The dataset is a sub-set of the larger one composed by 529 documents of EU Legislation.

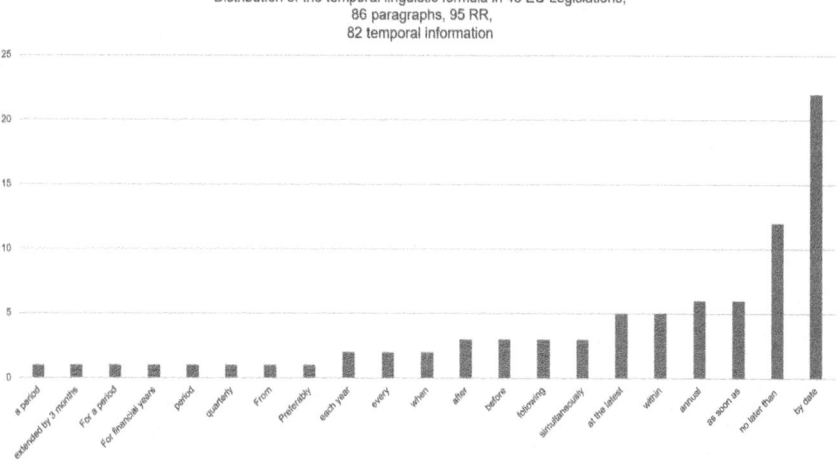

Fig. 3. Statistics of temporal linguistic formulae.

We can distinguish four macro-typologies of temporal parameters:

- Instant: By 1 July 2020, From 3 November 2013, No later than 8 December 2012. In this case we have this example:
- Interval: At the latest within 7 calendar days, From 2025 to 2028,
- Duration: Within 180 days, For 6 months, Not later than 10 years
- Frequency: Annual, Every year by the end of February.

In addition to these categories, we find the ending or starting of an interval unspecified or dependent on an external event (e.g., enter into force date of the regulation, the signature of an agreement, the accession of a country in the European Union). For this reason, we have two booleans for identifying these forms and to monitor over time the evolution of the external events (Figs. 4, 5, 6, 7, 8 and 9) .

9   Execution of Action Planned

The RR is a command to do something, but the execution happens in the real world and in a different dimension with respect to the meta-level of normative specifications written in the legal sources. Additionally, some temporal parameters depend on external events not self-contained inside of the legislative system

```
rrmv:atTime :TemporalEntity_1 [
        a :Instant;
        rrmv:before "2020-07-01"^^xsd:date;
        rrmv:hasFunction "deadline";
        oa:annotation "By 1 July 2020";


].
```

```
rrmv:atTime :TemporalEntity_1 [
        a :Instant;
        rrmv:after "2013-11-03"^^xsd:date;
        rrmv:hasFunction "deadline";
        oa:annotation "From  3 November 2013";


].
```

Fig. 4. Instant ttl representation.

```
rrmv:atTime :TemporalEntity_1 [
        a :Interval [
        rrmv:hasStart "2023-02-01"^^xsd:date;
        rrmv:before  :Duration_1 [
        rrmv:hasDuration "P7D"^^xsd:duration;
        ];
        rrmv:hasFunction "deadline";
        oa:annotation "At the latest within 7 calendar days;";

].
```

Fig. 5. Representation of Interval in ttl.

```
rrmv:atTime :TemporalEntity_1 [
        a:Duration [
        rrmv:starts "2011-04-24"^^xsd:date;
        rrmv:hasDuration "P5Y"^^xsd:duration;
        ];
        rrmv:hasFunction "deadline";
        oa:annotation "for a period of 5 years from 24 April 2011"

].
```

Fig. 6. Representation of Duration in ttl.

http://data.europa.eu/eli/reg/2005/396/2008-04-10

Article 33

Submission of the Annual Report on Pesticide Residues to the Committee

The Commission shall submit the Annual Report on Pesticide Residues to the Committee referred to in Article 45(1) without delay, for review and recommendations on any necessary measures to be taken regarding reported infringements of the MRLs set out in Annexes II and III.

```
rrmv:atTime :TemporalEntity_1 [
        a :Instant; [
            rrmv:isUnSpecified "1"^^xsd:Boolean;
            rrmv:hasFrequency [
                    rrmv:value "4"^^xsd:integer; (4 times)
                    rrmv:unit "P2Y"^^xsd:duration
            ]
        rrmv:hasFunction "deadline";
        oa: annotation "Annual Report on Pesticide Residues to the Committee referred to in Article 45(1) without
delay";

].
rrmv:Request_1 a rrmv:Request;
        eli:cites http://data.europa.eu/eli/reg/2005/396/2008-04-10/art_45/para_1
    .
```

Fig. 7. Representation of Frequency in ttl.

```
rrmv:atTime :TemporalEntity_1 [
        a :Duration [
        rrmv:start"????"^^xsd:date; -->rrmv:externalEvent "1"^^xsd:Boolean;
        rrmv:before "P180M"^^xsd:duration;
        ];
        rrmv:hasFunction "deadline";
        oa:annotation "Within 180 days of receipt of a recommendation from the evaluating competent authority";

] .<f
```

```
rrmv:atTime :TemporalEntity_1 [
        a :Duration [
        rrmv:start"????"^^xsd:date; -->rrmv:externalEvent "1"^^xsd:Boolean;
        rrmv:before "P10Y"^^xsd:duration;
        ];
        rrmv:isUnSpecified "1"^^xsd:Boolean;
        rrmv:hasFunction "deadline";
        oa:annotation "Not later than 10 years after the entry into force of this Regulation";

] .
```

Fig. 8. Representation in ttl of unspecified and external event case.

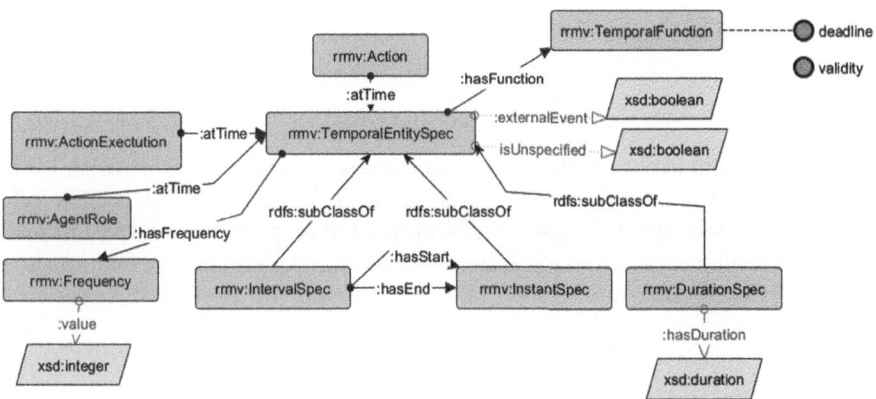

Fig. 9. Modelling of temporal linguistic formulae.

process. For this reason, it is necessary to have a mechanism for monitoring the real execution of the Action that could update the repository of RRs, tracking which ones have been completed or are in different statuses (e.g., suspended for COVID).

10   Evaluation

To evaluate our RRMV ontology, we have selected 48 European norms, for a total of 86 paragraphs, 96 RR, 82 temporal provision[23].

---

[23] The dataset is available here: https://gitlab.com/CIRSFID/eulegislation-reporting-requests.

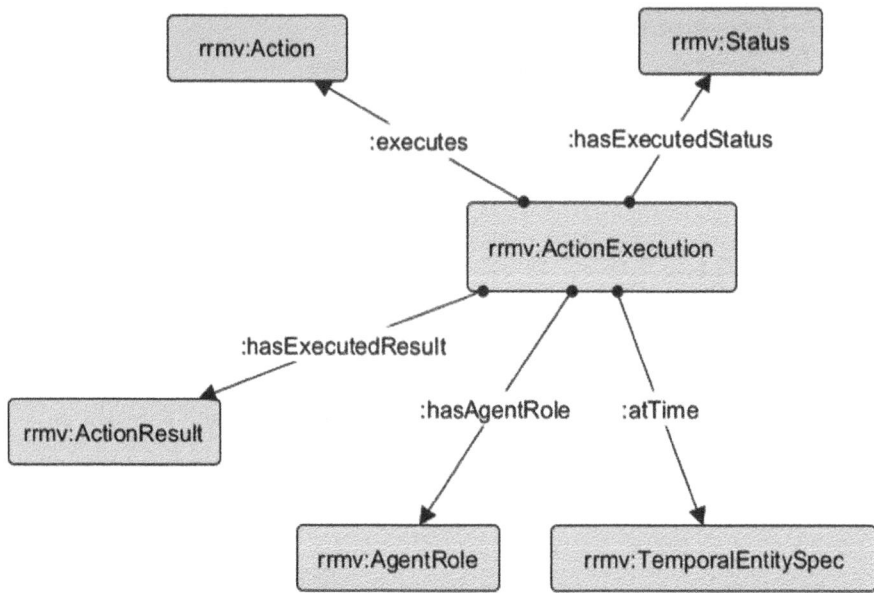

Fig. 10. Execution Module.

After the annotation in RDF, we have connected this repository with CEL-LAR. CELLAR is a repository of metadata concerning the EUR-LEX official European gazette. European Publications Office provides a SPARQL endpoint for querying the legal information, including the modificatory relationships between articles[24] and information in order to track the modifications for each article[25].

---

[24] https://op.europa.eu/en/web/cellar/cellar-data/metadata/knowledge-graph.
[25] https://graphs-rrmv-a4a999.gitlab.io/.

The Knowledge Graph of all the articles of the Directive 2014/65/EU of the European Parliament and the Council of 15 May 2014. In Fig. 10, the red nodes mean article modified, the orange nodes mean article with RR, and the green nodes means article with RR and modified (Fig. 11).

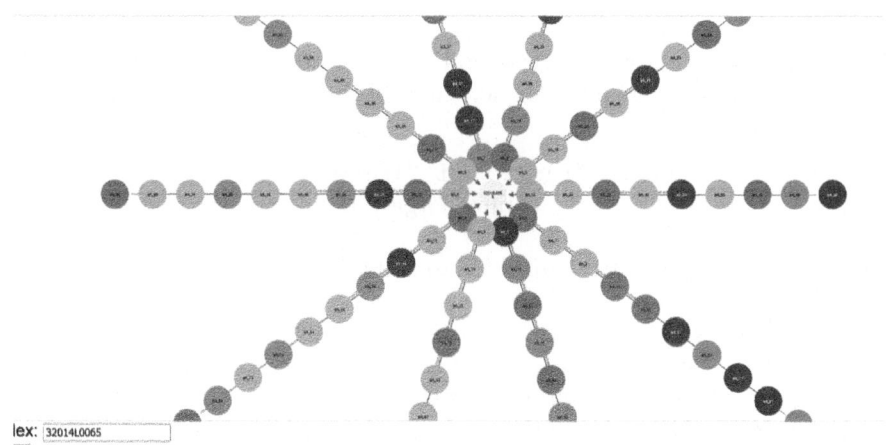

lex: 32014L0065

Fig. 11. Knowledge Graph Directive 2014/65/EU

In Fig. 11 KG can be navigated to explode the detail of RR, underlining the connection between RR and modificatory new legislation.

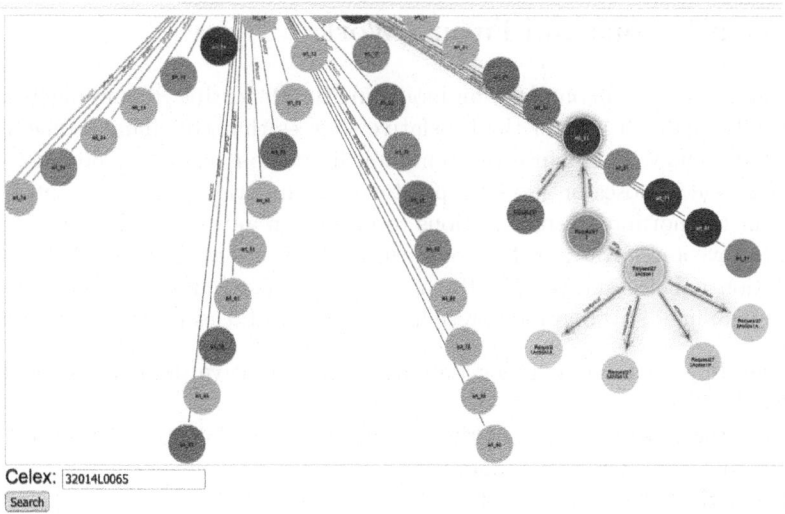

Celex: 32014L0065
Search

Fig. 12. Detail of the Knowledge Graph related to the art. 51 with an RR modified on 2024.

We have, in this manner, demonstrated the effectiveness of the RRMV to track the RRs over time, to answer to the queries of the competencies questions, and to cope with the goals under a functional point of view.

11   Queries

We have tested the ontology with several SPARQL queries to evaluate the Competencies questions. Here an example. "Give all the RRs that have frequency as TemporalEntity".

```
SELECT ?requirement ?text ?uri ?frequency ?unit
?value ?action ?result ?time ?agentRole ?agent ?date
WHERE {
?requirement rrmv:produces ?action ;
rrmv:hasAnnotation ?text ;
rrmv:hasFrequency ?frequency ;
rrmv:hasUri ?uri .
?frequency rrmv:hasTemporalEntity ?unit ;
rrmv:value ?value .
?action rrmv:hasResult ?result ;
rrmv:atTime ?time ;
rrmv:hasAgentRole ?agentRole .
?time cccev:starttime ?date .
?agentRole rrmv:forAgent ?agent .
}
```

12   Conclusions and Future Work

This paper presents an ontology for modelling the Reporting Requirements (RR), a specially-qualified part of the legislative sources that commands some agents to perform some actions in given temporal limitations. The convoluted legislative language imposes on model sophisticated temporal options to capture and represent the normative specifications to permit an automatic checking of these special provisions. Tracking RRs over time allows the monitoring of the Better Legislation policies and to offer to the decision-makers an effective tool for the policy planning. This ontology presented several obstacles that we have tackled:

- Integration with the existing ontologies in legislative domain like ELI and FRBR.
- Model the legal text and, in the meantime, the human being interpretation from the legal operators (annotation).
- Anchor the correct version of the legislative source.
- Represent the different temporal parameters.
- Associate the correct Agent paying a specific Role.

- Design an ontology reusable for different scenarios (e.g., publication, monitoring, policy building) and for different legislative systems (e.g., Member State legislation).

However, there are some challenges that we should develop in the future:

- Go in deep in the model of the Execution part.
- Better model the role of the normative references inside of each element when the link expresses temporal parameters.
- Detect the external events and report the changes in the RR.

Acknowledgment. This project is developed thanks to the cooperation with the JRC of the European Commission, SEMIC group, DG Informatics. In particular, we are deeply grateful to Cecile Guasch and Alessio Nardin of DIGIT for their valuable contributions to the current version of the RRMV ontology and for the constant support of the SORTIS project. This project is conducted with the support of the European Commission funds within ERC HyperModeLex. Grant agreement ID: 101055185.

References

1. Anim, J., Robaldo, L., Wyner, A.Z.: A SHACL-based approach for enhancing automated compliance checking with RDF data. Information **15**(12) (2024). https://doi.org/10.3390/info15120759. https://www.mdpi.com/2078-2489/15/12/759
2. Barabucci, G., Cervone, L., Palmirani, M., Peroni, S., Vitali, F.: Multi-layer markup and ontological structures in Akoma Ntoso. In: AICOL Workshops (2009). https://api.semanticscholar.org/CorpusID:10112235
3. Cimmino, A., Cano-Benito, J., GarcíÂɲa-Castro, R.: Open digital rights enforcement framework (ODRE): from descriptive to enforceable policies. Comput. Secur. **150**, 104282 (2025).https://doi.org/10.1016/j.cose.2024.104282. https://www.sciencedirect.com/science/article/pii/S0167404824005881
4. Kebede, M.G., Sileno, G., Van Engers, T.: A critical reflection on ODRL. In: AI Approaches to the Complexity of Legal Systems XI-XII: AICOL International Workshops 2018 and 2020: AICOL-XI@JURIX 2018, AICOL-XII@JURIX 2020, XAILA@JURIX 2020, Revised Selected Papers, pp. 48–61. Springer-Verlag (2020). https://doi.org/10.1007/978-3-030-89811-3_4
5. Palmirani, M., Liga, D.: Derogations analysis of European legislation through hybrid AI approach. In: Electronic Government and the Information Systems Perspective: 11th International Conference, EGOVIS 2022, Vienna, Austria, 22–24 August 2022, Proceedings, pp. 123–137. Springer-Verlag (2022). https://doi.org/10.1007/978-3-031-12673-4_9
6. Palmirani, M., Martoni, M., Rossi, A., Bartolini, C., Robaldo, L.: PrOnto: privacy ontology for legal reasoning. In: Kő, A., Francesconi, E. (eds.) EGOVIS 2018. LNCS, vol. 11032, pp. 139–152. Springer, Cham (2018). https://doi.org/10.1007/978-3-319-98349-3_11
7. Palmirani, M., Nuzzolese, A.G., Poggi, F., Nicholson, J., Estevez, J.: Tracking who reporting requests using hybrid AI. In: Proceedings of the 17th International Conference on Theory and Practice of Electronic Governance, ICEGOV 2024, pp. 139–146. Association for Computing Machinery, New York(2024). https://doi.org/10.1145/3680127.3680224

8. Palmirani, M., Vitali, F.: Akoma-Ntoso for legal documents. In: Sartor, G., Palmirani, M., Francesconi, E., Biasiotti, M.A. (eds.) Legislative XML for the Semantic Web: Principles, Models, Standards for Document Management, pp. 75–100. Springer Netherlands, Dordrecht (2011).https://doi.org/10.1007/978-94-007-1887-6_6
9. Peroni, S., Palmirani, M., Vitali, F.: UNDO: the united nations system document ontology. In: d'Amato, C., et al. (eds.) ISWC 2017. LNCS, vol. 10588, pp. 175–183. Springer, Cham (2017). https://doi.org/10.1007/978-3-319-68204-4_18

Digital Credentialing Framework for Continuing Professional Development: Global Practices and Integration

Pricilla Faye T. Simon[1,2], Chutiporn Anutariya[1]($^{\boxtimes}$), and Gaurav Dixit[2]($^{\boxtimes}$)

[1] Asian Institute of Technology, Pathum Thani, Thailand
{pricillafayesimon,chutiporn}@ait.ac.th
[2] Indian Institute of Technology Roorkee, Roorkee, India
gauravdixit.fdm@iitr.ac.in

Abstract. Digital credentialing offers a promising solution to enhance transparency, efficiency, and trust in Continuing Professional Development (CPD) systems. However, most existing frameworks are designed for education or e-governance and do not fully address the unique needs of CPD, such as credential validation, stakeholder coordination, and regulatory compliance. This study reviews existing frameworks and evaluates their relevance to CPD using six key criteria. Findings reveal significant gaps in lifecycle management, adoption strategies, and policy alignment. In response, a CPD-specific conceptual framework is proposed, incorporating stakeholder integration, secure technology infrastructure, validation mechanisms, and governance. The framework provides a structured foundation for implementing verifiable credentials in CPD and supports long-term goals in professional mobility and lifelong learning.

Keywords: Digital Credentialing · Continuing Professional Development (CPD) · Lifelong Learning · Digital Transformation

1 Introduction

Maintaining professional competence over time is a key aim of Continuing Professional Development (CPD), ensuring that professionals remain effective well beyond their initial qualifications. As part of this process, individuals engage in various learning activities such as seminars, workshops, online courses, and self-directed study. Rooted in the concept of lifelong learning, CPD encourages continuous improvement and adaptability in response to evolving industry demands. Regular participation also reinforces accountability and helps sustain public trust by ensuring practitioners stay informed and skilled. Yet despite differences in implementation across countries, the core purpose of CPD remains consistent: to support ongoing professional growth and excellence throughout a person's career. However, the way CPD is regulated varies widely among countries, often reflecting differences in professional standards, legal frameworks, and cultural perspectives on learning.

A. Kő et al. (Eds.): EGOVIS 2025, LNCS 16049, pp. 33–47, 2026.
https://doi.org/10.1007/978-3-032-02225-7_3

1.1 Continuing Professional Development

CPD is a structured form of lifelong learning designed to ensure that professionals maintain their competence and remain up-to-date in their fields. Though the structure and enforcement vary by discipline and region, CPD consistently aims to safeguard the quality and accountability of professional practice [1]. Regulatory bodies typically define the minimum number of CPD units required for license renewal, with professionals earning credits through various formal and informal learning methods. These activities are then assessed and converted into CPD points based on a matrix established by the licensing authority [2]. If requirements are unmet, some jurisdictions allow an extension period for compliance, reinforcing continuous development while upholding regulatory standards.

In many professional sectors, the structure of CPD involves three main stakeholders: the professional, the training provider, and the licensing organization. This setup is also reflected in the Philippine context, where professionals are expected to earn CPD units through accredited learning activities to renew their licenses. Training providers, on the other hand, are tasked with delivering CPD programs, issuing certificates, and reporting attendance to the licensing bodies. Meanwhile, organizations like the Professional Regulation Commission (PRC) are responsible for setting the CPD requirements, accrediting programs, and validating whether professionals have complied with the necessary units. Each stakeholder plays a critical role in ensuring that the process supports professional growth and regulatory compliance.

1.2 CPD Implementation

CPD requirements differ by country and profession. Some mandate them across all sectors, while others apply them selectively. This discussion centers on the healthcare field, particularly nursing, where CPD tends to be more heavily enforced. Given the rapid pace of medical innovation and the high stakes of public health, healthcare often acts as the forerunner in formalizing CPD structures.

CPD requirements differ widely in structure and intensity across countries, particularly in the healthcare sector. While Italy [4] mandates 150 credits over three years—suggesting a high workload, countries like South Africa [5] and Singapore [3] impose 15 points or hours annually, promoting continuous yearly engagement. These annual models enforce a stricter cadence, where professionals must meet CPD obligations each year or risk non-renewal of their licenses. Australia [6] follows a similar pattern, requiring 20 h annually for registered nurses. In contrast, the Philippines [7] and the United Kingdom [8] adopt a triennial system, requiring 45 CPD points and 35 h (20 of which must be participatory), respectively. These models allow flexibility, though they risk encouraging last-minute compliance near the end of the renewal cycle. The United States, exemplified by California's two-year cycle requiring 30 contact hours [9], offers a middle ground, balancing flexibility with accountability. Italy's model is notable not only for its volume but also for how deeply CPD is embedded into national policy, reflecting a strong commitment to structured lifelong learning.

The effectiveness of any CPD system hinges on collaboration among professionals, providers, and regulators. While professionals complete accredited activities and providers issue certificates or submit records, many countries still rely on manual, paper-based processes. These outdated systems cause inefficiencies, delays, and increase the risk of fraud. Without a secure, interoperable digital framework for credential verification, regulatory bodies face administrative burdens and reduced credibility, underscoring the urgent need for streamlined digital solutions.

1.3   CPD Technologies and Implementation Challenges

As CPD becomes increasingly vital for maintaining professional competence, various technologies have emerged to support the documentation, verification, and tracking of learning activities. Traditional paper-based documentation, still widely used in low-tech environments, requires licensees to submit physical certificates and training records for verification. While straightforward, this method is highly susceptible to fraud, especially when lacking security features like embossed seals or tamper-proof markers, and places a significant administrative burden on regulators [1]. In contrast, online portfolios allow professionals to manage their CPD records digitally, with some platforms integrating directly with training providers like MOOCs to receive digital credentials. However, these systems often face compatibility issues due to inconsistent credential formats, data standards, and a lack of integration with regulatory databases [10].

Other models, such as trainer submission systems, streamline verification by having CPD providers directly report attendance to the licensing body, allowing automatic crediting of CPD points. This approach reduces the risk of falsification and administrative delays but functions best in centralized or closed ecosystems where all training providers are accredited [11]. More recently, verifiable credentials (VCs) linked to decentralized identifiers (DIDs) have shown significant promise. These cryptographically secure credentials offer real-time verification without the need to contact the issuer and enhance data security and portability [12]. However, adoption remains limited due to a lack of technical capacity, unified standards, and enabling policies, especially in CPD-specific contexts. While these technologies offer improvements in isolation, fragmented implementation across platforms and providers continues to challenge the development of a cohesive and scalable CPD ecosystem [14].

1.4   Digital Credentialing

Digital credentialing involves the use of machine-readable digital documents to verify an individual's qualifications, achievements, or licenses. Unlike traditional paper-based credentials, digital formats are issued, stored, and shared electronically, offering advantages in terms of accessibility, remote verification, and integration with digital systems [15]. Institutions are increasingly adopting digital credentials to overcome the limitations of paper documents, such as physical degradation, loss, and vulnerability to forgery. However, this transition introduces new challenges, including cybersecurity risks, technological dependence, and unequal access—especially in underserved regions with limited internet connectivity or digital infrastructure [14].

Despite these challenges, digital credentials offer numerous benefits: they can be distributed quickly, stored in cloud systems, easily searched, and shared across platforms—enhancing both convenience and environmental sustainability. Their growing use is largely driven by the rise of online learning and micro-credentialing. Ramírez-Montoya et al. [10] observed that digital certificates serve as motivational incentives for learners completing MOOCs and short courses. To support trust and standardization, [14] proposed a comprehensive digital credentialing ecosystem composed of seven actors: users, providers, awarding bodies, quality assurance agencies, evaluators, verification entities, and convening organizations. By this, the stakeholders play crucial roles in ensuring the interoperability of credentials. Which is essential in a globalized professional and educational landscape.

2   Research Problem

In the current landscape of CPD, digital technologies have been increasingly adopted globally. However, there remains a lack of clarity on how does the existing digital credentialing systems can be effectively adapted to support proper CPD Implementation. Currently, practices vary widely across different countries. Although there are several frameworks that exist in licensing and e-governance, only few directly address the unique verification and coordination needed for CPD systems. This study explores how existing global practices and digital systems can be analyzed to create a framework that supports the use of digital credentials in CPD for license renewal.

3   Methodology

To explore the existing frameworks that are currently guiding the adoption of digital credentialing in CPD, this study employed a Systematic Literature Review (SLR) using the structured methodology proposed by Okoli and Schabram [16]. It mainly emphasized the theoretical and empirical rigor through eight detailed phases: planning, selection, extraction, quality appraisal, synthesis, and presentation. The review focused on literature that are of English Language and published between 2016 and 2024. Keywords used are: "Digital Credentials," "Verifiable Credentials," "CPD", and "Micro-Credentials". Search was done across databases like IEEE, Scopus, Web of Science, and search engine Google Scholar. These were then filtered through title and abstract screening. After a comprehensive screening, 10 studies were selected for in-depth analysis. These were chosen based alignment with credentialing, licensing, or document verification systems using digital credentialing systems in various international and regulatory contexts.

4 Results

4.1 Adoption of Digital Credentialing in CPD

The adoption and implementation of different digital credentialing systems for CPD is evidently seen in Table 1. It illustrates how different countries manage the submission and evaluation of CPD requirements, particularly in the context of digitization and integration. Predominantly, countries such as Singapore, South Africa, Australia, the United States, and the United Kingdom maintain a largely manual process despite utilizing digital submission portals. Professionals in these contexts would upload PDFs or images of CPD certificates, which are then subject to manual evaluation by regulatory bodies.

While this digital interface has improved accessibility, it fails to alleviate the burden on the administrative side to evaluate each credential. It is also vulnerable to inefficiencies and credential fraud, which is a wide concern in CPD systems [14]. The persistence of manual evaluation does indicate that regulatory systems are yet to fully capitalize on the use of fully digital verification infrastructure.

In contrast, countries like the Philippines and Italy has exhibited comparatively progressive approaches. This is evident by their incorporation of system-based grading mechanism into their CPD evaluation framework. The Professional Regulation Commission (PRC) of the Philippines employs a semi-automated model in which CPD providers upload attendance lists directly into an evaluation portal. This enables automated credit allocation for verified participants. Similarly, Italy's Commissione Nazionale per la Formazione Continua (CNFC) integrates partial automation in its review process. Blending system-graded assessments with manual oversight. These models represents and early effort toward the adoption of Digital Credentials within the CPD system. However, even in these cases, full adoption of cryptographically verifiable credentials, such as those adhering to the W3C's Verifiable Credentials standard, remains unrealized [12, 13].

One pathway to accelerate the full integration of digital credentials to CPD system is the implementation of a structured digital adoption framework. This will mainly address the technological, organizational, and policy related changes. Enabling regulatory bodies to systematically plan, deploy, and scale digital credentialing solutions.

4.2 Current Digital Adoption Framework

The digital adoption framework has long been a tool for organizations to guide the structured integration of technology into their operations, ensuring that digital tools are effectively integrated. It this context, it can facilitate the sustainable integration of digital credentialing across stakeholders such as licensing bodies, training providers, and professionals [17, 18].

To examine the applicability of existing digital transformation strategies to CPD, this study conducted a comparative analysis of ten adoption frameworks from diverse sectors. These include sectors like education, identity verification,

Table 1. CPD Submission and Evaluation Process by Country

Country/ Region	Regulatory Board	Process of Requirement Submission	Evaluation	Integration of DC in the Evaluation of CPD
ASEAN (Singapore)	Singapore Nursing Board	Upload PDF/Photo of CPD evidence	Manual Evaluation of Digital Document	No
ASEAN (Philippines)	Professional Regulatory Commission	1. CPD Provider uploads list of attendees to evaluation website 2. Upload PDF/Photo of CPD evidence	System-Graded CPD Points for verified attendees	Yes
Africa (South Africa)	South African Nursing Council	Upload PDF/Photo of CPD evidence	Manual Evaluation of Digital Document	No
Australia	Australia Health Practitioner Regulatory Agency	Upload v PDF/Photo of CPD evidence	Manual Evaluation of Digital Document	No
European Union (Italy)	Commissione Nazionale per la Formazione Continua	1. CPD Provider uploads list of attendees to evaluation website 2. Evaluated by CNFC	System-Graded CPD Points for verified attendees	Partially Automated
United States (California)	California Board of Registered Nursing	CEU Certificate Information (Manual input to the website)	Manual Evaluation of Digital Document	No
United Kingdom	Nursing & Midwifery Council	Upload Log Sheet of CPD taken and Evidences	Manual Evaluation of Digital Document	No

and public governance. Although not originally intended for CPD, these frameworks offer valuable structural elements and best practices for building a credentialing model suited to professional development [10,21]. Using evaluation criteria adapted from Harrington & O'Neill [17] and CPD-related literature, each framework was assessed on five key dimensions: stakeholder coordination, platform identification, strategy design, artifact management, and validation support. These are then mapped against a four-level matrix (see Table 2) to determine relevance and implementation readiness in the CPD context.

Table 2. Grading Scale for Digital Credentialing and Verification Framework

Level	Description
Not Identified	The framework does not mention or address this aspect at all.
General Mention	The framework acknowledges the aspect in a broad sense, using vague or general language without explanation or implementation detail.
Partially Specified	The framework includes specific elements related to the aspect, but lacks comprehensive explanation, structure, or actionable guidance.
Clearly Defined	The framework thoroughly addresses the aspect with clear components, structured processes, and practical or technical details that indicate readiness for implementation or replication.

Evaluation of Frameworks. One key aspect in building an effective Continuing Professional Development (CPD) system is the presence of a strong and well-defined adoption framework. As digital credentialing technologies advance, their adoption in professional licensing contexts must be guided by clear strategies and validated mechanisms. To explore this, ten existing frameworks across education, governance, and credential verification were compared, as presented in Table 3. While not all were designed specifically for CPD, they present valuable features that can inform the development of a tailored model.

This study applies five key criteria: (1) tri-stakeholder coordination, (2) technology platform identification, (3) adoption strategy design, (4) digital artifact management, and (5) support for artifact validation and recognition. These dimensions collectively reflect the structural integrity needed for a robust and scalable digital credentialing system.

Tri-Stakeholder Coordination. All ten frameworks reviewed acknowledge the importance of incorporating professionals, providers, and regulators in credentialing ecosystems. Their inclusion supports system transparency, aligned standards, and better oversight—essential qualities in CPD environments. This tri-stakeholder model creates accountability and enhances credential portability.

However, while this principle is well recognized, the detailed processes for how these actors interact remain vague in several models. For example, Balaban et al. (2019) and Joshi et al. (2018) recognize the need for coordination but fall short of explaining how data is shared or decisions are co-managed. This can be a significant hurdle in CPD implementation, which demands real-time collaboration for license verification and renewal.

Technology Platform Identification. Several frameworks like those by Mazumder et al. (2021), VS et al. (2016), and Satybaldy et al. (2022) excels in having robust digital infrastructure. These includes technologies like blockchain, self-sovereign identity protocols, and decentralized databased. Their platform does not only focus on being technically comprehensive but also being transparent in their configuration.

On the flip side, other frameworks like Joshi et al. (2018) and Balaban et al. (2019) offer general references to technology use. While the intention is positive, the lack of clarity in the system architecture may lead to implementation delays and confusion. Specially in the CPD context, where auditability and compliance are non-negotiable

Adoption Strategy Design. Selvaratnam et al. (2024) provided one of the most strategic outlines, incorporating phased rollouts, stakeholder training, and evaluation mechanisms. Their work stands out for addressing human and organizational aspects of digital change. This is key to ensuring a smooth transition in CPD adoption.

Conversely, some frameworks like Ivic et al. (2023) and Ghani et al. (2022) lean heavily into the technical domain but do not present comprehensive adoption pathways. These can pose as a challenges for real-world application. Where clear adoption strategy guides the organization in proper integration of the system.

Digital Artifact Management. Mazumder et al. (2021) and Satybaldy et al. (2022) demonstrate significant attention to the full credential lifecycle. From the issuance and user access to revocation and storage. Their emphasis on metadata use and secure access control presents a reliable approach for CPD contexts, which often demand records over extended periods.

Still, some models, like Ivic et al. (2023), reference credential storage only in passing. Without detailed retention policies or governance structures, these systems might struggle with scale or long-term data accuracy.

Support for Artifact Assessment, Validation and Recognition. Selvaratnam et al. (2024) and Iatrellis et al. (2024) contribute significantly by integrating assessment rubrics and linking credentials to formal qualifications. Their work is particularly relevant to CPD, where the recognition of professional learning activities must align with licensing benchmarks. Their frameworks offer insight into implementation of competency mapping and automated validation.

Others, like VS et al. (2016) and Joshi et al. (2018), do not elaborate beyond general document verification. While this is a good starting point, CPD systems require more nuanced validation layers to ensure that digital credentials reflect not just participation but skill attainment. Enhancing this area can significantly boost credibility and regulatory compliance.

Table 3. Analysis of Existing Frameworks for Digital Credentialing and Verification

Author	Tri-Stakeholder Coordination	Technology Platform Identification	Adoption Strategy Design	Digital Artifact Management	Support for Artifact Assessment, Validation & Recognition
Ivic, A., et al. (2023) [23]	Yes	Clearly Defined	Not Identified	General Mention	General Mention
Mazumder, M.M.H.U., et al. (2021) [21]	Yes	Clearly Defined	General Mention	Clearly Defined	Partially Specified
VS, R., et al. (2016) [24]	Yes	Clearly Defined	General Mention	Partially Specified	General Mention
Ghani, R.F., et al. (2022) [25]	Yes	Clearly Defined	General Mention	Partially Specified	Partially Specified
Satybaldy, A., et al. (2022) [22]	Yes	Clearly Defined	General Mention	Clearly Defined	Partially Specified
Mühle, A., et al. (2023) [13]	Yes	Clearly Defined	General Mention	Partially Specified	Partially Specified
Joshi, P.R., et al. (2018) [20]	Yes	General Mention	Partially Specified	Partially Specified	Partially Specified
Balaban, I., et al. (2019) [19]	Yes	Partially Specified	General Mention	Partially Specified	Partially Specified
Selvaratnam, R.M., et al. (2024) [18]	Yes	Partially Specified	Partially Specified	Partially Specified	Partially Specified
Iatrellis, O., et al. (2024) [26]	Yes	General Mention	Clearly Defined	General Mention	Partially Specified

While these existing frameworks offer valuable insights, they fall short in addressing the specific needs of CPD systems. There is a lack of clear mechanism for stakeholder coordination, comprehensive adoption strategies, and validation processes. These gaps underscore the need for a dedicated CPD-focused framework which ensures secure, scalable, and interoperable digital credentialing aligned with regulatory requirements.

4.3 Proposed CPD Digital Credentialing Conceptual Framework

Drawing from the findings of this study and in response to the gaps identified in current digital credentialing models, this paper puts forward a conceptual framework specifically tailored to the integration of verifiable digital credentials within CPD systems for professional license renewal. As visualized in Fig. 1, the framework integrates five essential domains: Stakeholder Integration, Technology Infrastructure, Credential Lifecycle Management, Validation & Recognition Layer, and Governance & Policy Alignment. This collectively form a dynamic system supporting secure, efficient, and transparent CPD credentialing. The proposed framework seeks to address this shortcoming by offering a holistic, secure, and scalable structure that can be adapted across different professional sectors.

Stakeholder Integration. In the CPD ecosystem, integration among professionals (learners), training providers (issuers), and regulatory bodies (verifiers) is essential to ensure the integrity, efficiency, and recognition of credentialing processes. However, current systems remain fragmented, often relying on partial digital tools like email submissions or PDF uploads that require manual verification, resulting in inefficiencies and heightened fraud risk. A fully integrated system requires interoperable infrastructure that enables real-time communication. For instance, allowing providers to directly submit validated CPD credits to a licensee's digital portfolio, accessible to regulators during license renewal. This integration becomes even more critical in cross-border contexts, such as within ASEAN or the EU, where the lack of system interoperability can hinder professional mobility and recognition of credentials. Therefore, a stakeholder-integrated framework aligned with international standards is essential to support both local coordination and global portability of CPD credentials.

Technology Infrastructure. Technology infrastructure is the foundation of any effective digital credentialing system, especially in Continuing Professional Development (CPD), where credentials must be secure, verifiable, and accessible over time. The proposed framework underscores the need for scalable, interoperable systems incorporating technologies such as blockchain, decentralized identifiers (DIDs), and encrypted databases to ensure reliability and trust. To be effective, this infrastructure must support cross-platform compatibility, long-term data retention, and stable performance across diverse digital environments. Equally important is ensuring accessibility in low-resource settings through lightweight, mobile-friendly designs and secure authentication features. A robust infrastructure not only enables efficient credentialing but also strengthens the system's credibility and inclusivity in professional development.

Credential Lifecycle Management. Credential Lifecycle Management encompasses the end-to-end process to which a digital credential experiences. It starts from the issuance, maintenance, updating, archiving, and revocation. With this, it is important that the records remain secure, verifiable, and accessible over extended periods. Which is crucial in licensing context which span years.

It is proposed that each credential should carry embedded metadata. Examples of these are learning outcomes, timestamps, issuing authority, and expiration. This can then be readily available for professionals and regulatory bodies to access. Furthermore, long-term data stewardship sets CPD systems apart from standard credentialing. Features like expiration tracking, automated renewal reminders, and secure audit trails are also important. More secure technologies can also be integrated like blockchain-based timestamping, and decentralized storage. Effective lifecycle management guarantees that CPD credentials remain trustworthy, compliant, and aligned with evolving professional standards.

Table 4. Proposed CPD Digital Credentialing Conceptual Framework

Component	Description	Key Features and Examples
Stakeholder Integration	Ensures that all concerns from stakeholders are taken into account for the improvement of the system. This results to a more integrated system between the stakeholders.	Seamless handover of credentials from training providers to professionals. Standardized accepted digital format for credentials
Technology Infrastructure	Refers to the technical backbone that ensures the CPD system is scalable, secure, and accessible across different environments.	Utilizes technologies such as blockchain, decentralized identifiers (DIDs), and encrypted databases; ensures cross-platform compatibility, lightweight mobile-ready design, and inclusive access for low-resource settings.
Credential Lifecycle Management	Covers the entire life of a digital credential from issuance to revocation, ensuring long-term usability and compliance.	Manages embedded metadata (e.g., timestamps, issuer, outcomes), enables expiration tracking, audit trails, secure archiving, and facilitates renewal and verification over multi-year licensing cycles.
Validation and Recognition	Ensures that issued credentials are both verifiable and recognized for professional mobility and regulatory purposes.	Employs machine-readable metadata for real-time validation, aligns credentials with national qualifications frameworks (NQFs) and international standards, and promotes acceptance by licensing bodies.
Governance and Policy Alignment	Provides regulatory and legal anchoring for the system, ensuring responsible implementation and cross-sector coordination.	Aligns with CPD laws and data protection regulations (e.g., GDPR), defines stakeholder responsibilities via standard operating procedures (SOPs), and fosters multi-level governance among regulatory agencies, government bodies, and accreditors.

Validation and Recognition Layer. The Validation & Recognition layer of the framework addresses two critical functions: confirming the authenticity and alignment of digital CPD credentials (validation), and ensuring their acceptance by regulatory bodies for licensure, advancement, or cross-border recognition (recognition). Most existing systems rely on manual validation or self-reported evidence, leading to inconsistencies and limited trust. To overcome this, the framework promotes the use of machine-readable metadata embedded in credentials—detailing issuer authority, learning outcomes, hours, and assessment methods—for automated, real-time validation. For broader recognition, credentials should align with national qualifications frameworks (NQFs) and, where possible, be interoperable with international standards to facilitate professional mobility. Through these mechanisms, this layer ensures that CPD credentials are both verifiable and widely accepted, reinforcing their value for career progression and regulatory compliance.

Governance and Policy Alignment. While technology provides the means to issue and verify credentials, it is governance and policy alignment that ensure these tools are implemented consistently, fairly, and in compliance with legal and professional standards. This layer anchors digital credentialing within the broader regulatory ecosystem by aligning practices with CPD legislation, national qualification frameworks, and data protection laws such as the Philippine Data Privacy Act or the EU's GDPR. A key gap in many existing frameworks is the weak integration of legal dimensions, which can hinder adoption despite technological readiness. To address this, the proposed framework introduces a multi-level governance model involving regulatory boards, government agencies, and accrediting institutions to promote participatory decision-making and cross-sectoral harmonization. It also emphasizes the creation of standard operating procedures (SOPs) to clearly define stakeholder roles and workflows. Embedding governance within the digital credentialing framework ensures not only legal compliance and institutional trust but also the adaptability of CPD systems to evolving professional requirements.

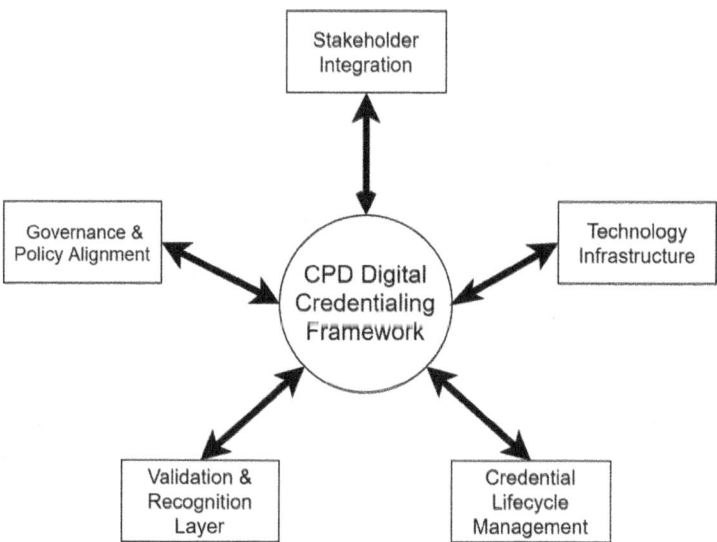

Fig. 1. Proposed CPD Digital Credentialing Conceptual Framework

The developed Conceptual framework offers a structured approach in implementing digital credentialing systems in CPD. The framework provides guiding principles that can support future policy formulation and the design of evaluation tools. Since the framework is general in nature, it allows for adaptation by various professional sectors. This promotes a more unified and holistic approach to managing CPD system as a whole.

4.4 Future Work

While the conceptual framework presented in this study establishes a foundational structure for digital credentialing in CPD, its full operationalization invites further scholarly exploration. Future research should focus on developing evaluative mechanisms that can systematically assess how institutions are progressing in adopting and institutionalizing the framework.

5 Conclusion

This study highlights the need for a dedicated framework to guide the integration of digital credentialing within Continuing Professional Development (CPD), addressing gaps not covered by existing systems in higher education or general credentialing. The proposed conceptual framework offers a structured, interoperable, and standards-aligned approach tailored to CPD's unique requirements—such as accurate tracking, fraud prevention, and dual support for learners and assessors. Emphasizing inclusivity, scalability, and adaptability, the framework serves as a practical foundation for institutions seeking to modernize their CPD processes. By clearly defining essential components and process areas, it supports the development of secure and effective credentialing systems that enhance the quality, transparency, and trustworthiness of professional development—ultimately ensuring alignment with the evolving needs of a dynamic global workforce.

Acknowledgments. This work was co-funded by the Department of Science and Technology (DOST), Philippines. The authors gratefully acknowledge the support provided in the pursuit of this research.

References

1. Murry, L.T., Hughes, P.J., Singh, R.M., Travlos, D.V., Engle, J.P.: Current and future opportunities and challenges in continuing pharmacy education: a 2024 update. Am. J. Pharm. Educ. **88**(10), 101281 (2024). https://doi.org/10.1016/j.ajpe.2024.101281
2. Grant, J., Zilling, T.: The good CPD guide: a practical guide to managed continuing professional development in medicine. CRC Press, Boca Raton (2017). https://doi.org/10.1201/9781315379623
3. Singapore Nursing Board. Criteria for the award of continuing professional education (CPE) points (2018)
4. Commissione Nazionale per la Formazione Continua. Criteri per l'assegnazione dei crediti alle attività ECM (2016)
5. South African Nursing Council. Continuing professional development framework for nurses and midwives in South Africa (2021)
6. Nursing and midwifery board of Australia. Registration standard: Continuing professional development (2016)

7. Professional Regulatory Commission. Professional regulatory commission res. 1032 s. 2017 (2017)
8. Nursing and Midwifery Council (NMC). The Code: Professional standards of practice and behaviour for nurses, midwives and nursing associates (2018). https://www.nmc.org.uk/globalassets/sitedocuments/nmc-publications/nmc-code.pdf
9. California Board of Registered Nursing: Nursing Practice Act - California Code of Regulation. Retrieved from (2018). https://www.rn.ca.gov/practice/npa.shtml
10. Ramirez Montoya, M.S., Martínez-Pérez, S., Rodriguez-Abitia, G., Lopez-Caudana, E.: Digital accreditations in MOOC-based training on sustainability: factors that influence terminal efficiency. Australasian J. Educ. Technol. **38**(2), pp. 162–180 (2022). https://doi.org/10.14742/ajet.7082
11. Merry, L., Castiglione, S.A., Rouleau, G.: Continuing professional development (CPD) system development, implementation, evaluation and sustainability for healthcare professionals in low- and lower-middle-income countries: a rapid scoping review. BMC Med. Educ. **23**, 498 (2023). https://doi.org/10.1186/s12909-023-04427-6
12. World wide web consortium (W3C): verifiable credentials data model 1.0: expressing verifiable information on the Web (Technical Report). W3C Recommendation (2019). https://www.w3.org/TR/vc-data-model/
13. Mühle, A., Assaf, K., Köhler, D., Meinel, C.: Requirements of a digital education credential system. In: 2023 IEEE Global Engineering Education Conference (EDUCON), Kuwait, pp. 1–10. IEEE (2023). https://doi.org/10.1109/EDUCON54358.2023.10125183
14. Chakroun, B., Keevy, J.: Digital credentialing: implications for the recognition of learning across borders. UNESCO, Paris (2018). https://doi.org/10.54675/SABO8911
15. European training foundation: Guide to Design, Issue and Recognise Micro-Credentials. European Training Foundation, Turin (2022). https://www.etf.europa.eu/sites/default/files/2023-05/MicroCredential%20Guidelines%20Final%20Delivery.pdf
16. Okoli, C.: A guide to conducting a standalone systematic literature review. Commun. Assoc. Inf. Syst. **37**, pp–pp (2015). https://doi.org/10.17705/1CAIS.03743
17. Harrington, T., O'Neill, S.: Adoption of e-portfolios for registered nurses and midwives professional registration and revalidation in Ireland. Irish J. Technol. Enhanced Learn. **6**(1), 138–153 (2021). https://doi.org/10.22554/ijtel.v6i1.100
18. Selvaratnam, R.M., Warburton, S., Parrish, D., Crew, S.: A maturity model for micro-credentialing and shorter forms of learning practice in Australasian universities. J. High. Educ. Policy Manag. **46**(4), 409–424 (2024). https://doi.org/10.1080/1360080X.2023.2299150
19. Balaban, I., Ravet, S., Soboďić, A.: EPortfolio Maturity Framework. In: Auer, M.E., Tsiatsos, T. (eds.) ICL 2018. AISC, vol. 917, pp. 473–484. Springer, Cham (2019). https://doi.org/10.1007/978-3-030-11935-5_45
20. Joshi, P.R., Islam, S.: E-government maturity model for sustainable e-government services from the perspective of developing countries. Sustainability **10**(6), 1882 (2018)
21. Mazumder, M.M.H.U., Islam, T., Alam, M.R., Al Haque, M.E., Islam, M.S., Alam, M.M.: A novel framework for blockchain-based driving license management and driver's reputation system for Bangladesh. In: Proceedings of the 2nd International Conference on Robotics, Electrical and Signal Processing Techniques (ICREST), pp. 263–268 (2021)

22. Satybaldy, A., Subedi, A., Nowostawski, M.: A framework for online document verification using self-sovereign identity technology. Sensors **22**(21), 8408 (2022). https://doi.org/10.3390/s22218408
23. Ivic, A., Stefanovic, D., Dakic, D., Vuckovic, T., Havzi, S., Sladojevic, S.: Conceptual framework for the development of an e-government licensing system. Access Sci. Bus. Innovation Digital Econ. **4**(2), pp. 313–330 (2023). https://doi.org/10.46656/access.2023.4.2(11)
24. VS, R., Raj, V.C., Eswaran, S., RU, S.: Optimization of digitalized document verification using e-governance service delivery platform (e-SDP). Int. J. Appl. Eng. Res. **11**(4), 2531–2539 (2016)
25. Ghani, R.F., Al-Karkhi, A.A.S., Mahdi, S.M.: Proposed framework for official document sharing and verification in e-government environment based on blockchain technology. Baghdad Sci. J. **19**(6 (Suppl.)), 1592–1592 (2022)
26. Iatrellis, O., Samaras, N., Kokkinos, K.: Towards a capability maturity model for micro-credential providers in European higher education. Trends High. Educ. **3**(3), 504–527 (2024)

Japan's Electronic Voting System: Causes of Failure and Keys to Success

Katsuhiro Musashi[✉]

Doshisha University, Kyoto 6620872, Japan
ktani@mail.doshisha.ac.jp

Abstract. In Japan, electronic voting was initially implemented by local governments in 2002, and by 2016, it had been used 25 times across 10 cities and towns. However, its use was suspended thereafter. In December 2024, electronic voting was reintroduced in Shijonawate City, Osaka Prefecture, marking its first deployment in eight years and attracting considerable attention. Electronic voting has played a significant role in expediting the vote-counting process and minimizing the occurrence of invalid votes. Nevertheless, it is costly and presents substantial risks, including potential election disruptions due to equipment malfunctions. In response to these concerns, Shijonawate City adopted a standalone electronic voting system, which records data on electromagnetic storage media without connecting the voting machine to a network, thus mitigating the risk of equipment failure. Additionally, while the city endeavored to reduce costs by employing general-purpose machines, the expenses associated with outsourcing to contractors escalated, necessitating financial assistance from the national government. This report, in light of the recent revival of electronic voting, will examine the prospects of implementing electronic voting in national elections and address the technical and legal challenges related to Internet voting, particularly for voters facing difficulties in accessing polling stations.

Keywords: standalone electronic voting system · guaranteed voting rights · Internet voting

1 Introduction

The Electronic Record Voting Act, which came into effect in 2002, introduced electronic voting in local elections in Japan, utilizing electronic recording voting machines. This legislation aims to ensure the fair and accurate conduct of elections while enhancing the efficiency and speed of vote counting, in line with the evolving information society. A bill for national elections was debated but ultimately abandoned in 2008. Since its initial use in Niimi City in 2002, electronic voting has been implemented 25 times in 10 municipalities, but ceased after 2016. However, electronic voting was carried out in Shijonawate City in December 2024, after an eight-year hiatus.

This report will analyze the effects of electronic voting in Japan on voter turnout, invalid votes, and election administration efficiency, based on previous implementations.

A. Kő et al. (Eds.): EGOVIS 2025, LNCS 16049, pp. 48–53, 2026.
https://doi.org/10.1007/978-3-032-02225-7_4

It will also examine the reasons behind the eight-year suspension of electronic voting, despite its benefits in enhancing voter participation, and explore the conditions that have made its resumption possible. Additionally, this report will consider the future development of electronic voting in Japan, focusing on the prospect of Internet voting. This study is based on publicly available documents from local election management committees and reports by the Ministry of Internal Affairs and Communications (MIC) study group. These sources were reviewed and analyzed to support the research.

2 Impact of Electronic Voting on Voter Behavior and Election Procedures

Remarkably, only 26 countries have adopted electronic voting for national elections, with 16, including Japan, incorporating it in local elections, positioning them as a minority [1]. The adoption of electronic voting in both national and local elections has been found to influence voter behavior, including changes in voter turnout, reductions in invalid votes, and shifts in the vote share of political parties. For example, electronic voting precincts in India [2], the United States [3], and Belgium [4] have been linked to lower voter turnout. Conversely, electronic voting has shown no significant effect on turnout in Brazil [5] or the Netherlands [6]. While evaluations of its impact on voter turnout vary, studies in India [7], Brazil, the United States [8], the Netherlands, and Belgium suggest that electronic voting can effectively reduce invalid votes. Regarding vote share, electronic voting has been shown that in Brazil, left-wing parties increased their votes by reducing invalid votes among impoverished and less educated demographics. In India, small parties experienced increased vote share. In this way, if the introduction of electronic voting has an impact on the vote share of political parties and candidates, it is expected that political parties for which a change to the status quo would be disadvantageous will be strongly opposed to the introduction of electronic voting.

In Japan, when comparing voter turnout before and after the introduction of electronic voting, it appears that the system does not consistently increase turnout. In fact, voter turnout tends to decrease in subsequent elections after electronic voting is introduced. The initial increase in voter turnout may be attributed to the heightened awareness and public relations activities surrounding the new system, which are not sustained over time.

On the other hand, electronic voting reduces the occurrence of invalid votes, as it does not require voters to write their names on the ballot. Instead, a touch panel allows for the selection of candidates, which prevents errors commonly associated with hand-written ballots. The use of electronic voting machines and audio guidance has also diminished the demand for Braille ballots. Moreover, electronic voting significantly reduces vote counting time; while paper ballots would take one to four and a half hours to count, electronic voting has reduced this time to approximately 20 min to one hour and 45 min.

As noted by a study group from MIC (2018), electronic voting in Japan has contributed to the prompt and accurate determination of election results, reflecting the true will of voters by eliminating questionable and invalid votes. It also proactively guarantees voters' rights by facilitating voting for those who face difficulties writing their ballots.

3   Reasons for Freezing Electronic Voting

Despite these benefits, by fiscal year 2024, all local governments except Shijonawate City—where a new ordinance was passed in July 2024—had suspended or abolished their electronic voting ordinances. Six of the 10 municipalities that had previously implemented electronic voting cited financial burdens as the primary reason for discontinuation. The cost of each voting machine, approximately 180,000 yen, was deemed prohibitive, particularly in financially strained local governments. Furthermore, municipalities that had introduced electronic voting in anticipation of its eventual national adoption were forced to suspend or abandon it due to the postponement of national electronic voting systems. Furthermore, Kani City and Ebina City decided to abolish or suspend the implementation of electronic voting due to concerns regarding its technical reliability, including issues with the electronic voting systems that resulted in lawsuits rendering elections invalid. Numerous local governments that had previously contemplated adopting electronic voting ultimately refrained from doing so, citing its lack of adoption in national elections and persistent doubts about its technological dependability. This, in turn, led to a considerable reduction in the demand for electronic voting systems, prompting the exit of electronic voting providers from the market and creating a situation where no businesses were available to lease such equipment. Rokunohe Town and Niimi City, which had continued utilizing electronic voting until recently, expressed their inability to maintain the practice due to the unavailability of suitable equipment. The aforementioned local governments ultimately withdrew from electronic voting, as they faced the significant risk of electoral errors and found the benefits insufficient to justify the associated financial burden.

In response to these challenges, MIC's study group (2018) proposed reducing costs by allowing the use of general-purpose equipment, such as affordable tablets, instead of dedicated electronic voting machines. This recommendation calls for a review of the technical specifications and certification processes for electronic voting systems that utilize such general-purpose devices. It also emphasizes the need to highlight the advantages of electronic voting, such as the elimination of questionable ballots and reduced vote counting times, as well as the accommodation of voters with visual impairments through voice guidance. Additionally, efforts to engage local governments, developers, and other stakeholders are needed to clarify costs through model cases and promote the adoption and development of electronic voting systems.

4   Movement to Resume Electronic Voting

In response to the aforementioned challenges, MIC revised the technical requirements for electronic voting systems in 2020, allowing the use of general-purpose devices like affordable tablets instead of requiring dedicated voting machines. This revision has prompted renewed interest from businesses, including those that had previously withdrawn, in re-entering the electronic voting market. To stimulate local governments' interest and encourage the development of electronic voting systems, MIC has emphasized the importance of publicizing the benefits of the technology, such as reducing questionable votes, shortening vote counting times, and accommodating voters with disabilities through voice guidance.

Shijonawate City implemented electronic voting in December 2024 for the first time in eight years, spurred by its commitment to advancing digital transformation. The city identified improvements in election administration efficiency and employee work processes through digitalization as key motivations for adopting electronic voting. The city's decision was supported by the selection of Kyocera to provide electronic voting and counting services, with the company developing its own system that uses encrypted information to ensure voter anonymity. The system was tested and evaluated by MIC and was deemed compliant with over 100 technical standards. In Shijonawate City's implementation, commercially available tablet terminals were used, with vote results recorded on USB drives and backup SD cards. These data storage devices were then transported to the counting station for tallying. Although the use of a networked system would have expedited vote counting, a stand-alone method was chosen to avoid the technical failures experienced in the 2003 Kani City election. The adoption of a stand-alone system, disconnected from any network, ensured that there were no equipment malfunctions. Additionally, the provision of 204 generic terminals, which could be swiftly replaced in the event of failure, contributed to system reliability. Despite the voter turnout rate for this election being 42.54%, a decrease from the previous election's 44.54%, the introduction of electronic voting effectively eliminated invalid and questionable ballots, thus enhancing the accuracy of the election results in reflecting public opinion. Regarding the vote-counting process, after providing detailed explanations to observers, the determination of results took one hour and forty minutes. Although the time required for this process remained largely unchanged, the number of staff involved in the counting was significantly reduced, from 88 to 27, representing a decrease of approximately one-third. However, the number of personnel at the polling stations was increased by 37, bringing the total to 117—1.5 times the previous staff number—to facilitate guidance and the release of passwords. Consequently, while the workload for vote counting was considerably diminished, this reduction was balanced by the increased efficiency in both voting and counting procedures. Despite remaining challenges, the meticulous planning and efforts of the city played a pivotal role in the successful execution of the process. The primary issue encountered was the substantial increase in costs, amounting to approximately 45 million yen, surpassing the previous election's cost of 16.6 million yen. Notably, the outsourcing fee paid to Kyocera, the provider of the tablet devices, alone accounted for 44.5 million yen. In contrast, the national subsidy system for implementing electronic voting remains limited, prompting Shijonawate City to request special grants from the national government to cover the full outsourcing fee as a model case post-election. MIC also plans to conduct a hearing with the city, and Shijonawate City will need to evaluate and disseminate the expertise and efficacy of this electronic voting system. Given the outcomes observed in Shijonawate City, significant attention is now directed toward the potential widespread adoption of electronic voting in other municipalities.

5   Future Challenges for Electronic Voting Systems

The stand-alone method employed by the electronic voting system in Shijonawate City aligns with the initial phase (where voters utilize electronic voting machines at designated polling stations) of the three-stage development process for electronic voting. At present, the second phase, which is currently restricted by law, involves online voting enabled by lifting the prohibition on network connections (where voters are permitted to vote at polling stations other than the designated ones). Ultimately, the third phase—Internet voting—is anticipated in the future, wherein voting at a physical polling station is not mandatory, and voters may cast their ballots using personal computers, smartphones, or other devices.

The outcomes of the current first-stage electronic voting reveal that the deployment of voting equipment based on general-purpose terminals has not necessarily resulted in a reduction of costs. Moreover, there remains a pressing need for expanded financial support from the national government. Regarding personnel reductions, it is anticipated that as voters and election management committees gain experience, a decrease in the number of staff required at polling stations will be possible.

Conversely, during the second stage of electronic voting, involving online voting, electronic voting machines at each polling station will be connected to electronic devices at the counting station through a dedicated line, with votes being tallied accordingly. This dedicated line will be secured to prevent breaches. As previously noted, voting at the polling station is assumed, thereby negating the need for an identity authentication system in the digital space. This configuration effectively sidesteps security concerns, such as those that may arise when voters cast their votes from personal devices like computers or smartphones in the third stage of Internet voting, and mitigates issues like the digital divide among individual voters. To enable voting at polling stations outside the designated locations in the second stage, it will be necessary to transition the voter list to an online format to facilitate identity verification and prevent multiple voting instances. The Public Election Law mandates that the data must be compared with records on paper or other mediums at the polling station, and online comparison served as an auxiliary measure. Consequently, a system reform was required to institutionalize online, real-time list comparison, which was achieved with the revision of the Public Election Law Enforcement Order in 2016. In response to this reform, local governments have begun implementing online comparison, though further security measures against voter register data leaks and financial adjustments are still necessary. For identity verification at polling stations outside designated areas, the use of My Number cards (individual identification cards) should be considered.

The report from MIC's study group suggests the potential for Internet voting in overseas elections, as well as further enhancements to domestic electronic voting. While domestic Internet voting remains a topic for future deliberation due to its implications for maintaining the fairness of elections and the principle of voting at polling stations on election day, the resumption of electronic voting enables progress toward Internet voting through the lifting of the network connection ban. To realize Internet voting, ensuring the technical security of voter and voting information is critical. In this regard, the adoption of blockchain technology is under consideration. Blockchain has been utilized in national elections in Estonia, and in a 2019 demonstration experiment in Tsukuba City, Internet voting was conducted using blockchain, My Number cards, and facial recognition technology, demonstrating the feasibility of voting remotely from a personal computer. The advantages of blockchain technology lie in its decentralized management of voting data through a distributed ledger, which prevents unauthorized tampering. Moreover, voting is protected by encryption with a private key, ensuring voter anonymity and preventing administrators from illegally casting votes on behalf of others [9].

Thus, while it is anticipated that technological advancements will address security challenges within the system, legal concerns such as the prevention of bribery, coercion, and illegal proxy voting must also be addressed. The principle of one person, one vote, along with secret balloting, can be safeguarded through the use of My Number cards, and the assurance of free will can be protected by incorporating a re-voting system. Conversely, Internet voting offers significant advantages in terms of providing equal voting opportunities, ensuring consistency between the number of votes cast and the number of votes counted, and improving the efficiency of the vote tallying process. Thus, once we have successfully navigated the technical and legal obstacles, it would be prudent to consider the implementation of electronic voting in national elections. Furthermore, provision should be made for internet voting to accommodate individuals who face challenges in voting in person, thereby ensuring the active safeguarding of citizens' right to vote.

References

1. Kawamura, K.: Electronic Voting and Electoral Governance in Japan. Keio University Press, Tokyo (2021)
2. Debnath, S., Kapoor, M., Ravi, S.: The Impact of Electronic Voting Machines on Electoral Frauds, Democracy, and Development. Brookings Institution, Washington, D.C. (2017)
3. Card, D., Enrico, M.: Does voting technology affect election outcomes? Touch-screen voting and the 2004 presidential election. Rev. Econ. Stat. **89**(4), 660–673 (2007)
4. Dandoy, R.: An analysis of electronic voting in Belgium: do voters behave differently when facing a machine? In: Caluwaerts, D., Reuchamps, M. (eds.) Belgian Exceptionalism. Belgian Politics between Realism and Surrealism, pp. 44–58. Routledge, Abingdon (2021)
5. Fujiwara, T.: Voting technology, political responsiveness, and infant health: evidence from Brazil. Econometrica **83**(2), 423–464 (2015)
6. Allers, M., Peter, K.: More evidence of the effects of voting technology on election outcomes. Public Choice **139**, 159–170 (2009)
7. Desai, Z., Alexander, L.: Technology and protest: the political effects of electronic voting in India. Polit. Sci. Res. Methods **9**(2), 398–413 (2021)
8. Ansolabehere, S., Charles, S.: Residual votes attributable to technology. J. Polit. **67**(2), 365–389 (2005)
9. Ohize, H.O., et al.: Blockchain for securing electronic voting systems: a survey of architectures, trends, solutions, and challenges. Clust. Comput. **28**(132), 1–39 (2025)

Digital Transformation
and E-Government Inclusion

Charting the Crossroads of Digital Sovereignty and Digital Transformation

Gideon Mekonnen Jonathan$^{(\boxtimes)}$ (iD)

Stockholm University, Borgarfjordsgatan 12, 164 55 Kista, SE, Sweden
gideon@dsv.su.se

Abstract. The global momentum of digital transformation within the public sector presents a paradox—while promising enhanced service delivery and operational efficiency, it simultaneously exposes governments to vulnerabilities stemming from reliance on transnational digital infrastructures and private technology providers. This study addresses the critical gap in understanding how digital transformation initiatives intersect with digital sovereignty concerns, particularly in low- and middle-income countries (LMICs). Employing a case study research strategy focusing on two LMICs, this study investigates the complex interplay between public sector digital transformation strategies and the preservation of national digital sovereignty. The findings highlight the urgent need for a coherent framework that aligns digital transformation goals with sovereignty objectives to mitigate risks related to data sovereignty (data control, cyber security), technological sovereignty, and policy autonomy. The findings of the study contribute to a nuanced understanding of the challenges and opportunities in achieving successful but sovereign digital transformation in LMICs contexts.

Keywords: Digital Sovereignty · Digital Transformation · Data Sovereignty · Technological Sovereignty · Policy Autonomy

1 Introduction

Digital transformation in the public sector is increasingly recognised as a critical driver for improving governance and citizen engagement [1]. Governments across the globe are adopting advanced digital technologies, including cloud computing, artificial intelligence (AI), and big data analytics, to enhance service delivery and streamline administrative processes. This development has also generated growing interest among researchers in exploring the implications of digital transformation in relation to governments' responsibility to ensure citizens' and national interests are maintained. One topic of discourse is the relationship between digital transformation in the public sector and digital sovereignty. In the Global South, particularly in Sub-Saharan Africa, countries are adopting digital technologies to improve public service delivery, promote transparency, and stimulate economic growth. However, this transformation also raises critical questions

A. Kő et al. (Eds.): EGOVIS 2025, LNCS 16049, pp. 57–71, 2026.
https://doi.org/10.1007/978-3-032-02225-7_5

about the control and governance of digital infrastructure, data, and platforms—central components of digital sovereignty [2]. Digital sovereignty, which refers to "....*the control of data, software, standards and protocols, processes, hardware, services and infrastructures, in short, for the control of the digital*" [3, p. 370] has been an important point of discourse in many countries. The concern from those calling for a closer look at the rapid digital transformation is often because digital transformation is predicated on the utilisation of transnational digital infrastructures and the services of private technology providers, raising profound concerns about digital sovereignty [4]. According to Floridi [3], the issue of digital sovereignty comes to light when states, as protectors of both national and individual sovereignty (i.e., the ownership of choices and data), act to exercise their power to regulate the digital. This contrasts with the firm's responsibility (i.e., while maintaining profitability) to design, produce, sell and maintain everything digital.

It is often argued that for both actors (states and private firms), the struggle is between pursuing the application of emerging technologies for innovation and improved efficiency and maintaining national control over digital assets that matter to the integrity of individual citizens and nations. That is why policymakers across countries seek the best ways of dealing with the opportunities and challenges of emerging technologies [2]. However, striking a balance necessitates a rigorous examination of the interplay between digital transformation strategies and digital sovereignty objectives [3], considering the contextual setting [2]. Therefore, this study attempts to elucidate the complexities of this relationship, addressing the pressing need for a framework that enables governments to realise the benefits of digital transformation while safeguarding their sovereign interests, with a specific focus on the Low- and Middle-Income Countries (LMICs) context. Kenya and Liberia, two countries in the sub-Saharan region, were selected for the study.

1.1   Background and Study Setting

The Global South nations, particularly in sub-Saharan Africa, have recognised that the leverage of emerging technologies can have tremendous potential in enabling transformations to combat poverty, economic disparity, and bad public governance. To this end, governments are actively integrating digital technologies to improve public service delivery, promote transparency, and stimulate economic advancement. However, this transformative endeavour has also raised several questions regarding the control and governance of digital infrastructure, data, and platforms—integral elements of digital sovereignty [2]. The concerns from prior studies related to digital sovereignty include data localisation, regulatory autonomy, and the potential for digital colonisation [5,6]. Moreover, as a concept, digital sovereignty extends beyond mere infrastructural control to encompass the ability to shape digital norms and standards, ensuring that technological development aligns with national values and priorities [7]. However, researchers also acknowledge that the tension between digital transformation and digital sovereignty is exacerbated by the varying capacities and regulatory frameworks within LMICs, where the balance between adopting transformative emerging technologies and ensuring sovereign control is particularly delicate [6]. In these settings, maintaining a careful equilibrium between embracing transformative emerging technologies—essential for economic and social development— and exercising effective sovereign control over digital assets and infrastructures becomes particularly challenging [5,6].

This heightened vulnerability stems from several interrelated factors. Firstly, according to the World Bank [8], LMICs frequently encounter substantial resource constraints, including limited financial capacity, inadequate digital infrastructure, and a shortage of skilled personnel, which collectively hinder their ability to cultivate and sustain independent digital ecosystems. Consequently, they may become overly reliant on external technology providers and international digital infrastructures, thereby risking the erosion of their digital autonomy [9]. Secondly, regulatory frameworks in many LMICs remain underdeveloped, lacking the sophistication and comprehensiveness needed to effectively govern the rapidly evolving digital landscape [10]. Such regulatory immaturity often results in critical gaps, undermining efforts to enforce data protection standards, mitigate cyber security threats, and uphold national sovereignty in digital governance [11].

The selection of Kenya and Liberia as case studies is based on their contrasting yet complementary characteristics, which offer a unique opportunity to examine the complex relationship between digital transformation and digital sovereignty. Kenya is widely acknowledged as a frontrunner in digital innovation across Africa, having implemented ambitious public sector digitisation projects such as Huduma Kenya, the eCitizen platform, and the forthcoming Maisha Namba digital ID system. Its relatively advanced ICT infrastructure, coupled with a dynamic tech ecosystem and growing engagement with data protection and platform governance issues, positions it as a significant case for examining how a nation with substantial digital capabilities navigates the complexities of digital sovereignty [12]. The rapid adoption of mobile money, for example, has propelled the nation to the forefront of fintech innovation, generating a wealth of data that demands robust governance frameworks [13]. In contrast, Liberia represents a lower-income, post-conflict context where digital transformation is still in its nascent stages and heavily reliant on international support. According to the International Telecommunication Union (ITU) [14], Liberia's National ICT and Digital Economy Strategy (2022-2027) articulates an aspiration to construct a modern digital state, yet it confronts substantial obstacles related to infrastructure development, capacity building, and cyber security governance. The nation's experience provides a critical perspective on how digital sovereignty is conceptualised and operationalised in a resource-constrained environment, where external dependencies and capacity limitations significantly influence digital policy and implementation. The challenges faced by Liberia are reflective of broader issues in post-conflict settings where rebuilding state capacity is intertwined with digital development [15].

This comparative research design allows for the exploration of how digital sovereignty is understood, contested, and operationalised in diverse African governance contexts. By examining these two distinct cases, the study aims to analyse how geopolitical dependencies, institutional capacity, and regulatory frameworks shape national approaches to digital transformation. Kenya's proactive approach to digital innovation, coupled with its growing engagement in regional and international digital governance forums, offers insights into how a nation can leverage its digital capabilities while asserting its sovereignty. Conversely, Liberia's reliance on international aid and its ongoing efforts to build a robust digital infrastructure highlight the challenges of achieving digital sovereignty in a context marked by significant developmental constraints. We argue that our research approach aligns with comparative research methodologies that seek to understand the impact of context on policy outcomes. By comparing and contrasting the experiences of Kenya and Liberia, the study will provide a nuanced understanding of the factors that influence the relationship between digital transformation and digital sovereignty in the African context. It will also contribute to the broader scholarly discourse on digital governance in the Global South, particularly LMICs, offering insights into the challenges and opportunities associated with achieving sovereign digital development.

1.2   Research Problem and Aim

The extant literature predominantly addresses digital transformation in the public sector through the lens of efficiency, innovation, and user-centric design [1]. Conversely, discussions on digital sovereignty are often confined to geopolitical or data governance contexts, particularly in the Global North [3, 16]. This compartmentalisation results in a paucity of studies that explicitly investigate the interdependencies between digital transformation strategies and digital sovereignty outcomes, particularly in empirical, cross-national, or sector-specific contexts, and especially in lower-income settings, where states may have less control over technological choices and are often reliant on foreign vendors and donors. Moreover, only a few empirical studies have explored how digital sovereignty concerns manifest within public sector digital transformation efforts in African countries.

We argue that the intersection between the two domains—digital transformation and digital sovereignty—remains theoretically underdeveloped and empirically underexplored, especially in contexts where state capacity, infrastructure, and regulatory frameworks are still evolving. Thus, the aim of this study is to explore the complexities of the relationship between digital transformation and digital sovereignty. The point of departure for our study is the recognition of the need for coherent strategies that empower governments to tap the advantages of digital transformation while safeguarding their sovereign interests, with a specific focus on LMICs. Thus, our study focusing on Kenya and Liberia provides empirical insights into the practical challenges and potential solutions for achieving sovereign digital transformation. Specifically, we examine how these two nations navigate the trade-offs between adopting external digital solutions and building indigenous digital capacity while assessing the impact of international digital governance regimes on their national digital sovereignty. We argue that this study contributes to furthering our understanding of how global digital norms interact with localised realities and how this impacts the ability of LMICs to craft effective and sovereign digital transformation strategies.

The following research questions guide our study: *How do public sector digital transformation initiatives in Kenya and Liberia reflect or challenge the principles of digital sovereignty?* and *What political, infrastructural, and institutional factors shape the pursuit of digital sovereignty in the public sectors of Kenya and Liberia?*

2   Related Studies

2.1   Digital Sovereignty

In an era defined by increasing digital interconnectedness and geopolitical fragmentation, the concept of digital sovereignty has ascended to a position of critical importance. Even though there is no clear definition [2], in broader terms, digital sovereignty encapsulates the capacity of a nation or organisation to govern its digital infrastructure, data flows, and technological ecosystems autonomously [16]. This concept has undergone a significant evolution, expanding beyond its initial roots in debates concerning internet governance to encompass a broader spectrum of concerns, including data control, cyber security, and technological self-sufficiency [7]. The central element of the various definitions and descriptions is that sovereignty is a function of a certain form of established, maintained or even expanded power [2].

The academic debates and the discourse among practitioners indicate that the framing of digital sovereignty has shifted away from predominantly geopolitical contexts, focusing on data control and internet governance [3]. The phenomenon now encompasses a more nuanced understanding, recognising its multidimensional nature. In the extant literature, these dimensions include (1) *data sovereignty*, which focuses on the control a nation exerts over data generated within its borders, including its storage, processing, and transfer, (2) *technological sovereignty*, which refers to the ability to develop, regulate, and maintain critical technologies, thereby reducing dependence on external actors, and (3) *regulatory sovereignty*, i.e., the autonomy of a nation to formulate and implement digital policies and regulations that align with its national laws and priorities [16]. This evolution signifies a shift from a purely geopolitical perspective towards a more comprehensive understanding of digital sovereignty as a crucial aspect of national governance and technological autonomy.

2.2   Digital Transformation of the Public Sector in LMICs

Digital transformation in the public sector has emerged as a critical priority for governments worldwide, particularly in LMICs in the Global South. While developed nations have long leveraged digital technologies to enhance public service delivery, LMICs are recently turning to digital solutions to address inefficiencies within their public sector—improving citizen engagement, and promoting transparency [17]. However, digital transformation within LMICs faces unique challenges, including inadequate infrastructure, limited digital literacy, and financial constraints [18]. Despite these barriers, initiatives such as Kenya's e-Citizen platform and Rwanda's Irembo have demonstrated the potential of digital transformation to streamline service delivery and foster government accountability. The reliance on digital technology is not merely about automating services; it also represents a fundamental rethinking of how public institutions operate in an era where citizens expect more accessible and efficient services.

However, the discourse on digital transformation in LMICs is complicated by structural and contextual factors that differentiate it from Global North experiences. For instance, while supranational frameworks like the Tallinn Declaration on eGovernment emphasise the benefits of digital governance, LMIC governments must navigate additional hurdles such as data sovereignty concerns, reliance on foreign technology providers, and fragmented policy environments [15,18]. The digital divide between urban and rural populations also poses a significant challenge, as millions of citizens still lack access to reliable internet and digital services. Furthermore, the absence of clear frameworks on how digital transformation should be implemented in public administration means that many governments in LMICs are adopting a trial-and-error approach, often influenced by donor priorities rather than homegrown strategies [15,18]. Therefore, while digital transformation presents a pathway towards improved governance, its success in LMICs depends on a holistic approach. This approach necessitates investment in infrastructure, local capacity building, and regulatory reforms tailored to these countries' socio-economic realities.

3   Research Methodology

This study employed a qualitative research approach, which was deemed appropriate for its suitability in revealing the factors related to the phenomenon under investigation. A comparative qualitative case study strategy was adopted, allowing us to gain a rich and nuanced understanding of a phenomenon within its natural setting [19]. This approach is well-suited because the research aims to explore digital transformation and digital sovereignty in two countries. The strategy facilitates the analysis of experiences, first-hand accounts, and detailed insights from the diverse stakeholders directly involved in shaping, implementing, or critiquing public sector digital initiatives in the countries chosen for the study [19].

3.1   Data Collection and Analysis Methods

The data collection for this study involved conducting semi-structured interviews with a range of stakeholders in Kenya and Liberia. In Kenya, interviews were conducted with one representative from seven different organisations—*the Ministry of ICT and the Digital Economy, the ICT Authority, the Office of the*

Data Protection Commissioner, the Ministry of Interior, a Local Cloud Services Provider, a University, and *a Hi-Tech multinational company* providing service to the Public Sector in the country. In Liberia, eight interviews were conducted with selected interviewees from the same number of organisations—*the Ministry of Posts and Telecommunications, the Ministry of Finance and Development Planning, the Liberia Telecommunications Authority, the Liberia Digital Economy Programme (UNDP/AU project), a University, the Center for Transparency and Accountability in Liberia, a Local ICT firm* working on public contracts, and *the World Bank Liberia Digital DE4A Initiative.* A purposive sampling approach was used to select participants with relevant expertise and responsibilities, ensuring alignment with the research objectives. Snowball sampling complemented our strategy to identify actors who were not publicly visible but were influential in implementation processes or advisory roles.

Thematic analysis, a widely used qualitative data analysis method, was selected for this study. This method was chosen due to its inherent flexibility, as it is not constrained by a specific theoretical or epistemological framework [20]. The coding and theme development were guided by the study's aim and research questions. The analysis followed the six-phase process outlined by Braun and Clarke [20], i.e., familiarisation with the data, generating initial codes, searching for themes, reviewing themes, defining and naming themes, and producing the report.

4   Results and Discussions

This section presents the study's findings analysing how digital transformation initiatives in the public sectors of Kenya and Liberia align with—or challenge—the principles of digital sovereignty. It also examines the political, infrastructural, and institutional factors that shape the pursuit of digital sovereignty in each context.

4.1   Digital Sovereignty in Kenya's and Liberia's Public Sector Digital Transformation

Kenya's Mixed Approach to Digital Sovereignty. Kenya has embraced digital transformation with vigour, as evidenced by flagship initiatives such as the Huduma Kenya integrated service delivery platform and the eCitizen portal, which aim to streamline public service delivery through digitisation. These efforts have enhanced access and efficiency. However, according to our interviewees, these initiatives have also shown critical dependencies on foreign technology providers, particularly in cloud services and digital payment systems. This is consistent with the findings of prior studies [21]. As one of the interviewees at the Ministry of ICT and the Digital Economy acknowledges, Kenya *"continues to rely significantly on foreign companies and cloud services for certain vital infrastructure and software solutions,"* including *"Microsoft Azure, AWS, and Google*

Cloud for hosting some government platforms". This reliance raises pressing concerns about data jurisdiction, control, and the risk of external surveillance or manipulation [22].

On the other hand, the Kenyan government has taken tangible steps towards asserting digital sovereignty. For instance, respondents mention that the enactment of the Data Protection Act (2019) and the formulation of the National Digital Master Plan (2022-2032) reflect a growing policy emphasis on data localisation, privacy protection, and cyber security. This finding is consistent with prior studies indicating a heightened awareness of sovereignty risks [23]. As the respondent from the Data Protection Commissioner (ODPC) states, digital sovereignty means that Kenya has the *"legal and regulatory authority to govern how data is collected, stored, and processed within its borders"*. However, according to our interviewees, implementation challenges stemming from fiscal constraints, capacity gaps, and uneven enforcement continue to hinder their full realisation. Specifically, the response from our interviewee from the Ministry of ICT and the Digital Economy lists challenges such as a *"lack of local expertise in AI, cloud computing, and cyber security"* and funding limitations, where *"public-sector digital transformation projects often rely on donor funding"*. This is consistent with broader findings that even relatively advanced digital economies must constantly negotiate the balance between innovation and sovereign control [2].

Liberia's Limited Capacity and External Dependencies. The analysis of our interview suggests that Liberia's digital transformation remains nascent, marked by fragmented efforts and significant reliance on external actors. For instance, the Liberia Telecommunications Authority's e-government Strategy outlines a vision for digital governance but is constrained by limited institutional capacity and infrastructural underdevelopment. According to our interviewee at the Ministry of Posts and Telecommunications of Liberia, the country faces challenges such as a *"lack of adequate data centres and broadband coverage"*. Thus, many digital initiatives are externally funded and executed, often by international donors or private foreign technology firms. Prior studies indicate that this has resulted in digital systems lacking interoperability and local oversight, weakening state control and accountability [24]. The respondent from the Ministry of Finance and Development Planning of Liberia highlighted that insufficient local expertise and financial limitations lead to a consistent reliance on externally funded projects and consultants. This reliance, he noted, compromises the ability to make independent choices.

Another issue identified in the literature in relation to digital sovereignty in Liberia is that the country has yet to establish a comprehensive legal framework for data protection, leaving citizen data vulnerable to misuse and foreign exploitation [25]. Our analysis also confirms this regulatory vacuum, which, combined with resource scarcity, severely hampers the state's ability to govern its digital space effectively. As the interviewee at the Liberia Telecommunications Authority noted, the country faces challenges in enforcing the policies that are in place because "*many government agencies lack the technical capacity to implement these policies fully*". This example demonstrates how constrained state capacity heightens exposure to external digital dominance and underscores the difficulties post-conflict states face in developing sovereign digital governance structures [8].

In sum, our findings reveal that both Kenya and Liberia have made noteworthy progress in digital transformation. However, their trajectories reflect divergent levels of engagement with digital sovereignty principles, shaped by differing national capacities, policy orientations, and geopolitical dependencies.

4.2   Political, Infrastructural, and Institutional Factors Shaping Digital Sovereignty

The result of our study suggests that three key factors played a significant role in shaping the degree to which Kenya and Liberia are able to assert digital sovereignty—political leadership, infrastructural development, and institutional capacity.

Political Factors—Leadership and Policy Frameworks. In Kenya, relatively stable governance and a leadership that is generally supportive of technological innovation have facilitated the formulation and adoption of forward-looking digital policies. However, as prior studies suggest, political interference—particularly in ICT procurement and implementation—can undermine these efforts, leading to inefficiencies and eroding public trust [26]. As our interviewee from the Ministry of ICT and the Digital Economy notes, decisions on technology adoption in public services follow a "*multi-stakeholder process*" with consideration for "*policy alignment*" and "*technical feasibility and security assessments*", but also "*public-private partnerships (PPPs) and procurement processes guided by regulatory frameworks.*" This suggests the role of politics in influencing these processes. In other words, sustained political will, detached from vested interests, is therefore critical for advancing sovereign digital development. The interviewee from the Citizen project argues that solutions must meet "*cost-effectiveness, security, and sustainability*" requirements and that they "*prioritise local solutions where possible*" but sometimes rely on international expertise. This also suggests that political influence is necessary to consistently prioritise these factors, particularly when local solutions might be more expensive or less readily available.

Liberia's political context presents more substantial challenges. As found in prior studies, the country's post-war fragility, frequent leadership transitions, and policy discontinuities have stymied the development of a coherent digital sovereignty agenda [27]. According to the respondent from the Liberia Telecommunications Authority, "*political instability and corruption have been significant barriers*" to digital development. Additionally, the dominance of donor-driven projects often results in externally imposed priorities that do not align with local needs or long-term sovereignty goals. For instance, the interviewee from the

Ministry of Finance and Development planning said, *"...because of limited local expertise and financial constraints, we often rely on donor-funded projects and external consultants to guide these choices, which sometimes limits our autonomy in decision-making"*.

Infrastructural Factors—Connectivity and Local Capabilities. Kenya benefits from comparatively advanced digital infrastructure, including an expansive fibre-optic network and innovation ecosystems like Konza Technopolis. These assets provide a strong foundation for achieving greater digital self-reliance. Nevertheless, prior studies have shown that reliance on undersea cables, such as TEAMS and foreign-owned data centres, introduces external points of vulnerability [28]. According to the respondent from the Ministry of ICT and the Digital Economy, Kenya is actively working to reduce this dependence by *"developing local cloud infrastructure"* and *"encouraging open-source adoption in government systems"*. However, the interviewee from the Citizen project also acknowledges the current reliance on foreign cloud providers like *"AWS, Microsoft Azure, and Google Cloud."* This duality reflects the paradox of digital sovereignty in an interconnected world: complete autonomy is often technically and economically impractical. As the participant from the Office of the Data Protection Commissioner notes, *"a strong data protection law and enforcement mechanisms, can improve the country's chances to have control over its digital assets and citizen information"*.

Liberia, by contrast, faces acute infrastructural deficits in its pursuit of digital transformation. For instance, prior studies indicate that internet access is patchy outside the capital, Monrovia, and often relies on foreign mobile network operators and satellite providers [14]. As the respondent from the Ministry of Post and Telecommunications of Liberia stated, *"one of the biggest challenges is infrastructure—Liberia still lacks adequate data centres and broadband coverage to support digital transformation fully."* These infrastructural constraints not only limit public access to digital services but also inhibit the state's ability to govern its digital space, rendering sovereignty goals aspirational rather than actionable. The interviewee from the Ministry of Finance and Development Planning also acknowledges *"infrastructure deficits—reliance on foreign-hosted platforms"* as a major challenge.

Institutional Factors—Regulations and Human Capital. Our analysis indicates that Kenya's institutional landscape, including specialised agencies such as the Office of the Data Protection Commissioner, serves as a key enabler of digital governance. However, prior studies indicate that enforcement remains inconsistent, and regulatory frameworks often struggle to keep pace with rapidly evolving technologies [8,30]. According to the interviewee from the Office of the Data Protection Commissioner, Kenya faces challenges such as a *"shortage of experts in data protection, cyber security, and digital forensics"* and *"some ministries still operate in silos, making data governance enforcement inconsistent"*.

This highlights the significance of institutional agility and sustained investment in regulatory capacity to maintain digital sovereignty.

In Liberia, institutional fragility is more pronounced. The country faces acute shortages of skilled personnel in areas such as cyber security, ICT regulation, and digital policy design [8]. The absence of robust oversight mechanisms not only limits effective governance but also makes it difficult to challenge the dominance of powerful foreign actors. According to the respondent at the Liberia Telecommunications Authority, the country faces challenges such as a *"lack of human capacity and technical expertise"* and *"many government agencies lack the technical capacity to fully implement these policies"*. Thus, strengthening institutions and capacity development are critical for realising digital sovereignty. In the respondent's own words, *"we need digital literacy programmes badly if we are to digitally transform our nation in our terms"*.

4.3   Cross-Country Analysis

The findings suggest that both Kenya and Liberia recognise digital sovereignty as a desirable objective, yet their strategies diverge due to contextual differences. Kenya demonstrates greater agency in managing the trade-offs between digital transformation and sovereignty. Its hybrid approach—embracing external technologies while incrementally building domestic capacity—offers a potential model for other LMICs. In contrast, Liberia's limited institutional capacity and high external dependency hinder its ability to pursue sovereign digital development, illustrating the vulnerability of weaker states in the global digital order.

This contrast foregrounds a critical question: *Can LMICs pursue digital sovereignty without slowing the pace of digital development?* Kenya's experience suggests a phased approach is feasible, whereas Liberia's case highlights the risks of dependency without domestic capacity. These dynamics echo the broader critique of digital colonialism, where the adoption of digital tools by LMICs is frequently accompanied by a loss of autonomy and extractive data practices [5, 6, 13].

4.4   Recommendations for Strengthening Digital Sovereignty

The findings of this study highlight that while Kenya and Liberia face divergent challenges in asserting digital sovereignty, both countries can adopt targeted strategies to mitigate external dependencies, build domestic capacities, and enhance governance of their digital ecosystems. The recommendations below are tailored to each country's context, while also identifying shared priorities for strengthening sovereignty in the digital domain.

4.5   Kenya—Reinforcing Data Localisation and Investing in Domestic Cloud Infrastructure

Kenya should bolster its data localisation policies by mandating that sensitive public sector and citizen data be stored within national borders, preferably on locally managed infrastructure. While the 2019 Data Protection Act and the National Digital Master Plan (2022-2032) already emphasise local data hosting [6,30], enforcement remains uneven, and several public services continue to depend on infrastructure provided by foreign cloud service providers such as Amazon Web Services and Microsoft Azure [21]. The extant literature underscores the strategic importance of data localisation as a mechanism to enhance state control over data flows, improve accountability, and reduce exposure to extraterritorial surveillance or legal regimes such as the U.S. CLOUD Act [6,30]. Investing in domestic cloud infrastructure—whether through public-private partnerships, national data centres, or community-based alternatives—can also stimulate local tech industries, enhance cyber security, and create jobs [33]. Moreover, countries such as India and Brazil offer instructive examples where state-led infrastructure investments have reinforced both digital capacity and regulatory sovereignty [32].

4.6   Liberia—Developing a Comprehensive Digital Sovereignty Strategy and Prioritising Local Capacity

Liberia urgently needs to develop a comprehensive digital sovereignty strategy that articulates a long-term vision for controlling and governing its digital infrastructure, platforms, and data. Such a strategy should be informed by participatory processes involving civil society, the private sector, and regional partners. It must address regulatory gaps—particularly in data protection, cyber security, and digital procurement—and should be backed by legislation and institutional reforms. A central component of this strategy should be the prioritisation of local capacity-building. As the literature on state capacity in post-conflict settings shows, weak institutions are often ill-equipped to govern complex digital ecosystems [33]. Donor support should be restructured to focus on sustainable capacity development, including training for civil servants, investment in local tech ecosystems, and the establishment of national research and policy units on digital governance. As prior studies point out, externally imposed digital systems without local ownership can entrench dependency rather than support long-term transformation in the context of African digital development [6,30].

Donor partnerships should, therefore, be evaluated not only on technical outcomes but also on their contribution to local agency, control, and institutional development. The concept of "digital public infrastructure" (DPI) provides a useful lens here—emphasising interoperable, inclusive systems that are owned and governed by public institutions rather than foreign tech firms [33].

4.7   Shared Priorities—Enhancing Cyber Security and Promoting Digital Literacy

Both Kenya and Liberia must strengthen their cyber security frameworks to safeguard digital infrastructure, public data, and user trust. Cyber security is foundational to digital sovereignty, as vulnerabilities can expose national systems to foreign manipulation, espionage, or ransomware attacks [34]. Kenya's existing cyber security strategy needs periodic updates and greater funding for implementation, while Liberia must develop a comprehensive national cyber security framework aligned with regional and international standards [14].

In addition, both countries should invest significantly in digital literacy programmes to empower citizens to participate safely and meaningfully in digital public services. Low levels of digital literacy not only limit uptake of digital platforms but also increase susceptibility to misinformation, cybercrime, and data exploitation [4]. Programmes should target marginalised groups and be integrated into national education curricula and public awareness campaigns. Digital literacy also supports democratic participation, civic agency, and accountability in digital governance processes. As the extant literature suggests, digital sovereignty is not solely about state control but also about equipping individuals with the knowledge and tools to navigate and shape digital systems [2,3].

5 Concluding Remarks

This study sought to investigate the alignment of public sector digital transformation initiatives in Kenya and Liberia with the principles of digital sovereignty. By examining two distinct national contexts within sub-Saharan Africa, the research aimed to elucidate the political, infrastructural, and institutional factors that influence the pursuit of digital autonomy in LMICs. Utilising qualitative data gathered through semi-structured interviews with key stakeholders, this research contributes to the burgeoning body of scholarly work on digital governance, sovereignty, and state capacity in the Global South.

The findings reveal divergent trajectories in Kenya and Liberia's approaches to digital sovereignty, despite both nations embracing digital transformation as a strategic policy objective. Kenya has adopted a hybrid strategy, leveraging foreign technological infrastructure while concurrently investing in regulatory frameworks, such as data protection legislation and national digital planning. However, persistent challenges remain, including implementation gaps and continued reliance on foreign cloud infrastructure. In contrast, Liberia faces more pronounced sovereignty vulnerabilities, driven by limited institutional capacity, underdeveloped infrastructure, and a high degree of dependence on external actors for funding and technical expertise. The comparative analysis underscores that digital sovereignty is not a binary state but rather a spectrum, shaped by a nation's political commitment, institutional resilience, and capacity to regulate and develop digital infrastructure.

While this study provides valuable insights, it is not without limitations. The primary reliance on case studies and qualitative interviews introduces constraints regarding generalisability. The sample size, necessarily limited by time and logistical considerations, makes the findings interpretive rather than broadly generalisable. Furthermore, the use of interviews may be subject to the positionality and biases of respondents, particularly within politically sensitive environments where participants may exhibit self-censorship or provide overly optimistic accounts. Additionally, although the research aimed to capture a range of stakeholder perspectives—including government officials, civil society representatives, and ICT professionals—the voices of rural communities and marginalised groups remain underrepresented.

Future research could address these limitations in several ways. Firstly, broader comparative studies across multiple LMICs could facilitate the identification of regional patterns and typologies of digital sovereignty. Secondly, the integration of mixed-methods approaches—including survey data, policy analysis, and digital infrastructure mapping—would strengthen the empirical foundation for understanding sovereignty dynamics. Thirdly, longitudinal studies tracking the evolution of digital sovereignty over time would offer valuable insights into how states adapt to rapidly evolving technological and geopolitical landscapes. Finally, there is a need for deeper inquiry into the lived experiences of citizens within digital governance systems, particularly concerning data rights, algorithmic decision-making, and trust in state-managed digital platforms.

In conclusion, this study emphasises the significance of digital sovereignty within the political economies of digital transformation. It calls for nuanced, context-sensitive strategies that balance the imperatives of development with the principles of autonomy, equity, and accountability in the digital age.

References

1. Mergel, I., Edelmann, N., Haug, N.: Defining digital transformation: results from expert interviews. Gov. Inf. Q. **36**(4), 101385 (2019)
2. Glasze, G., et al.: Contested spatialities of digital sovereignty. Geopolitics **28**(2), 919–958 (2023)
3. Floridi, L.: The fight for digital sovereignty: what it is, and why it matters, especially for the EU. Philos. Technol. **33**, 369–378 (2020)
4. Van Dijck, J., Poell, T., De Waal, M.: The platform society: public values in a connective world. Oxford University Press (2018)
5. Couldry, N., Mejias, U.A.: Data colonialism: rethinking big data's relation to the contemporary subject. Telev. New Media **20**(4), 336–349 (2019)
6. Kwet, M.: Digital colonialism: us empire and the new imperialism in the global south. Race class **60**(4), 3–26 (2019)
7. Hintz, A., Dencik, L., Wahl-Jorgensen, K.: Digital citizenship in a datafied society. John Wiley and Sons (2018)
8. WorldBank: Digital economy diagnostic liberia. In: Digital Economy for Africa Initiative. The World Bank (2020)
9. Zwitter, A., Hazenberg, J.: Decentralized network governance: blockchain technology and the future of regulation. Front. Blockchain **3**, 12 (2020)
10. Ozumba, A., Olaniyi, T., Mohammed, S.: Adoption of big data technologies for the digital transformation of public agencies in the global south (GS). Int. J. Sustain. Energy Dev. **10**(1), 465–469 (2022)
11. Adu Amoah, L.G.: Global digital political economy and its concerns: is digital imperialism the elephant in the room? Glob. Polit. Econ. **4**(1), 89–101 (2025)
12. De Stadler, E., Hattingh, I.L., Esselaar, P., Boast, J.: Over-thinking the protection of personal information act. Juta (Pty) Limited (2021)
13. Donner, J., Tellez, C.A.: Mobile banking and economic development: linking adoption, impact, and use. Asian J. Commun. **18**(4), 318–332 (2008)

14. International Telecommunication Union: Global Cybersecurity Index 2022: ITU Publications (2023)
15. Heeks, R.: Decent work and the digital gig economy: a developing country perspective on employment impacts and standards in online outsourcing, crowdwork, etc. Development Informatics Working Paper **71** (2017)
16. Pohle, J., Thiel, T.: Digital sovereignty. internet. Policy Rev. **9**(4), 1–19 (2020)
17. Luna-Reyes, L.F., Gil-Garcia, J.R.: Digital government transformation and internet portals: the co-evolution of technology, organizations, and institutions. Gov. Inf. Q. **31**(4), 545–555 (2014)
18. Heeks, R., et al.: The principles of digital transformation for development (dx4d): systematic literature review and future research agenda. MIOIR Working Paper Series (2023)
19. Yin, R.K.: Case study research and applications: design and methods. Sage Publications (2017)
20. Braun, V., Clarke, V.: Using thematic analysis in psychology. Qual. Res. Psychol. **3**(2), 77–101 (2006)
21. Ndungu, N., Oguso, A.: Digital technology and innovation in Africa: leapfrogging in finance. In: Technological Leapfrogging and Innovation in Africa, pp. 89–111. Edward Elgar Publishing (2023)
22. Calzati, S.: 'Data sovereignty' or 'data colonialism'? exploring the Chinese involvement in Africa's ICTs: a document review on kenya. J. Contemp. Afr. Stud. **40**(2), 270–285 (2022)
23. Venske, T.: Navigating digital sovereignty in Africa: a review of key challenges and constraints. The Africa Governance Papers **1**(4) (2023)
24. Haßler, B., Brugha, M., Muyoya, C., Mitchell, J., Hollow, D., Jackson, A.: Donor organizations and the principles for digital development: a landscape assessment and gap analysis. In: Principles for Digital Development. Jigsaw and Open Development and Education (2018)
25. House, F.: Freedom on the Net: Liberia (2023). https://freedomhouse.org
26. Tsuma, V.I., Kanda, M.: Factors affecting the adoption of e-procurement systems among international non-governmental organisations in Kenya. Int. J. Acad. Res. Acc. Finance Manag. Sci. **7**(2), 164–176 (2017)
27. Mensah, R., Cater-Steel, A., Toleman, M.: Factors affecting e-government adoption in Liberia: a practitioner perspective. Electron. J. Inf. Syst. Developing Countries **87**(3), e12161 (2021)
28. Atintande, M.: Digital communication in Africa at crossroads: from physical exploitation in the past to virtual dominance now. In: Langmia, K., Lando, A. (eds) Digital Communications at Crossroads in Africa. Palgrave Pivot, Cham
29. Otele, O.: Kenya's data protection regime: challenges and future prospects. J. African Politics **1**(1), 66–88 (2021)
30. Chander, A., Lê, U.P.: Data Nationalism Emory LJ **64**, 677 (2014)
31. UNCTAD: Digital economy report 2021: cross-border data flows and development. United Nations Conference on Trade and Development (2021)
32. DeNardis, L.: The internet in everything. Freedom and security in a world with no off switch. Yale University Press (2020)
33. Aziz, M.: Implementing ICT for governance in fragile states–a case study of Afghanistan. In: E-Governance, A Global Journey, pp. 93–106. IOS Press (2012)
34. UNDP: Digital public infrastructure: Action plan for inclusive and open digital systems (2023)
35. Broeders, D.: The public core of the internet: an international agenda for internet governance. Amsterdam University Press (2016)

Exploring the Strategy of E-Government Inclusion in Developing Countries

Gaffar Hafiz Sagala$^{(\boxtimes)}$ ⓘ and Dóra Őri ⓘ

Department of Information Systems, Institute of Data Analytics and Information Systems,
Corvinus University of Budapest, Budapest, Hungary
gaffar.sagala@stud.uni-corvinus.hu, dora.ori@uni-corvinus.hu

Abstract. E-government has the potential to facilitate citizens' access to public services in a more flexible form without reducing its effectiveness. However, developing countries face a digital divide problem in its implementation. This study aims to identify the theoretical background of the digital divide in the e-government context and propose alternative solutions to improve e-government inclusion in developing countries. We utilize co-citation analysis and a systematic literature review (SLR). From the literature review findings, we categorize the problem into four perspectives: information systems, infrastructure, end-user, and organizational perspectives, and we propose the related strategic solution. Furthermore, we propose four research agendas focusing on an evaluation study of existing e-government initiatives, encouraging multiple channels of e-government services, a social mobilization strategy to facilitate e-government inclusion, and social media utilization to promote e-government adoption. This study contributes to organizing knowledge regarding the digital divide and its alternative solution that could be followed up through various research agendas.

Keywords: e-government · digital divide · developing country · social inclusion

1 Introduction

Researchers indicate that the digital divide of e-government services is happening in various countries. The digital divide refers to the individuals left behind in the digital revolution, which leads to the digital access gap [1]. At the same time, digital inclusion refers to the activities that allow citizens and disadvantaged groups to have access and skills to use information and communication technologies (ICTs), enabling them to participate in and enjoy the information society [2]. The inequality issue of access to digital technology becomes critical as it potentially excludes citizens from the benefits of e-government services [3]. Researchers found various factors contributing to the digital divide and issues related to e-government services. Gauld et al.'s [4] research in Australia and New Zealand indicates that respondents with older age and lower education tend to be reluctant to use sophisticated 'transactional' e-government services. Pérez-Morote et al.'s [5] research in European Countries highlighted the existence of a digital divide as they found that e-government usage is positively affected by citizens' trust in

A. Kő et al. (Eds.): EGOVIS 2025, LNCS 16049, pp. 72–87, 2026.
https://doi.org/10.1007/978-3-032-02225-7_6

government, educational levels, and income. Reddick et al.'s [6] research in Canada identified that the digital divide affects access to e-government, particularly among women and older people, who prefer using the phone for assistance. Abu-Shanab's [7] research on Jordanians indicates that the level of awareness of the e-government initiatives and citizen familiarity with the e-government application contribute to e-government adoption. The previous studies indicate that the digital divide is a global issue that should be addressed by optimizing equal access to digital services for diverse citizens with appropriate information systems services.

In developing countries, the digital divide may escalate as the socioeconomic demography, geographical landscape, and digital infrastructure inequality issues are more challenging [8, 9]. Additionally, the lack of digital literacy and awareness further complicates the challenges of e-government services' inclusion in developing countries [9, 10]. Therefore, we argue that digital divide issues regarding e-government initiatives would be more intense in developing countries. Consequently, the strategy to address these problems may differ from those in developed countries.

Previous studies have proposed improvements in digital competence training [1], cohesive e-government training [11], specialized learning activities for older citizens [12], and raising citizen's awareness of e-government services [7]. However, the proposed strategy remains general and does not yet cover the holistic digital divide problem related to e-government initiatives in developing countries. We argue that scholars need a comprehensive point of view to generate holistic alternative solutions that are useful as references for further research, policy-making, and developing strategies to increase e-government inclusion. Therefore, this study aims to 1) Identify the theoretical background of the digital divide in e-government implementation through co-citation analysis of the published articles, 2) Investigate the theoretical perspective of solving the digital divide problem in implementing e-government in developing countries through systematic literature review, and 3) Propose a research agenda for the e-government inclusion strategy in developing countries.

This study provides insights into understanding the e-government inclusion problem in developing countries and its alternative solution. This study also proposes future research agendas for further investigation related to digital divide and to obtain empirical data for evidence-based policy-making. That insight could contribute to government bodies addressing the digital divide problem. The following sections of this article will cover the research method, findings, future research agenda, and conclusion.

2 Research Method

This study uses co-citation analysis to understand the theoretical background of the digital divide problem in e-government implementation and a systematic literature review (SLR) to identify the problems causing the digital divide in e-government implementation in developing countries and alternative solutions from primary articles. Co-citation analysis will help researchers understand the developing knowledge patterns in the related issue [13, 14]. Meanwhile, SLR facilitates researchers to conduct evidence-based reviews through relevant and credible academic literature [15]. We use multiple approaches because we try to provide strategic recommendations to bridge the digital divide in e-governance based on credible references that serve as a reference for research in related fields [15, 16].

2.1 Article Selection Protocol

The primary articles in this study were collected from the Scopus database. We considered the Scopus database because it has credibility in listed articles from various reputable journals. We conducted two stages of article selection, the first as input for co-citation analysis and the second as input for SLR. The article selection steps are presented in Fig. 1. In the identification step, we applied a general search key without specifically addressing the developing country to collect a greater number of articles, which is important to get more representative results of co-citation analysis. We performed the following search key: (TITLE-ABS-KEY("e-government" OR egovernment OR "electronic government") AND TITLE-ABS-KEY ("digital divide" OR "digital inclusion")) AND (LIMIT-TO(SUBJAREA,"BUSI") OR LIMIT-TO(SUBJAREA,"SOCI") OR LIMIT-TO(SUBJAREA,"ECON") OR LIMIT-TO(SUBJAREA,"DECI")). This search resulted in 452 documents. Furthermore, in the screening step, we limited to only journal and proceeding papers, and English-written documents were included in the analysis. The screening process left 330 included documents for co-citation analysis. Furthermore, for the SLR stage, we added one more search key at "TITLE-ABS-KEY" with the word "developing country," which left 39 articles for review. Finally, in the eligibility step, we applied inclusion and exclusion criteria focusing on the topic discussed. The collected document should contain a discussion regarding the problem of the digital divide in the e-government implementation and propose an alternative solution to solve the digital divide problem. Documents that do not directly discuss that information were excluded from the primary articles to be reviewed. The last steps left 20 documents that were included in the review process.

2.2 Data Analysis

In the first phase, we applied co-citation analysis to identify the theoretical background to understand the digital divide phenomenon in the implementation of e-government. We used R Studio with a biblioshiny package to perform co-citation analysis on the 330 screened articles. Furthermore, we reviewed the co-citation articles, particularly articles with high betweenness centrality, to identify the related articles' theoretical background and research findings. After that, we highlighted the key topic and described the findings. In the second phase, we applied a SLR to deepen our understanding of the digital divide related to e-government implementation in developing countries. This phase aimed to identify the specific problem of the digital divide in developing countries and identified the alternative solution proposed by the primary articles to improve e-government inclusion in developing countries. Scholars argue that SLR could help researchers gain a comprehensive mapping of knowledge, which is significant in providing insight and guidance for researchers, practitioners, and policymakers to act on further research and practical solutions to improve e-government inclusion [15, 16]. Finally, we proposed a future research agenda that can be conducted to generate relevant strategies to bridge the digital divide issue and promote e-government inclusion in developing countries.

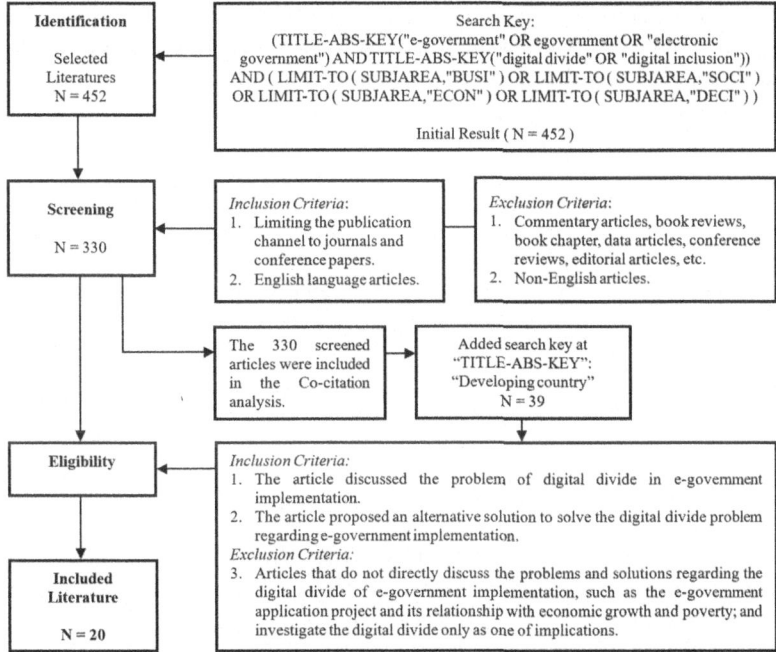

Fig. 1. Article Selection Protocol

3 Findings

3.1 Co-citation Analysis

The co-citation analysis results are presented in Table 1 and Fig. 2. The co-citation analysis is an effective approach to identify the significant references of the literature in the research front, which indicates the foundation of the concept regarding the digital inclusion of e-government services. Co-cited documents are the two or more documents that are cited by the paper from the research front, which are selected published papers from the academic database [13]. Different groups of co-citation patterns of the paper in the research front will lead to different clusters. The co-citation clustering would cluster the older papers and could not cluster the most recent papers because they have not yet been cited [13]. In the current study, the result indicates that the co-citation literature is distributed into four clusters. However, the current study is limited to reviewing the co-citation articles with significant betweenness scores. Therefore, we focus the review on the twenty documents in Cluster 1 and Cluster 2.

According to the literature review on Cluster 1, Bélanger and Carter [17] argue that the digital divide may hinders some populations from benefiting e-government services, highlighting disparities in access and skills [17]. Furthermore, Bélanger and Carter [18] indicate that government agencies should consider the disposition of trust to develop trust in the government and provide reliable e-government services. It was critical because trust in the government negatively affects perceived risk and usage intentions of e-government [18]. Consistently, Colesca and Dobrica [20] highlight the importance of user engagement and service accessibility, stating that it is critical for tailored e-government services to meet diverse user needs. Colesca and Dobrica [20] found that perceived usefulness, ease of use, information quality, and system quality are critical factors in encouraging user engagement in e-government services.

Table 1. Co-Citation Analysis

No.	Node	Cluster	Btwnss	Closeness	Page Rank	Topic
1	Belanger F. 2009	1	260,01853	0,007462	0,076234	Digital divide on e-government services
2	Carter L. 2005	1	250,39284	0,007352	0,069777	Trust and risk on e-government services
3	Norris P. 2001	1	108,21449	0,006024	0,031476	E-government adoption
4	Colesca S.E. 2008	1	14,61144	0,005681	0,027539	E-government acceptance
5	Davis F.D. 1989–2	1	41,83727	0,006329	0,021919	TAM
6	Mossberger K. 2003	1	100,02568	0,007142	0,030237	Virtual inequality
7	Taipale S. 2013	1	31,21547	0,006024	0,036308	Socioeconomic demographic
8	Ferro E. 2011	1	44,25075	0,006024	0,023440	IT skills acquisition
9	Akman I. 2005	1	10,83204	0,005747	0,014945	Socioeconomic demographic
10	Belanger F. 2008	1	89	0,003205	0,023829	E-government trust
11	Layne K. 2001	2	388,19411	0,007299	0,035107	Stages of e-government development
12	Rogers E.M. 1995	2	58,70149	0,006451	0,029452	Diffusion of innovation
13	Davis F.D. 1989–1	2	18,51545	0,005988	0,019478	TAM
14	Okunola O.M. 2017	2	86,34119	0,006369	0,041343	Socioeconomic demographic
15	Morris M.G. 2000	2	39,49443	0,006211	0,024761	Technology adoption
16	Venkatesh V. 2003	2	67,55558	0,006451	0,021656	UTAUT

(continued)

Table 1. (*continued*)

No.	Node	Cluster	Btwnss	Closeness	Page Rank	Topic
17	Chen Y.N. 2006	2	49,90438	0,006289	0,020626	E-government success strategy
18	Ebbers W.E. 2016	2	21,66504	0,005464	0,018878	Channel of online service
19	Fornell C. 1981	2	15,70457	0,006211	0,021139	SEM
20	Ma L. 2018	2	21,03459	0,006289	0,015573	E-government demand

Additionally, Taipale [21] found that socio-demographic factors, such as education, having children, and place of residence significantly influence e-service usage [21]. Gender and income were also found to be moderating factors in the relationship between internet usage and e-government services [21]. Akman et al. [23] also found that gender and education levels significantly correlate with e-government usage. In this case, Warschauer [19] emphasized that technology alone cannot guarantee social inclusion or educational improvement. Therefore, government agencies should also pay attention to the importance of socially mobilizing technology for effective educational reform in e-government services. [19]. Moreover, Ferro et al. [22] reveal that self-learning is significant for acquiring basic IT skills. Ferro et al. [22] propose three distinct approaches in IT skills acquisition leading to different user needs, such as "the athletes", "the laidback", and "the needy", which is critical to guide the development of effective digital inclusion policies.

According to literatures in Cluster 2, the co-citation analysis results indicate that co-citation articles lie in the theory on the Technology Acceptance Model (TAM) proposed by Davis et al. [24], the Diffusion of Innovations theory by Rogers [25], and the Unified Theory of Acceptance and Use of Technology (UTAUT) formulated by Venkatesh et al. [26]. Carter and Bélanger [27] explore factors influencing citizen's adoption of e-government services, integrating models from Technology Acceptance and Diffusion of Innovation. Carter and Bélanger [27] found that key predictors include perceived ease of use, compatibility, and trustworthiness. Carter and Bélanger [27] argue that government agencies should develop citizen-centered online services related to their e-government. Furthermore, Davis's [28] research indicates strong correlations between perceived usefulness, ease of use, and actual usage behaviors. Consistently, Rogers [25] discusses the diffusion of new technologies, emphasizing the importance of perceptions in adopting innovations. Rogers [25] argues that achieving a critical mass is essential for the successful diffusion of technology. However, Morris and Venkatesh [29] argue that different age groups have different approaches to technology adoption. Furthermore, Venkatesh et al. [26] review eight key factors of technology acceptance, develop a unified acceptance model, and empirically validate its efficacy, proposing a revised framework for understanding technology acceptance.

However, several co-citation articles highlight various aspects of e-government adoption beyond the technology acceptance features. Layne and Lee [30] discuss the chaotic nature of e-government initiatives and their challenges for public administrators. Layne and Lee [30] propose a 'stages of growth' model for fully functional e-government to cope with the technological and organizational challenges in each stage of e-government development. Chen et al. [31] identify key factors for successful e-government implementation, particularly in developed versus developing countries, and propose a framework for e-government strategies. Furthermore, Okunola et al. [32] highlight the impact of demographic, socioeconomic, and locational factors on Internet access and e-government experience and argue that the government should address those issues for citizen empowerment. Ebbers et al. [33] found that digital skills are less relevant for channel uptake but affect satisfaction with online services. However, in this context, Ebbers et al. [33] indicate that the e-government service provides a registration process online, while consultation processes are provided offline. Ma and Zheng [34] highlight the importance of understanding the demand side of e-government, suggesting that merely supplying e-government functions does not guarantee increased citizen engagement.

Based on co-citation articles, we can reflect that the development of e-government should fulfill the criteria for technology acceptance, such as usefulness, ease of use, enjoyment, quality of information, and quality of service. However, when implementing e-government, government agencies should develop appropriate strategies that encourage citizens to access the application, improve technological literacy, facilitate the learning process, and provide appropriate internet infrastructure and technical support according to the demographic, socioeconomic, and locational factors of the targeted users (citizens). This underscores the need for a comprehensive understanding of the demand side of e-government, influenced by the objective of providing e-government services and the needs and capabilities of citizens to adopt related technology, which differ among social groups [34]. The urgency of this task cannot be overstated, as it is crucial for the successful adoption and utilization of e-government. Additionally, Fornell and Larcker [35] are identified as one of the co-citation articles. It indicates the use of structural equational modelling in the growing research regarding e-government.

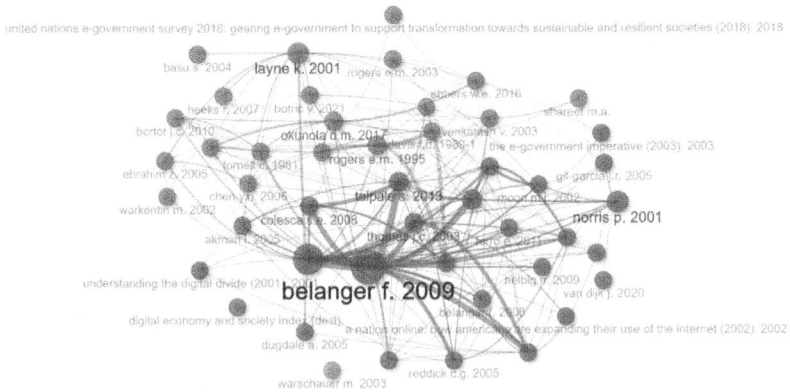

Fig. 2. Co-Citation Map

3.2 Systematic Literature Review

Based on the main articles, several factors contribute to the digital divide, posing a challenge to e-government inclusion in developing countries. Based on the research findings of the primary literature, we categorized the problem and solution into four perspectives, including the information systems perspective, the infrastructure perspective, the end-user perspective, and the organizational perspective. These categorizations aimed to deliver a comprehensive point of view on the digital divide issue that is critical to develop appropriate strategies to improve e-government inclusion in developing countries. The optimal adoption of e-government services simultaneously improves the effectiveness of digital investment in the public sector. The literature review summary is observable in Table 2.

Information Systems Perspective. The primary articles found a lack of adoption of e-government [36]. According to the co-citation articles, previous studies have investigated the e-government issue through TAM [28], Diffusion of Innovations [25], and UTAUT [26] frameworks. Those frameworks are consistently found in the SLR phase, which indicates that the adoption issue contributes to user experience with the e-government information systems, which leads to acceptance or resistance behavior. The key issues proposed by the primary articles are user satisfaction [37], information systems usability regarding the ease of use issue [38], and lack of qualifications regarding the feature and service quality of the e-government information systems [39]. Regarding these findings, the digital divide issues should consider the information systems perspective to solve the problem of e-government acceptance and continuous adoption among citizens in general.

We found several alternative solutions proposed by the primary articles to address the information systems issues, such as improvement in information systems compatibility [36], system quality [37], relative advantage in security and privacy [40], service quality, ease of use [38], and a transparent regulatory framework and implementation strategy [39]. The compatibility of information systems to the specific task of related e-government services will lead to perceived usefulness among citizens and significantly impact the adoption of related e-government services [36]. System quality refers to the extent to which the e-government application works appropriately with minimum constraint to provide a smooth working experience when citizens use the e-government services [37]. Consistently, Arshad and Khurram [38] highlight the ease of use issue that should be improved to encourage various backgrounds of citizens to adopt e-government services easily. Perceived ease of use would stimulate low digital literacy users to intend to use the e-government service and continue using it when they get a convenient experience. Moreover, Alomari et al. [40] highlighted security and privacy issues that the e-government application should cover. It would facilitate trust in the e-government service regarding personal data security [36, 40, 41]. Finally, Garad and Qamari [39] propose a clear regulatory framework and implementation strategy for developing and implementing e-government information systems. That proposed solution could be applied to improve existing e-government information systems by focusing on improving certain functions or features to improve compatibility, usefulness, ease of use, and security and privacy features.

Table 2. SLR Findings: Digital Divide Problems and Proposed Solutions

No.	Digital Divide Problems	Proposed Solutions
1	*Information Systems Perspective*	
	• Lack of E-government adoption [36] • User satisfaction [37] • Usability (Ease of use) [38] • Lack of qualifications [39]	• Improve compatibility [36] • Improve system quality [37] • Improve e-service quality (regarding ease of use) [38] • Improve relative advantage in security and privacy [40] • Clear regulatory framework/implementation strategy [39]
2	*Infrastructure Perspective*	
	• Broadband internet access/Low internet access [6, 42] • Low access to technology/digital tools [9, 32] • Weak technological infrastructure [39, 43] • Channel of government service [6]	• Equally distributed internet infrastructure [6, 32, 36, 42] • Improve technology adoption [6, 32, 42] • Distributed technology availability [36] • Improvement of technology infrastructure [39, 43] • Multiple channels of e-government service [6]
3	*End-User Perspective*	
	• Socio-economic factors/income and education disparities [6, 9, 32, 42] • Low computer/digital literacy [9, 10, 43] • Lack of awareness about service [10, 37] • Social exclusion problem [44] • Cultural norms [45] • Gender gap [7, 9, 38] • Locational factors [32] • Digital divide and trust [41] • Lack of e-government adoption/resistance to change [36, 38, 40]	• Adequate training to improve digital literacy/self-efficacy [10, 41, 46] • Technical support [10, 41] • Individual and community/Citizen empowerment (resource building) [41, 44, 47] • Mobile phone proliferation and telecenters [48] • Attention to local and cultural contexts [41] • Attention to digital convergence [44] • Generating trust [36] • Social influence, word of mouth (WoM), and benefiting social network [36, 38, 40]
4	*Organizational Perspective*	
	• Institutions, leadership, resources, and organizational factors [49] • Apprehensiveness towards technology, preferring manual processes over electronic ones [50] • Significant digital divide (even on advance e-government services) [51]	• Leadership approach and good governance [49] • Managing knowledge-based resources effectively [51] • Clear strategy of e-government implementation [50]

Digital Infrastructure Perspective. Infrastructure is one of the most significant aspects that primary researchers highlight regarding the digital divide issue in developing countries. The critical issue regarding infrastructure is the equalization of infrastructure availability, which leads to unequal access to digital infrastructure. Primary researchers found low internet infrastructure [6, 42], low technological infrastructure [39, 43], low access to the internet, technology, and digital tools [9, 32], and a limited channel of government service [6] escalated the digital divide in e-government service.

Therefore, the previous studies highlight the need for internet access that is evenly distributed from urban to rural areas [9, 32]. Providing equal access to the internet demands reliable internet infrastructure throughout the country [6, 32, 36, 42]. Furthermore, to ensure digital inclusion, the government should facilitate technology availability [36]. In many cases, citizens in rural areas lack technology ownership or have limited access to digital tools. In some cases, citizens have ownership of the technology but do not realize the potential of its usability for accessing e-government services. Therefore, government agencies could facilitate access to technology with two alternative strategies: 1) technical facilitation by facilitating citizens in accessing technology with a digital device provided by the government in specific service points in governmental offices, and 2) technical support by facilitating learning to adopt e-government services with the citizens' own device [6, 32, 42]. Additionally, regarding access to e-government services, the government could provide multiple channels of e-government service, which could be accessed through mobile applications, governmental offices (service points), or telephone services [6]. Those proposed solutions imply the needs of e-government information systems that accommodate a multichannel approach to enhance accessibility and promote digital inclusion [6]. The facilitation of digital devices and technical support would lead to further investment in e-government services. However, it is considerably commensurate as the government can deliver inclusive public goods and services, and the efficiency would simultaneously be increased due to the effective data gathering from digital devices.

End-User Perspective. The primary articles have significantly highlighted end-user issues as contributors to the digital divide concerning e-government services in developing countries. It leads to the argument that end-user issues are the most significant issue, which implies the digital divide. We use the term end-user to represent citizens who use the e-government service. According to the primary articles, we found complex problem that comes from the end-user perspective, including socio-economic factors (income and education disparities) [6, 9, 32, 42], gender gap [9, 38, 45], locational factors [32], social exclusion problem [44], low computer and digital literacy [9, 10, 43], resistance to change [36, 38, 40], lack of awareness about service [10, 37], cultural norms [45], and trust [41].

Socioeconomic factors are the identical problems in developing countries, such as the gap in income, educational background, and social support, that lead to social exclusion in the use of digital technologies and digital literacy to optimize the use of digital tools. Consistent with the co-citation article, Warschauer [19] stressed that technology alone does not ensure social inclusion or educational improvement. Therefore, the government should initiate social mobilization of technology for effective educational reform aimed at e-government services inclusion and user engagement that meet diverse user needs

[19, 20]. Additionally, locational factors also become identical issues in developing countries as the development of infrastructure is not equally implemented, particularly in rural areas. Those situations exclude the end user from the availability of e-government services due to unawareness of such technology, inability to access such digital devices, and resistance to adoption due to a lack of digital literacy. Moreover, several primary articles found the gender gap and cultural norms to be significant contributors to the digital divide problem. These norms may discourage certain groups from engaging with digital technologies.

In this case, firstly, the government should give appropriate attention to developing an appropriate strategy through policy research to improve inclusive access to e-government that specifically addresses the socioeconomic and demographic issues. Those strategies should focus on social inclusion in e-government services. The government should improve access to digital literacy among its citizens so that they can get e-government services wherever they are and whatever their social and economic circumstances are. Practically, the government should give appropriate attention to digital convergence in local contexts [44], facilitate adequate training to improve digital literacy [10, 36, 41], and facilitate technical support [10, 41]. Secondly, the government should empower individuals or communities to support the government agenda regarding e-government inclusion in terms of publication, social influence, social network, and social support to distribute access to technology and knowledge in using e-government [38, 40, 41, 44, 47]. Thirdly, the government could exploit digital tools to improve citizens' awareness of e-government services through mobile phone proliferation and telecenters [48]. This strategy would be effective for digitally literate citizens. Finally, to address cultural norms issues, governments should give appropriate attention to cultural infrastructure [41], generating trust in the government that using e-government would not interrupt cultural norms [36].

Organizational Perspectives. Apriliyanti et al. [49] indicate that organizational factors regarding the digital divide of e-government services are rarely investigated. Therefore, Apriliyanti et al. [49] propose that the government should give appropriate attention to institutions, leadership, resources, and organizational factors in the e-government project and its implementation that promotes e-government inclusion. The government should develop a clear strategy for e-government implementation, addressing specific aspects that certain areas face [50]. To do this effectively, governments should conduct evaluation studies to identify the root causes of the digital divide based on their unique circumstances. This approach will help the government develop targeted strategies to enhance e-government inclusiveness. Finally, Chatfield and Alhujran [51] highlight the critical role of the government in managing knowledge-based resources effectively to create e-government services that meet the needs of citizens.

4 Future Research Agenda

According to the co-citation analysis and SLR findings, we formulate four research agendas outlined as follows:

1. *Policy research of e-government service implementation.* The digital divide issue in the existing e-government services needs to be identified beyond the theoretical point of view. Government bodies and stakeholders should conduct evaluation research to identify the root of problems, followed by policy studies to develop appropriate regulations and strategies for delivering access to e-government to all groups of citizens. This study should address the information system, infrastructure, end-user, and organizational perspectives. The government and stakeholders can highlight the specific problem from one of those perspectives so that the strategic solution is specific and right on target.

2. *Exploring strategies to distribute technology access through multiple channels of e-government services that address diverse targeted users.* In developing countries, socio-economic factors are the main challenges to bridge the inclusion of e-government services. However, a massive investment in digital infrastructure is expensive and time-consuming. Meanwhile, e-government services can help the government carry out specific tasks, and their accessibility is crucial. Therefore, providing e-government service channels through e-government service centers in village offices and social mobilization to provide access to e-government services can be an alternative while waiting for the digital infrastructure to cover rural areas. In this case, a practical strategy should be explored to ensure that it effectively encourages social inclusion in accessing e-government services. Scholars and the government could collaboratively apply action research to design the strategic implementation of hybrid services of e-government and continuously improve the service during the study cycle through the evaluation and revision phases until the best practices are discovered.

3. *Exploring social mobilization strategy enabling communities to deliver social influences in improving e-government adoption.* Individual and community empowerment is one of the alternative strategies to improve digital inclusion. At the same time, we also found that social influence is a critical factor in encouraging end-users to adopt e-government services. In this case, governments need specific strategies to mobilize the community to help them influence citizens to adopt e-government services. Researchers could adopt digital marketing and soft marketing strategies for this agenda. For example, further researchers could investigate the strategic role of the community task force in helping the government deliver access to e-government services. Community task force could function as social support to help digitally illiterate citizens utilize e-government services through home services or ambassadors in promoting the e-government services to the communities. However, the effectiveness of this approach should be further investigated through action research or an experimental research agenda.

4. *Developing a training strategy for e-government usage through social media platforms.* One of the problems identified in the SLR findings is that users or citizens are unaware of the availability of e-government services, and there is low technical knowledge of how to use e-government services and their benefits. Even though digital literacy becomes a problem in developing countries. However, the unoptimized use of personal digital devices also becomes a significant problem regarding e-government adoption. Therefore, distributing knowledge through soft training would facilitate the publication, introduction, and learning process of certain e-government services. In

this case, social media would be a potential platform as it facilitates broad access to citizens. Design research in developing appropriate infographics, user guidance, tutorials, and service features of certain e-government services is needed to teach the prospective user to operate the e-government feature appropriately.

5 Conclusion

The current studies consistently found that socioeconomic demographic and geographical factors become significant constraints of e-government services inclusion, and their impact on the digital divide escalates linearly in developing countries with the escalation of socioeconomic demographic and geographical problems themselves. Furthermore, the problem of infrastructure availability, digital literacy, and technology acceptance has also been found to be a constraint to e-government adoption among citizens in developing countries. We also found that gender gap and cultural norm issues contribute to the resistance to adopting e-government services. In this case, we categorized the problem into four perspectives, including: information systems, infrastructure, end-user, and organizational perspective, and proposed the related strategic solution. Based on those findings, we proposed four research agendas focusing on an evaluation study to identify relevant problems of the digital divide faced by the government, encourage multiple channels of e-government services to facilitate social inclusion, social mobilization strategy as community empowerment to facilitate e-government inclusion, and social media utilization to facilitate publication, introduction, and training strategy for e-government usage. This research agenda is critical to developing appropriate strategies for bridging the digital divide regarding the implementation of e-government services. The inclusion of e-government services is critical to ensuring the benefits of public goods investment.

This study contributes to organizing knowledge regarding the digital divide problem and its alternative solution that could be followed up through various research agendas. This study has limitations in the method that limits the research findings to published literature. This study needs further validation of the proposed concept and further empirical research to ensure the proposed solution effectively works in specific communities and addresses e-government service inclusion problems.

Acknowledgement. This study is funded by the EKÖP scholarship, number EKOP-CORVINUS-25-3-9, with the support of the National Research, Development, and Innovation Fund provided by the Ministry of Culture and Innovation, Hungary, as part of the University Research Scholarship Program announced for the 2025/2026 academic year.

References

1. Morte-Nadal, T., Esteban-Navarro, M.A.: Digital competences for improving digital inclusion in e-government services: a mixed-methods systematic review protocol. Int J Qual Methods **21**, 1–9 (2022)

2. Adam, I.O., Dzang, A.M.: Bridging the global digital divide through digital inclusion: the role of ICT access and ICT use. Transform. Gov. People Process Policy **15**(4), 580–596 (2020)
3. Heeks, R.: Digital inequality beyond the digital divide: conceptualizing adverse digital incorporation in the global South. Inf. Technol. Dev. **28**(4), 688–704 (2022)
4. Gauld, R., Goldfinch, S., Horsburgh, S.: Do they want it? Do they use it? The "demand-side" of e-government in Australia and New Zealand. Gov. Inf. Q. **27**(2), 177–186 (2010)
5. Pérez-Morote, R., Pontones-Rosa, C., Núñez-Chicharro, M.: The effects of e-government evaluation, trust and the digital divide in the levels of e-government use in European countries. Technol. Forecast Soc. Change. **2020**(154), 119973 (2019)
6. Reddick, C.G., Abdelsalam, H.M.E., Elkadi, H.A.: Channel choice and the digital divide in e-government: the case of Egypt. Inf. Technol. Dev. **18**(3), 226–246 (2012)
7. Abu-Shanab, E.A.: E-government familiarity influence on Jordanians' perceptions. Telemat. Inform. **34**(1), 103–113 (2017)
8. Addo, A., Senyo, P.K.: Advancing e-governance for development: digital identification and its link to socioeconomic inclusion. Gov. Inf. Q. **38**(2), 101568 (2021)
9. Ariansyah, K., et al.: Digital inclusion for all? A gender-disaggregated analysis of e-government service use in Indonesia. Transform. Gov. People Process Policy **17**(4), 655–72 (2023)
10. Dwivedi, Y.K., Sahu, G.P., Rana, N.P., Singh, M., Chandwani, R.K.: Common services centres (CSCs) as an approach to bridge the digital divide: reflecting on challenges and obstacles. Transform. Gov. People Process Policy. **10**(4), 511–525 (2016)
11. Chohan, S.R., Hu, G.: Strengthening digital inclusion through e-government: cohesive ICT training programs to intensify digital competency. Inf. Technol. Dev. **28**(1), 16–38 (2022)
12. Botrić, V., Božić, L.: The digital divide and e-government in European economies. Econ. Res. Istraz. **34**(1), 2935–2955 (2021)
13. Boyack, K.W., Klavans, R.: Co-citation analysis, bibliographic coupling, and direct citation: which citation approach represents the research front most accurately? J. Am. Soc. Inf. Sci. Technol. **61**(12), 2389–2404 (2010)
14. Small, H.: Co-citation in the scientific literature: a new measure of the relationship between two documents. J. Am. Soc. Inf. Sci. **24**(4), 265–269 (1973)
15. Okoli, C.: A guide to conducting a standalone systematic literature review. Commun. Assoc. Inf. Syst. **37**(1), 879–910 (2015)
16. Webster, J., Watson, R.T.: Analyzing the past to prepare for the future: writing a literature review. MIS Q. xiii--xxiii (2002)
17. Bélanger, F., Carter, L.: The impact of the digital divide on e-government use. Commun. ACM **52**(4), 132–135 (2009)
18. Bélanger, F., Carter, L.: Trust and risk in e-government adoption. J. Strateg. Inf. Syst. **17**(2), 165–176 (2008)
19. Warschauer, M.: Dissecting the "digital divide": a case study in Egypt. Inf. Soc. **19**(4), 297–304 (2003)
20. Colesca, S.E., Dobrica, L.: Adoption and use of e-government services: the case of Romania. J. Appl. Res. Technol. **6**, 204–217 (2008)
21. Taipale, S.: The use of e-government services and the Internet: the role of socio-demographic, economic and geographical predictors. Telecomm. Policy. **37**(4–5), 413–422 (2013)
22. Ferro, E., Helbig, N.C., Gil-Garcia, J.R.: The role of IT literacy in defining digital divide policy needs. Gov. Inf. Q. **28**(1), 3–10 (2011)
23. Akman, I., Yazici, A., Mishra, A., Arifoglu, A.: E-government: a global view and an empirical evaluation of some attributes of citizens. Gov. Inf. Q. **22**(2), 239–257 (2005)
24. Davis, F.D., Bagozzi, R.P., Warshaw, P.R.: User acceptance of computer technology: a comparison of two theoretical models. Manage. Sci. **35**(8), 982–1003 (1989)

25. Rogers, E.M.: Diffusion of innovations: modifications of a model for telecommunications. Die Diffus von Innov der Telekommunikation 25–38 (1995)
26. Venkatesh, V., Morris, M.G., Davis, G.B., Davis, F.D.: User acceptance of information technology: toward a unified view. MIS Q. 425–78 (2003)
27. Carter, L., Bélanger, F.: The utilization of e-government services: citizen trust, innovation and acceptance factors. Inf. Syst. J. **15**(1), 5–25 (2005)
28. Davis, F.: Perceived usefulness, perceived ease of use, and user acceptance of information technology. MIS Q. Manag. Inf. Syst. **13**(3), 319–339 (1989)
29. Morris, M.G., Venkatesh, V.: Age differences in technology adoption decisions: implications for a changing work force. Pers. Psychol. **53**(2), 375–403 (2000)
30. Layne, K., Lee, J.: Developing fully functional e-government: a four stage model. Gov. Inf. Q. **18**(2), 122–136 (2001)
31. Chen, Y.N., Chen, H.M., Huang, W., Ching, R.K.H.: E-government strategies in developed and developing countries: an implementation framework and case study. J. Glob. Inf. Manag. **14**(1), 23–46 (2006)
32. Okunola, O.M., Rowley, J., Johnson, F.: The multi-dimensional digital divide: perspectives from an e-government portal in Nigeria. Gov. Inf. Q. **34**(2), 329–339 (2017)
33. Ebbers, W.E., Jansen, M.G.M., van Deursen, A.J.A.M.: Impact of the digital divide on e-government: expanding from channel choice to channel usage. Gov. Inf. Q. **33**(4), 685–692 (2016)
34. Ma, L., Zheng, Y.: Does e-government performance actually boost citizen use? Evidence from European countries. Public Manag. Rev. **20**(10), 1513–1532 (2018)
35. Fornell, C., Larcker, D.F.: Structural Equation Models with Unobservable Variables and Measurement Error: Algebra and Statistics. Sage Publications Sage CA, Los Angeles, CA (1981)
36. Kumar, R., Sachan, A., Mukherjee, A.: Direct vs indirect e-government adoption: an exploratory study. Digit. Policy Regul. Gov. **20**(2), 149–162 (2018)
37. Idoughi, D., Abdelhakim, D.: Developing countries e-government services evaluation identifying and testing antecedents of satisfaction case of Algeria. Int. J. Electron. Gov. Res. **14**(1), 63–85 (2018)
38. Arshad, S., Khurram, S.: Gender difference in the continuance intention to e-file income tax returns in Pakistan. Inf. Polity. **26**(2), 147–155 (2021)
39. Garad, A., Qamari, I.N.: Determining factors influencing establishing e-service quality in developing countries: a case study of Yemen e-government. Int. J. Electron. Gov. Res. **17**(1), 15–30 (2021)
40. Alomari, M.K., Sandhu, K., Woods, P.: Exploring citizen perceptions of barriers to e-government adoption in a developing country. Transform. Gov. People Process Policy **8**(1), 131–150 (2014)
41. Mousavi, S.A., Pimenidis, E., Jahankhani, H.: Cultivating trust - an electronic-government development model for addressing the needs of developing countries. Int. J. Electron. Secur. Digit. Forensics **1**(3), 233–248 (2008)
42. Pazmiño-Sarango, M., Naranjo-Zolotov, M., Cruz-Jesus, F.: Assessing the drivers of the regional digital divide and their impact on eGovernment services: evidence from a South American country. Inf. Technol. People **35**(7), 2002–2025 (2022)
43. As-Saber, S., Hossain, K., Srivastava, A.: Technology, society and e-government: in search of an eclectic framework. Electron. Gov. **4**(2), 156–178 (2007)
44. Muganda, N., Van Belle, J.P.: Towards a nomadic e-government co-evolutionary framework (NECE) for building knowledge infrastructures for African countries. Creat Glob Econ through Innov Knowl Manag Theory Pract - Proc 12th Int Bus Inf Manag Assoc Conf IBIMA 2009. 1–3:1125–32 (2009)

45. Abu-Shanab, E., Al-Jamal, N.: Exploring the gender digital divide in Jordan. Gend. Technol. Dev. **19**(1), 91–113 (2015)
46. Gaur, A., Kumar, M.: A systematic approach to conducting review studies: an assessment of content analysis in 25 years of IB research. J. World Bus. **53**(2), 280–289 (2018)
47. Al-Sammarraie, M.K.F., Rasheed, M.M., Faieq, A.K.: Determinants of the long term factors and effects of sustainability on usage of electronic government services: evidence from the kingdom of Saudi Arabia. Int. J. Econ. Perspect. **10**(4), 622–633 (2016)
48. Rahman, T., Khan, N.A.: Reckoning electronic government progress in Bangladesh. Int. J. Public Adm. **35**(2), 112–121 (2012)
49. Apriliyanti, I.D., Kusumasari, B., Pramusinto, A., Setianto, W.A.: Digital divide in ASEAN member states: analyzing the critical factors for successful e-government programs. Online Inf. Rev. **45**(2), 440–460 (2021)
50. Moatshe, R.M., Mahmood, Z.: Implementing eGovernment projects: challenges facing developing countries. In: Proceedings of the European Conference e-Government, ECEG., pp. 464–72 (2012)
51. Chatfield, A.T., Alhujran, O.: A cross-country comparative analysis of e-government service delivery among Arab countries. Inf. Technol. Dev. **15**(3), 151–170 (2009)

The Digital Transformation of Census in Iraq: Challenges and Opportunities

Rozha Kamal Ahmed[1,3,4(✉)], Dara Rashid Mahmud[2], Silvia Lips[3], and Dirk Drahiem[3]

[1] Sulaimani Polytechnic University, Sulaimaniyah, Iraq
[2] Ministry of Planning in the Kurdistan Region of Iraq, Erbil, Iraq
dara.khoshnaw@gov.krd
[3] Tallinn University of Technology, Tallinn, Estonia
rozha.ahmed@spu.edu.iq,
{rozha.ahmed,silvia.lips,dirk.drahiem}@Taltech.ee, rozha.ahmed@ega.ee
[4] e-Governance Academy, Tallinn, Estonia

Abstract. The census process is a critical foundation for national data collection, policymaking, and government planning. The digitization of the census process offers significant potential to improve accuracy, data integrity, and efficiency. This research examines the digital transformation of the census process in Iraq as a case study. The main objective is to evaluate the benefits and obstacles encountered in the application of digital tools throughout the census operation of 2024. Data were gathered from a triangulation of various sources. Conducting interviews with 150 census enumerators in Sulaimaniyah, Kurdistan region of Iraq, provided comprehensive information on the process, supplemented by document analysis and direct observation to enhance the research findings. The findings indicate numerous advantages, including improved time efficiency, data accuracy, user-friendliness, and increased data security. The research concurrently highlighted numerous significant challenges, including technological infrastructure issues, software limitations, administrative inefficiencies, and concerns about public trust. In light of these findings, the study offers a set of practical recommendations to improve future Iraqi censuses. This first study on the digital transformation of the census process in Iraq seeks to inform policymakers, government officials, and researchers, providing essential knowledge to facilitate future improvements.

Keywords: Census · Digital Transformation · Challenges · Opportunities · Iraq · Kurdistan

1 Introduction

Censuses are a cornerstone of national planning, providing essential data on population size, demographics, economic characteristics, and social context, as well

A. Kő et al. (Eds.): EGOVIS 2025, LNCS 16049, pp. 88–102, 2026.
https://doi.org/10.1007/978-3-032-02225-7_7

as assessing the needs of local communities [11,35]. Census represents a statistical operation designed to count and collect information on the entire population of a country [3,11,16,30,33,35,43]. It serves as a vital tool for governments in designing policies, allocating resources, and monitoring development in all sectors.

Traditionally, censuses have been conducted using paper surveys and manual data collection methods [3,28,43]. Although these methods were important in the past, they are now considered slow and complicated, needing many workers to collect data in the field, and can be expensive, especially in areas with security and logistical issues [3,16,35,43].

Recently, the global shift toward digital transformation has provided new possibilities for modernizing data collection processes, including national censuses. Modern census methods, such as online surveys, mobile data collection tools, and integrated databases, present enhanced efficiency, timeliness, and precision. Many countries are beginning to adopt these innovations to meet the growing demand for current and reliable demographic data in an increasingly dynamic world [6,21,22,30,35,39,43].

This study aims to explore the digital transformation of census data collection in Iraq as a first preliminary research in this domain, with a focus on the opportunities it presents and the challenges it involves. As Iraq considers shifting to digital methods for its national census, it is essential to understand its implications. Consequently, this study addresses the following two central research questions:

- RQ1: What benefits can digital census methodologies bring to Iraq's governance and policymaking?
- RQ2: What barriers may Iraq face in adopting digital census methods?

The significance of this study lies in its potential to inform policymakers, government agencies, and researchers about the practical considerations of the digital transformation of census taking in Iraq. By exploring both potential and challenges, this research contributes to a broader discourse on how technology can improve data-driven decision-making and public administration in developing countries.

The study is structured as follows. Section 2 provides related work and highlights global trends in the implementation of digital transformation in census taking. Section 3 outlines the research methodology, detailing the research design, data collection methods, and data analysis approach. Section 4 presents the case description and provides an overview of the state of digitalization in Iraq, in particular, with the census process. Section 5 presents and discusses the key findings, focusing on the opportunities and challenges identified in Iraq's pursuit of digital census transformation, as well as recommendations for improvement. Finally, Sect. 6 concludes the study and, in addition, discusses its limitations and outlines potential directions for future research.

2   Background and Related Work

Census taking enables systematic collection and analysis of data on a country's population. Valid census information is vital for policymakers in planning long-term strategies and public services [46]. Different methods are available for census taking, depending on the country's resources and needs. This section provides an overview of census-taking methods based on the available academic literature.

Historically, the most well-known methods for population count are *de jure* and *de facto* methods [41]. According to the first scenario, the legal residence of the people is considered, regardless of their actual physical presence at the time of the census. In the second case, the actual physical presence during the census is counted [5].

Census taking can also be achieved through direct interviews when trained enumerators visit households and conduct interviews [23]. However, this time-consuming process is nowadays less used and has been replaced in many cases by self-enumeration. Therefore, some countries, like the US, UK, and Australia, have also used self-enumeration, where the census forms are filled out on paper or online by the households themselves [7,40].

More recently, countries have used existing government records (e.g., tax, health, and education data) for census taking, which is more cost-effective and less intrusive from the person's perspective [19,27]. In some countries, census data are collected continuously over time in segments rather than all at once. This method is called a rolling census, and for example, France has shifted since 2004 from the traditional decennial census to this new method [17,32].

In addition to traditional census, register-based census and rolling census, many European countries (e.g. Germany, Poland, Italy, Estonia, Latvia, Lithuania, etc.) prefer a combined approach, where the register information is combined with other available data sources such as existing surveys or sample surveys conducted ad hoc for the census [43]. In addition, Valente proposes alternative and innovative approaches to census-taking, focusing on data quality, costs, and organization [44].

All previously described census-taking methods have their pros and cons and related challenges. Regardless of the particular method, it is always a question of how to obtain a complete count [18]. Some works highlight several other census-related challenges, from financial and confidentiality challenges [1,38] to sensitive concerns related to the count of ethnic minorities [15].

Based on the literature, there has been a clear shift from traditional census methods to greater use of registers and their combined use with sample surveys. The review of the existing literature also showed that the main challenges in census taking are related to cost effectiveness, privacy concerns, collaboration, availability, and accessibility [38]. These challenges have prompted countries to make methodological developments and to find new alternative technologies and sampling methods in census taking.

When it comes to specifically census-taking practices in Iraq, the digital transformation of census-taking is a relatively new concept, with no significant prior literature or documented studies that address this specific area. As the country begins to modernize its data collection systems, particularly in the context of national censuses, there is a clear gap in academic and policy-oriented research on the subject. This study seeks to fill this gap by exploring the opportunities and challenges associated with implementing digital census methodologies in Iraq. By examining both the potential benefits and the practical barriers, the research provides valuable insights that can inform future strategies for digital governance and data-driven policymaking in the country.

3   Research Approach

3.1   Research Methodology

As the digital transformation of census taking is an underexplored area in Iraq, with no prior literature or documented studies that address this specific transition, this study adopts an exploratory case study approach as its primary methodology. This approach is especially appropriate for examining emerging context-specific phenomena where the boundaries between the phenomenon and its real-life setting are not clearly defined and are new [34, 47, 48].

3.2   Data Collection

The triangulation of multiple data sources was used to improve the validity and depth of the study by capturing diverse perspectives on the research subject. As noted in [34, 48], triangulation is particularly valuable in case study research, which allows cross-verification of findings and reduces the risk of bias associated with relying on a single source. Consequently, this study relied on the following data sources:

- In-depth interviews serve as the main data source in this case study, providing access to the experiences and perspectives of individuals directly involved in the digital census process, which may not be fully captured through other data sources [34]. A total of 150 participants were selected using purposeful sampling, a technique that involves identifying and selecting individuals who are especially knowledgeable about or experienced with the phenomenon [14, 20, 36, 37, 45]. The participants were the enumerators who acted as the end users of the system. This approach ensured the collection of information-rich data that are relevant to the research objectives. The sample size was determined based on the principle of data saturation, the point at which no new information or themes emerge from the data [8, 13, 14, 24, 36, 37, 45]. To monitor data saturation, the study employed a constant comparative method and systematic coding procedures during data analysis [9, 36]. This iterative process involved continuously comparing new data with existing codes and themes to identify any emerging patterns or discrepancies. Such a rigorous analytical approach improved the credibility and depth of the findings. Furthermore, participants have been informed that the interviews will be anonymous and that their identity will be kept confidential, and they have been clearly and transparently informed about the study, its procedures and its methodology.

- In this study, document analysis was also considered a vital qualitative data source, which involved systematically reviewing and interpreting printed and electronic materials to uncover meaning, gain understanding, and arrive at conclusions relevant to the research objectives. Document analysis was used to supplement the data obtained from other sources, providing a comprehensive understanding of the digital transformation of the census taking process in Iraq. The analysis encompassed a variety of sources, including current literature on technological applications in census processes, official publications, policy documents, and reports available on the Ministry of Planning's websites and other relevant online platforms.
- Direct observation is a fundamental qualitative data source that allows the collection of real-time data on behaviors, interactions, and environmental factors that may not be accessible through other methods; it also enables researchers to gain a complete understanding of phenomena within their natural contexts [34]. In this study, the second author served as a direct observer, engaged in the process intensively, and provided continuous supervision. This participation facilitated the collection of precise data, providing insight into the practical challenges and contextual factors that influence the adoption of digital census methodologies.

3.3   Instrument

The authors used a structured interview approach through a standardized set of open-ended questions presented in a consistent order to each participant. The interview protocol was meticulously designed to obtain rich qualitative data. It comprised four open questions aimed at capturing detailed narratives and personal experiences related to the census process. In addition, three demographic questions were included to provide context to participants' responses, such as their gender, age, and education level. The interviews were conducted after the completion of the digital census implementation phase between December 2024 and January 2025. This timing allowed participants to reflect comprehensively on the entire process, providing informed feedback on both the implementation and the results of the digital transformation.

3.4   Data Analysis Procedure

This study utilized the RQDA package (R-based qualitative data analysis) for qualitative data analysis, which provides features such as text coding, memo writing, and data retrieval for efficient management and analysis [10].

Thematic analysis was used to find, analyze, and summarize data as themes. This method effectively captures qualitative data, facilitating a comprehensive understanding of participants' experiences and perspectives [12,34].

3.5 Validity and Reliability Check

The research design adhered to established validity and reliability criteria, as outlined by Yin [47,48] and presented in Table 1, to ensure the robustness and credibility of this exploratory case study on the digital transformation of census collection in Iraq.

Table 1. Validity and reliability check by criteria

Criteria to check	Description
Construct validity	The study employed interviews, direct observations, and document analysis. This combination of data sources provided a comprehensive overview of the digital census process and reduced biases.
Internal validity	This exploratory study examined digital transformation context. Thus, causal connections were not the main objective. However, the study's approach minimized biases and ensured report credibility.
External validity	The extensive description of the study's techniques and context allows future research to reproduce it in similar environments, increasing generalization potential.
Reliability	It created a rigorous case study process and database of all obtained data. These resources ensure that the study's procedures are followed and that other researchers can evaluate and verify the results, ensuring reproducibility.

4 Case Description: Digital Transformation in Iraq and Census Overview

Digitalization in the public sector involves using digital technologies to transform public services, governance, and decision-making [42]. Public sector digitalization brings benefits such as greater efficiency, transparency, cost savings, and stronger citizen engagement, at the same time, it presents challenges including digital divides, security risks, institutional resistance, and regulatory gaps [2,42]. This broader understanding of digitalization provides essential context for Iraq's transition to a digital census.

The UNDP Digital Landscape Assessment report for Iraq highlights the evolving journey of Iraq to digital transformation, particularly in the context of national planning, governance and public service delivery. With a history marked by conflict and instability, Iraq faces numerous structural and political challenges, including a fragile economy, weak institutional frameworks, and inconsistent service delivery. Despite these obstacles, the country has shown a growing awareness of the importance of digital and ICT-driven initiatives as part of its larger development goals, as reflected in strategic frameworks such as Iraq Vision 2030.

Early efforts toward digital governance began in 2004 through international collaborations aimed at rebuilding institutional capacity. Since then, Iraq has implemented several key initiatives, including the development of digital infrastructure and national identification systems.

As presented in Fig. 1, Iraq's position in the United Nations E-Government Development Index (EGDI) for 2024 [42] reflects both its ongoing efforts and the considerable challenges that remain in its journey to digital transformation. Ranked 148th globally with a score of 0.4572, Iraq trails significantly behind the world average and leading nations such as Denmark (0.9847), Singapore (0.9691) in the region, and Saudi Arabia (0.9602) in its subregion. Although Iraq's EGDI score has gradually improved over the years, from 0.0000 in 2003 to 0.4572 in 2024, the country remains below both regional and subregional averages, signaling the need for continued investment in digital infrastructure, policy, and citizen engagement.

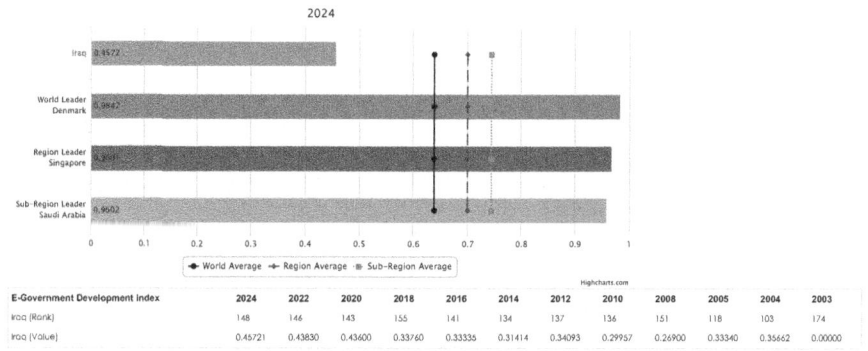

Fig. 1. E-government development index 2024 [42]

At the heart of the Iraqi e-Governance initiative lies the UR Portal[1], the official digital gateway of the Republic of Iraq. Serving as a centralized platform for public services, it unifies the offerings of various government institutions into a single user-friendly interface, streamlining access, and promoting transparency, efficiency, and accessibility. As of the latest figures, the portal hosts 6,900,078 registered users and offers 1,040 services in total, of which 585 are available online, while 455 services remain paper-based. These numbers indicate a significant shift toward digital engagement among citizens; however, they also underscore the ongoing need to accelerate the full transition from traditional manual processes to comprehensive digital service delivery.

---

[1] https://ur.gov.iq/.

In addition, Iraq has progressed in implementing digital technology to modernize the census collection process. Using technology improves accuracy, efficiency, and transparency in the process while addressing problems such as rural areas and displaced individuals. In contrast to previous censuses that utilized paper-based approaches, Iraq's 2024 census is the country's first total electronic population count in almost 40 years [4,25,26,29,31].

The 2024 census represents a significant advancement in Iraq, utilizing advanced digital technology to ensure thorough coverage, encompassing marginalized and difficult-to-access communities, including internally displaced individuals (IDPs) [31]. This effort represents a significant milestone for Iraq in creating a comprehensive database that will support policies designed to meet the needs of individuals and promote sustainable economic and social growth [25,26]. Furthermore, the digital census process enables significant advancements in data accuracy, timeliness, and granularity, which are particularly important for governance and policymaking. Improved data quality and real-time data accessibility allow the development of evidence-based policies and the allocation of resources to promptly address emerging social needs and demographic trends [1,17,32,38,44]. The transition to a digital census is a critical foundation for modern, data-driven public administration in Iraq, where planning and governance have historically encountered challenges as a result of fragmented or outdated data sources [25,26].

The 2024 census, conducted over two consecutive days (20–21 November 2024), required preparations that involved training more than 120,000 census workers assigned to survey the population and housing. The census used electronic tablets and digital forms, facilitating direct data transmission to the central data center in Baghdad. This shift from conventional paper-based approaches indicates significant progress, facilitating more precise and efficient data collection and processing [25,26].

5 Findings

As presented in Table 2, the demographic profile of the participants indicates a well-balanced representation in terms of gender, with 77 females (51.3%) and 73 males (48.7%), suggesting an inclusive sampling approach. The age distribution reveals that a significant majority of respondents (76.7%) fall into the age group of 21–30, followed by 22.0% in the range of 31–40. Very few participants were under 21 years old or over 40 years old, each comprising only 0.7% of the sample. Regarding educational background, most of the participants (78.0%) hold a bachelor's degree, reflecting a highly educated group. Furthermore, 16. 0% have a High Diploma, while the remaining respondents include holders of secondary education (4.0%), Diplomas (1.3%), and a single participant with a Master's degree (0.7%). This demographic composition suggests that the study predominantly involves young and educated individuals, which is aligning well with the context of research on digital transformation.

Table 2. Participants' demographic data

Gender	Count (%)	Age Group	Count (%)	Education	Count (%)
Female	77 (51.3%)	Under 21	1 (0.7%)	Secondary	6 (4.0%)
Male	73 (48.7%)	21–30	115 (76.7%)	Diploma	2 (1.3%)
		31–40	33 (22.0%)	Bachelor	117 (78.0%)
		Above 40	1 (0.7%)	High Diploma	24 (16.0%)
				Master	1 (0.7%)

5.1 Advantages of Digital Transformation in the Census Process

The responses reflect a broadly positive perception of the digital transformation of the census process, highlighting strengths across twelve key dimensions as follows:

Ease of Use: The system was perceived as intuitive and user-friendly, with simplified interfaces and data entry options. The interviewees praised the convenient design, indicating that the system lowered the barrier for technology use, even among non-tech-savvy users. The ease of use and a user-centered design approach were effective in encouraging adoption and ensuring smooth operation among various field personnel.

Time Efficiency: The interviewees widely acknowledged the significant time-saving aspect of the digital census. 95 out of 150 responses emphasized faster data entry, faster task completion, and the ability to gather large volumes of data in minimal time. Time efficiency not only enhances worker productivity but also allows for faster decision-making based on timely data. This theme reflects improved operational efficiency, which is a cornerstone benefit of digital systems in large-scale data collection.

Data Security and Protection: A protection against unauthorized access and secure storage were another key advantage highlighted by the majority of interviewees. 50 interviewees emphasized data confidentiality, and no instances of data leakage were reported during the processes, indicating a high level of trust in the system's security protocols. This trust is essential for public participation and for the protection of sensitive citizen information.

Location and Navigation Features: The inclusion of the global positioning system (GPS) and location tracking features was particularly valued by 70% of the respondents. The integration of geolocation added precision to data collection and supported geographic equity in census coverage. Improved logistic efficiency, reduced the chances of missing households, and allowed revisits when necessary.

Modern Digital Approach: Most of the interviewees considered this new digital method a modern and digital approach. The replacement of paper with tablets has been frequently cited as a mark of development and modernization.

Automated Features: Nearly 60% of the interviewees saw automation as a facilitator of error reduction, data consistency, and smooth workflow. Automated logic ensures standardized data while reducing the cognitive load on field workers. They stated that the system would not allow users to proceed with incomplete or incorrect entries.

Information Organization: 81 of 150 respondents explicitly appreciated the structured and systematic format of the digital platform. Organized information helped maintain clean data records and facilitated easier review and processing, as well as boosted post-collection efficiency and eased data analysis.

Demographic Insights: The interviewees recognized that the digital tools improved the ability to collect more and deeper demographic data and population data, including unemployment rates, educational levels, and demographic distributions. According to the responses, this reflects how digitization enables data richness, helping more informed policy-making.

Data Transfer and Accessibility: In terms of data transfer and accessibility, the interviewees noted that the system allowed instant data sharing, real-time accessibility, and faster publication of results. This feature greatly improved the relevance and timeliness of census findings, and finally, it supports responsive governance and proactive resource allocation.

Future Data Applications: Several participants noted the potential to use the collected data in long-term planning, government programs, and even employment prospects for census workers. They clearly highlighted that the digital census serves not only as a data collection tool but also as an investment in future governance infrastructure.

Cost Effectiveness: 62% of the people enumerators said that digital tools appeared to lower overall census costs by needing fewer resources than traditional methods and cutting out paper expenses; this suggests that digital methods could be a more sustainable option in the long run, especially for administrations with limited resources.

Data Accuracy and Integrity: 92 out of 150 interviewees highlighted error prevention, real-time validation, and data accuracy as key advantages. The built-in system checks, provides alerts for inconsistencies, and restricts access to sensitive functions to ensure high data quality.

5.2   Challenges of Digital Transformation in the Census Process

While the digital transformation of the census process was largely considered a positive and forward-thinking initiative, the responses of the interviewees also revealed several critical challenges that affected implementation and effectiveness. These challenges can be grouped into five main categories as described below.

Technical Infrastructure: 65 of 150 enumerators noted obstacles relevant to technical infrastructure issues. They explained that frequent server crashes and system slowdowns were common, disrupting work and causing delays. Poor internet connectivity, especially in remote areas, made it difficult to transmit data in real time.

Hardware Limitations: Hardware limitations were also considered another significant challenge, as tablets often ran slowly and some users reported lag or freezing. Battery life was a concern during long workdays and difficulty accessing data.

Software and System Design: 15 responses particularly highlighted issues relevant to software and system design. System crashes, VPN issues, and data syncing problems were recurring. Some users also found parts of the interface confusing or inefficient, affecting their ability to work smoothly.

Administrative and Process Issues 10% of the respondents were unsatisfied with the process administration; they said rapidly changing instructions created confusion and many felt they weren't properly trained. The workload was unevenly distributed, and poor planning led to a lack of preparation for unexpected problems.

Public Trust and Engagements: several enumerators encountered issues with public trust and understanding during data collection. Some citizens were hesitant to share information, fearing it could affect their government support. Others had concerns about privacy or were unfamiliar with digital processes, leading to mistrust or resistance.

5.3   Opportunities and Recommendations

Drawing on insights from the participants, Table 3 outlines key recommendations to address identified challenges and help build a more effective and efficient digital census system.

To sum up, both research questions of this study were systematically addressed, and the findings provide a more thorough, foundational approach

Table 3. Key recommendations for future digital census efforts

Recommendation Area	Actions
Strengthen technical infrastructure	Invest in robust server capacity, reliable internet connectivity, and updated hardware to prevent technical disruptions and ensure seamless data collection, especially in remote areas.
Enhance planning and training	Improve project management by providing clearer guidelines to enumerators and ensuring equitable workload distribution. Conduct comprehensive training on digital literacy and troubleshooting to build confidence in using digital tools.
Prioritize user experience and public engagement	Simplify system interfaces for both enumerators and citizens. Communicate transparently with the public about data privacy, the purpose of the census, and its benefits to foster trust and participation.
Improve data governance and quality	Establish clear policies for data management, storage, and access. Implement mechanisms for real-time data validation and error prevention. Incorporate ethical guidelines, including informed consent and protection of personal information.
Promote data-driven policymaking	Develop institutional processes to systematically integrate digital census data into governance, planning, and public service delivery at national and local levels. Foster collaboration between the statistical office and key ministries to promote evidence-based decision-making.
Ensure long-term sustainability and institutional learning	Retain and re-engage trained personnel for future census cycles. Document lessons learned and best practices to inform and improve future digital census initiatives.

that combines operational insights with wider governance implications, in contrast to prior studies [6, 21, 22, 30, 35, 39, 43]. As such, it contributes a uniquely holistic understanding of digital census implementation in a developing country context and provides practical guidance for future improvements.

6   Conclusion

Iraq's digital transformation of the census process represents a significant step toward advancing national data collection. This study highlights key lessons learned, including both the advantages and challenges encountered during implementation. In addition, it offers practical recommendations to help guide future digital census efforts and ensure a more effective and trusted process.

However, this study is not without limitations. Data collection was constrained by the lack of publicly accessible national data, making it difficult to obtain a fully comprehensive view of the census process across Iraq. In addition, the scope of interviews was limited to census enumerators from Sulaimaniyah city in the Kurdistan region due to accessibility challenges. While this provided valuable insights into operational and technical aspects of the digital census, it may not fully reflect experiences in other regions or capture broader national dynamics. Furthermore, perspectives from other key stakeholders—such as policymakers, government data users, and the public were not included. As a result, the study may not fully assess how digital census data are informing governance and policymaking, nor gauge public perceptions of trust, privacy, and data use. Future research should address these gaps by engaging a wider range of stakeholders and expanding geographical coverage to support a more comprehensive understanding of the digital census's impact on governance and society.

Despite the limitations of the study, this work underscores Iraq's remarkable progress in modernizing its census process through digital transformation. The lessons learned from this study provide a valuable foundation for future improvements. Through continuous investment, constant innovation, and enhanced collaboration with all stakeholders, Iraq is well positioned to further develop its digital census capabilities. The authors are confident that Iraq's experience can serve as an example of how technology can improve data-driven governance and promote more inclusive, transparent, and successful public administration, both in Iraq and the broader region.

References

1. Abowd, J.M., Hawes, M.B.: Confidentiality protection in the 2020 us census of population and housing. Ann. Rev. Stat. Appl. **10**(1), 119–144 (2023)
2. Afiyah, S.: The impact of e-government services, citizen participation, and transparency on public trust in government. Global Int. J. Innovative Res. **2**, 1246–1261 (2024). https://doi.org/10.59613/global.v2i6.200
3. Al-Lawati, A.H., Barbosa, L.S.: Towards a register-based census in Oman. In: 13th International Conference on Theory and Practice of Electronic Governance (ICEGOV 2020), pp. 823–826 (2020). https://doi.org/10.1145/3428502.3428631
4. Aljazeera: Iraq conducts first national census in nearly 40 years (2024). https://www.aljazeera.com/news/2024/11/20/iraq-conducts-first-national-census-in-nearly-40-years
5. Anderson, B.A., Silver, B.D.: There are two ideal types of total population counts, the de facto and the de jure. the former comprises all the people actually present in a given area at a given time. the latter is more ambiguous. it comprises all the people who" belong" to a given area at a given time by virtue of legal residence, usual residence, or some similar criterion. 2 consistent with the distinction between de facto and de jure population, the soviet. Sov. Stud. **37**(3), 386–402 (1985)
6. Beltadze, D.: Enumeration via Internet - Estonian experience. Stat. J. IAOS **32**(4), 563–568 (2016). https://doi.org/10.3233/SJI-160971
7. Bhatnagar, M.: Identifying the identified: the census, race, and the myth of self-classification. Tex. J. on CL CR **13**, 85 (2007)
8. Boddy, C.R.: Sample size for qualitative research. Qual. Market Res. **19**(4), 426–432 (2016)
9. Bowen, G.A.: Naturalistic inquiry and the saturation concept: a research note. Qual. Res. **8**(1), 137–152 (2008)
10. Chandra, Y., Shang, L.: An RQDA-based constructivist methodology for qualitative research. J. Cetacean Res. Manag. **20**(1), 90–112 (2017)

11. Christen, V., Groβ, A., Fisher, J., Wang, Q., Christen, P., Rahm, E.: Temporal group linkage and evolution analysis for census data. In: Advances in Database Technology - EDBT, vol. 2017, pp. 620–631 (2017).https://doi.org/10.5441/002/edbt.2017.83

12. Clarke, V., Braun, V.: Teaching thematic analysisâĂŕ: overcoming challenges and developing strategies for effective learning associate professor in sexuality studies department of psychology faculty of health and life sciences university of the west of England Coldharbour lane Br. Psychologist **26**(2), 120–123 (2013)

13. Cleary, M., Hayter, M., Horsfall, J.: Data collection and sampling in qualitative research: does size matter? J. Adv. Nurs. 473 –475 (2012)

14. Coyne, I.T.: Sampling in qualitative research. purposeful and theoretical sampling; merging or clear boundaries? J. Adv. Nurs. **26**(3), 623–630 (1997)

15. Csata, Z., Hlatky, R., Liu, A.H.: How to head count ethnic minorities: validity of census surveys versus other identification strategies. East Eur. Polit. **37**(3), 572–592 (2021)

16. Dias, C.A., Wallgren, A., Wallgren, B., Coelho, P.S.: Census model transition: contributions to its implementation in Portugal. J. Official Stat. **32**(1), 93–112 (2016). https://doi.org/10.1515/JOS-2016-0004

17. Durr, J.M.: The French new rolling census. Stat. J. U. N. Econ. Comm. Eur. **22**(1), 3–12 (2005)

18. Farley, R.: The importance of census 2020 and the challenges of getting a complete count. Harvard Data Sci. Rev. **2**(1), 1–8 (2020)

19. Griffin, R.A.: Potential uses of administrative records for triple system modeling for estimation of census coverage error in 2020. J. Official Stat. **30**(2), 177–189 (2014)

20. Guest, G., Namey, E.E., Mitchell, M.L.: Collecting Qualitative Data: A Field Manual for Applied Research. SAGE Publications, Ltd, Los Angeles (2017).https://doi.org/10.4135/9781506374680

21. Harun, M.S., Ali, N.M., M.A Khan, N.L.: 2020 Asia — Pacific Statistics Week The Use of Mobile Positioning data to Measure Visitors of a Multisport Events : 2020 Asia — Pacific Statistics Week A decade of action for the 2030 Agenda : Statistics that leaves no one and nowhere behind. 2020 Asia–Pacific Statistics Week, United Nations **1**, 15–20 (2020)

22. Ii, N., Dewi, L.P., Wibowo, A., Immanuel, N.M.A.: E-census implementation: a case study in Naikoten II, Kupang, Indonesia. In: 4th Engineering Science and Technology International Conference (ESTIC 2018), vol. 248, p. 5 (2018)

23. Kukutai, T., Thompson, V., McMillan, R.: Whither the census? continuity and change in census methodologies worldwide, 1985–2014. J. Popul. Res. **32**, 3–22 (2015)

24. Malterud, K., Siersma, V.D., Guassora, A.D.: Sample size in qualitative interview studies: guided by information power. Qual. Health Res. **26**(13), 1753–1760 (2016)

25. Ministry of Planning in Iraq: (2024). https://mop.gov.iq/en

26. Ministry of Planning in the Kurdistan Region of Iraq: (2024). https://krso.gov.krd/en

27. Mule Jr, V.T., Keller, A.: Administrative records applications for the 2020 census. Adm. Rec. Surv. Methodol. 205–229 (2021)

28. Nair, P.L.: Population and housing census Malaysia 2010 new approaches and technological advancements. Matematika **29**(1), 169–176 (2013)

29. News, T.N.: Iraq launches first national census in nearly four decades (2024). https://www.thenationalnews.com/news/mena/2024/11/20/iraq-launches-first-national-census-in-nearly-four-decades/

30. Paynter, J., Peko, G.: Census 2006 : capitalising on IT. In: 20th Annual Conference of the National Advisory Committee on Computing Qualifications (NACCQ 2007), pp. 217–221 (2015)
31. Release, P.: First census in over three decades begins in Iraq, backed by UNFPA expertise (2024). https://iraq.un.org/en/283979-first-census-over-three-decades-begins-iraq-backed-unfpa-expertise
32. Roux, V.: The French rolling census: a census that allows a progressive modernization. Stat. J. IAOS **36**(1), 125–134 (2020)
33. Roychowdhury, K., Jones, S., Arrowsmith, C., Reinke, K., Bedford, A.: The role of satellite data in census: case study of an Indian State. Proc. Asia Pac. Adv. Netw. **30**, 207 (2010). https://doi.org/10.7125/apan.30.23
34. Runeson, P., Host, M., Rainer, A., Regnell, B.: Case Study Research in Software Engineering. John Wiley & Sons, Inc, Hoboken (2012)
35. Sahar, A.Y.: Central Statistics Bureau, S.O.K.: Contact Center and Internet Data Collection for the 2011 Kuwait General Census. Technical report (2011)
36. Saunders, B., et al.: Saturation in qualitative research: exploring its conceptualization and operationalization. Qual. Quant. **52**(4), 1893–1907 (2018)
37. Sim, J., Saunders, B., Waterfield, J., Kingstone, T.: Can sample size in qualitative research be determined a priori? Int. J. Soc. Res. Methodol. **21**(5), 619–634 (2018)
38. Skinner, C.: Issues and challenges in census taking. Ann. Rev. Stat. Appl. **5**(1), 49–63 (2018)
39. Sturgeon, T.J.: In: Proceedings 59th ISI World Statistics Congress, 25–30 August 2013, Hong Kong (Session STS024) p.1550 (2013)
40. Taeuber, C., Hansen, M.H.: Self-enumeration as a census method. Demography **3**(1), 289–295 (1966)
41. Thorvaldsen, G.: Away on census day. Hist. Methods **39**(2) (2006)
42. United Nations Department of Economic and Social Affairs, U.: UN E-Government Knowledgebase (2024). https://publicadministration.un.org/egovkb/en-us/Data/Country-Information/id/80-Iraq
43. Valente, P.: Census taking in Europe: how are populations counted in 2010? Popul. Soc. **467**, 1–4 (2010)
44. Valente, P.: Innovative approaches to census-taking: overview of the 2011 census round in Europe. In: Statistical Methods and Applications from a Historical Perspective: Selected Issues, pp. 187–200 (2014)
45. Van Rijnsoever, F.J.: (I Can't Get No) saturation: a simulation and guidelines for sample sizes in qualitative research. PLoS ONE **12**(7), 1–17 (2017)
46. Wilson, R., Hasanali, S., Sheikh, M., Cramer, S., Weinberg, G., Firth, A., Weiss, S., Soskolne, C.: Challenges to the census: international trends and a need to consider public health benefits. Public Health **151**, 87–97 (2017)
47. Yin, R.K.: Case Study Research Design and Methods, vol. 1. SAGE, 4 edn. (2009)
48. Yin, R.K.: Case Study Research: Design and Methods. SAGE (2014)

AI in E-Government

GenAI in Public Sector Transformation: Balancing Promise and Prudence

Gideon Mekonnen Jonathan$^{(\boxtimes)}$ (ID) and Shengnan Han (ID)

Stockholm University, Borgarfjordsgatan 12, Kista, 164 55 Stockholm, Sweden
{gideon,shengnan}@dsv.su.se

Abstract. Generative Artificial Intelligence (GenAI) is a subject of intense interest among researchers and practitioners in the public sector, offering the potential to transform public administration through automation and improved efficiency. However, there is a lack of comprehensive synthesis in the growing body of literature that explores this technology's multifaceted impact on the sector. To contribute to the expanding discourse and address the existing gap, this research undertook a synthesis of 25 recent studies, analysing the potential benefits, challenges, and strategies for effective GenAI implementation in public organisations. The findings of our study indicate that while GenAI presents opportunities to streamline bureaucratic processes, enhance service delivery, and support improved decision-making, organisations face a variety of challenges in its implementation. The most commonly cited challenges include ethical concerns, regulatory compliance, data privacy, workforce resistance, and issues related to transparency. These findings underscore the need for robust AI governance frameworks, human oversight of GenAI systems, organisational readiness strategies, and continued investment in AI literacy. Further research is required to deepen our understanding of GenAI and how public organisations can best realise its benefits. To this end, we propose longitudinal studies to evaluate specific GenAI applications and their long-term impact, the development of governance frameworks, and methods to improve GenAI explainability and mitigate bias in public administration contexts.

Keywords: Generative AI · AI Governance · Public Administration · Public Organisations · Public Service Delivery

1 Introduction

1.1 Background

Generative Artificial Intelligence (GenAI) has become one of the transformative phenomena in the current digital transformation era, rapidly shaping industries and redefining creative processes. GenAI leverages machine learning models at its core to facilitate the creation of a diverse array of complex content encompassing textual, visual, and code-based outputs through the sophisticated analysis of extensive training datasets [1]. Researchers argue that the rapid proliferation of GenAI tools is speeding up the current digital transformation, fundamentally altering the way we work, create, and interact

© The Author(s), under exclusive license to Springer Nature Switzerland AG 2026
A. Kő et al. (Eds.): EGOVIS 2025, LNCS 16049, pp. 105–121, 2026.
https://doi.org/10.1007/978-3-032-02225-7_8

with each other [2]. The development is exemplified by the emergence of groundbreaking models like DALL-E 2, GPT-4, and Copilot, each pushing the boundaries of what's possible with AI. Given the wide application of the technology and its increasing adoption, it is no surprise that there is heightened anticipation of GenAi's favourable benefits, demonstrating a potent capacity to automate intricate tasks, refine decision-making protocols, and substantially augment productivity across a spectrum of sectors [3]. The assumption is that the capability of GenAI is driven by a sophisticated analysis of training datasets, which makes it possible for these models to learn underlying patterns and structures, enabling them to replicate and adapt, creating novel outputs [1].

Within the public sector contexts, the adoption of AI-driven technologies, including digital assistants, chatbots, and other GenAI applications, is increasingly attracting the attention of practitioners. The rationale is that the appropriate use of these tools has the potential to streamline bureaucratic procedures, enrich interactions with citizens, and optimise the overall efficiency of public service delivery. However, integrating AI into the operational framework of the public sector is not without its attendant challenges. It encounters significant impediments, including the navigation of ethical considerations, adaptation to regulatory complexities, management of workforce adaptation, and the surmounting of technological constraints [4]. As governments across the globe attempt to modernise their public service offerings and enhance responsiveness, the strategic adoption of GenAI technologies is increasingly taking a pivotal role, necessitating a delicate balance between fostering innovation and upholding the imperative of maintaining public trust and ensuring equitable service delivery.

According to researchers within the Information Systems (IS) and public administration disciplines, GenAI studies must address important contextual issues. Firstly, GenAI applications are expected to be explainable and transparent to maintain public trust [5]. The argument is that organisations in the public sector are subject to more stringent scrutiny and accountability standards. Thus, the research on GenAI applications within the sector should further our understanding of how the technology affects the decision-making processes. Secondly, research is needed to understand how GenAI can mitigate or perpetuate the existing inequalities and help us propose effective strategies for inclusive design and implementation [6]. It is worth noting that public organisations serve a diverse population and must ensure equitable use of GenAI, avoiding algorithmic bias. Thirdly, the complex legal and regulatory environments where public organisations operate also call for studies exploring the potential legal challenges of GenAI applications [7].

1.2 Research Problem

Despite the growing body of literature surrounding the transformative role of AI in public administration within the scientific community and publications in practitioner outlets, there is a lack of prior studies synthesising the adoption of GenAI. A closer look into the extant literature indicates that a substantial proportion of prior studies on the topic of GenAI have been fragmented in nature, often concentrating on specific aspects of the technology such as governance [8], ethical concerns [9], or sector specific implementations within narrowly defined areas such as healthcare [10]. These observations demonstrate the need for comprehensive research highlighting the determinant factors, benefits, and challenges of GenAI adoption across the public sector. This paucity of knowledge is unfortunate since the benefit of such a scholarly undertaking is no mere academic exercise but a work that has paramount significance for the provision of evidence-based guidance to governments and organisations in the public sector. Moreover, we also argue that organisations in the public sector operate in different internal and external contexts from their counterparts in the private sector, which has implications for the application of GenAI. For instance, the adoption of emerging technologies, including GenAI, should be designed and deployed in alignment with what Moore [11] referred to as the public value (i.e., prioritising ethical concerns, fairness, accountability and transparency). To this end, it is reasonable that we need to further our understanding of GenAI and its application within the public sector, considering the unique context of public administration.

1.3 Research- Aim and Questions

This study investigates the opportunities, challenges, and strategic considerations surrounding the adoption of GenAI in the public sector. By synthesising insights from recent research on GenAI implementation in public organisations, our aim is to identify and categorise the key factors that influence its successful adoption for improving public service delivery. The findings will further our understanding and provide practical insights, along with effective strategies for implementation. The following research question is formulated to guide our study: *What are the anticipated benefits, key challenges, and effective strategies for mitigating these challenges associated with the adoption of generative AI in public organisations?*

The remainder of the paper is structured as follows. Section two outlines the research methodology employed, detailing the literature search strategy and the procedure for synthesising the selected articles. Section three presents and discusses the findings of the review. Finally, section four concludes the paper by discussing the implications of the findings for both research and practice and proposing potential directions for future research.

2 Research Methodology

To cover the breadth of literature on GenAI within the public sector, a targeted search was conducted for peer-reviewed articles published in journals and conference proceedings in the IS and related domains according to the Preferred Reporting Items for Systematic Reviews procedure (PRISMA) [12]. The point of departure for our search was the databases known to index reputable journals and conference proceedings—ACM Digital Library, AIS e-library, IEEEXplore, Scopus, SpringerLink, and Web of Science. This approach is intended to improve the probability of capturing relevant studies published in various outlets, reflecting diverse perspectives and applications of GenAI within the public sector. Besides, the selection of these databases, renowned for their rigorous indexing and extensive coverage, guarantees the retrieval of high-quality, peer-reviewed articles.

Given the burgeoning research interest in GenAI, a strategic approach utilising combinations of keywords was deemed appropriate to identify relevant literature consistent with the specific aims and context of the study. The search string—(("*Generative AI* " OR "*Digital Assistant*" OR "*Virtual Assistant*" OR "*AI Assistant*" OR "*Conversational AI* " OR "*Chatbot*") AND ("*Public Sector*" OR "*Public Administration*" OR "*Public Service*" OR "*Government*") AND ("*Work Productivity*" OR "*Task Performance*" OR "*Automation*" OR "*Employee Efficiency*") AND ("*Artificial Intelligence*" OR "*AI* " OR "*AI-powered Systems*" OR "*Machine Learning*"))—was applied to the titles, abstracts, and author-supplied keywords within each database.

Even though GenAI is a topic that has attracted the attention of researchers across disciplines, our approach to the literature search resulted in a manageable volume of articles for the review. Thus, a time restriction in the form of the year of publication was not necessary. However, inclusion and exclusion criteria were used to appraise the relevance of the study. Complete peer-reviewed publications (journal articles and conference proceedings) focusing on GenAI adoption within the specific context of public organisations were considered relevant for our review. On the other hand, the following exclusion criteria were applied: book chapters, incomplete articles and articles published in languages other than English.

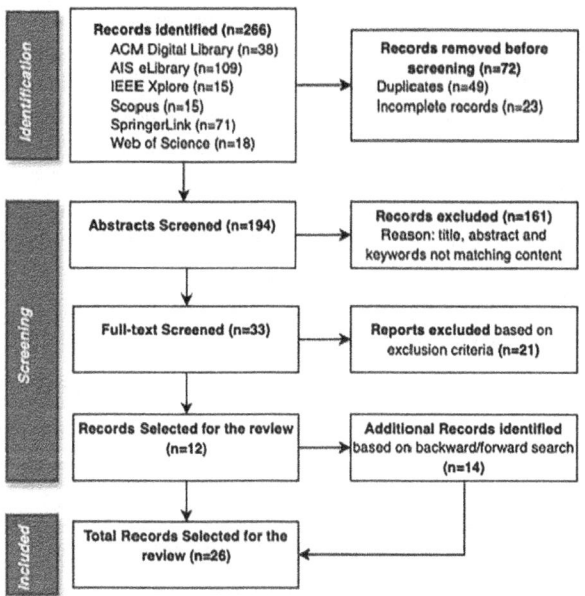

Fig. 1. The Literature search and appraisal process according to PRISMA.

As illustrated in Fig. 1, the systematic search of the relevant literature identified 26 studies. This corpus comprised 17 peer-reviewed journal publications and 9 conference proceedings. It is worth noting that the final list of studies selected for this review contains those identified not only through the initial database searches but also through supplementary forward and backwards citation searches conducted [13] after the initial full-text screening phase. A rigorous screening process was implemented to ensure the integrity of the review. Initially, duplicate records retrieved from the various databases were removed. Subsequently, incomplete records, including those lacking full text, papers without finalised results, and records missing essential metadata, were excluded. A preliminary screening of abstracts was then performed to identify and remove articles that did not align with the review's scope. Finally, a thorough full-text screening was conducted, and articles were excluded based on the pre-established exclusion criteria.

A structured data extraction process was employed to facilitate a comprehensive understanding of the reviewed studies and effectively address the research question of this study. The following information was systematically extracted, labelled, and coded for each study: publication type (journal article or conference proceeding), author(s), research methodology, central concepts, research questions, hypotheses, research objectives, key findings, and concluding remarks. However, the full texts of the selected studies were meticulously examined, allowing for a thorough analysis and subsequent categorisation of the contents into emergent thematic areas. This study adopts a concept-driven approach, wherein key concepts serve as the organising framework for synthesising and presenting the findings. According to Webster and Watson [13], this approach ensures that the analysis is focused and directly relevant to the research question, providing a coherent and insightful overview of the existing literature.

3   Results and Discussions

Of the 25 papers included in this review, 19 were published after OpenAI's release of ChatGPT in November 2022, demonstrating the rapid proliferation of research on this subject. The analysis of these studies indicates a widespread recognition of GenAI's potential to revolutionise public sector operations, offering improvements in efficiency, citizen engagement, and policy development. However, the adoption of this technology presents a range of challenges that necessitate careful consideration and management. This discussion elaborates upon the key themes identified in the literature, incorporating anticipated benefits, challenges, and strategies to provide a comprehensive understanding of GenAI within the context of public administration. A Concept matrix showing the reviewed papers and the main concepts is shown as an appendix.

3.1   GenAI Adoption in the Public Sector and Anticipated Benefits

GenAI is rapidly permeating the public sector, with applications emerging across public administration. Based on the findings of our review, this section highlights the common motivations for organisations in the public sector to adopt GenAI.

Enhancing efficiency through automation is one of the key themes we found in the extant literature. Researchers argue that the potential for GenAI to automate tasks and improve operational efficiency is widely recognised among researchers and practitioners in public organisations. Several studies [14–16] found that GenAI can significantly reduce administrative burdens by automating repetitive tasks such as document processing, report generation, and email responses. This automation, in turn, frees civil servants to focus on more complex and strategic roles, ultimately improving productivity and service delivery. For instance, Bhuyan et al. [10] illustrate the value of GenAI in healthcare administration, where it can automate patient record-keeping and alleviate clinician burnout. This suggests that similar benefits can be extended to other areas of the public sector, such as social services, education, and environmental management. Moreover, Jackson and Panteli [17] also argue that GenAI solutions can enhance inter-agency collaboration by improving communication and data-sharing across government departments. This could lead to more streamlined and coordinated public services, reducing redundancy and improving overall efficiency.

Enhancing public service accessibility and citizen engagement is another anticipated benefit of GenAI that is found in the literature. According to the findings of recent studies [16, 18, 19], GenAI promises to revolutionise citizen interactions with public services through AI-driven chatbots and virtual assistants. These tools can provide 24/7 support, answer frequently asked questions, and guide citizens through complex processes, ensuring efficient and accessible public services. Furthermore, Hernandez Gonzalez [20] also points out the potential for AI-driven legal assistance, which could simplify legal documentation for citizens and improve access to justice. GenAI can empower citizens to navigate legal processes more effectively by automating routine legal tasks and providing personalised guidance.

Another interesting benefit of GenAI is its role in *supporting decision-making and policy formulation*. Researchers argue that GenAI offers powerful tools for data analysis, prediction, and decision-making support. For instance, according to Hill et al. [21] and Nikiforova et al. [22], GenAI can be trained to identify policy trends, forecast socio-economic shifts, and support evidence-based policymaking. These studies suggest that GenAI can provide policymakers with invaluable insights supporting them in making more informed decisions by analysing large datasets and identifying patterns. Maragno et al. [23] also found that GenAI can generate multiple scenarios showing the potential outcomes of a policy across different demographic groups, geographic regions, or economic conditions. Moreover, GenAI can also analyse patterns from historical data and predict potential impacts on various stakeholders, helping identify unintended consequences before implementation. This allows policymakers to understand possible outcomes, identify unintended consequences, and refine policies before they are enacted. Such simulations can lead to more effective and impactful policies, ultimately benefiting citizens and society as a whole.

Beyond these key areas listed above, the literature also suggests further potential benefits of GenAI in the public sector. For instance, Beltran et al. [24] and Jalali and Hongsong [25] found that GenAI could *improve data security and privacy management* through advanced encryption and blockchain integration. This is crucial in an era of increasing cyber threats and data breaches. Similarly, other studies [26, 27] also suggest that GenAI *can play a significant role in workforce transformation*, offering intelligent assistance to help public sector employees adapt to digitalisation. For instance, GenAI can empower employees to acquire new skills and embrace new technologies by providing personalised training and support, ensuring a smooth transition to a digital-first public sector.

3.2   Challenges that Limit the Realisation of GenAI Benefits

Despite its transformative potential, the adoption of GenAI comes with a complex interplay of challenges that could hinder its successful implementation. These challenges found in the studies reviewed can be broadly categorised into four key areas: technological, ethical, legal, and organisational.

Despite its rapid development and adoption across organisations in various industries, GenAI is considered an emerging technology. Thus, it is challenging for public organisations to establish stable implementation strategies or fully understand what GenAI can and cannot do reliably. It is, therefore, not surprising that various *technological challenges* were found in the literature. For instance, one of the recurring technological issues in the reviewed studies was the propensity of GenAI models to "hallucinate," generating factually incorrect or nonsensical outputs [21, 28, 29]. This is considered a significant concern in public administration and legal contexts, where inaccurate information could lead to misinterpretations, errors, and flawed decision-making with grave consequences. Furthermore, GenAI models often require access to sensitive data, raising concerns about privacy breaches and the potential exposure of confidential information, particularly in areas such as citizen data processing and public records management [22, 24, 25]. Another technological barrier found in the studies was the language limitations of current GenAI models, which often exhibit biases towards dominant languages due to training data limitations [18–20]. This can create barriers to equitable access and effective service delivery in multilingual public service environments. Finally, the lack of interoperability and seamless integration across disparate public sector information systems poses a significant challenge to deploying GenAI solutions effectively [16, 23]. This can lead to data silos, workflow inefficiencies, and hinder the realisation of GenAI's full potential.

Ethical consideration is one of the recurring topics raised in the studies reviewed. Given the stringent scrutiny and expectation of the public sector to operate in the public's best interest, ethical considerations are paramount when designing and deploying GenAI in the public sector. Unfortunately, our analysis indicates that GenAI models can, for instance, inherit and amplify biases present in their training data, leading to discriminatory outcomes and exacerbating existing inequalities [10, 30, 31]. Prior studies also suggest that public organisations are expected to address challenges to ensure fairness and mitigate bias, requiring careful data curation, algorithmic transparency, and ongoing monitoring. Researchers recognise that it is the "black box" nature of many GenAI models that is the culprit of ethical challenges, as it makes it difficult to understand how they arrive at their conclusions [4, 8, 9]. Unless efforts succeed in overcoming this lack of transparency, the adoption of GenAI can undermine public trust, hinder accountability, and make it challenging to justify future AI-driven decisions. Furthermore, according to Vainionpää et al. [32] and Papageorgiou et al. [33], the use of GenAI in public decision-making raises questions about accountability and responsibility. Thus, it is crucial to establish clear lines of responsibility for AI-generated outputs and ensure that human oversight remains a central component of the decision-making process [17, 21].

Legal challenges are among the critical concerns raised in the extant GenAI studies. Researchers argue that the evolving legal landscape surrounding AI in general and GenAI in particular presents challenges for public sector adoption of the technology.

For instance, regulations like the European AI Act, with their stringent requirements for AI use in public administration, necessitate careful consideration of compliance and governance frameworks [32, 33]. However, given the technology's evolving nature and application, ensuring adherence to data protection laws, AI-specific regulations, and ethical guidelines is challenging but essential for responsible GenAI deployment. The various legal challenges organisations face when adopting GenAI relate to the complex questions regarding intellectual property and copyright ownership of AI-generated content [24, 28].

Organisational challenges can also impede the successful adoption of GenAI and the realisation of anticipated benefits in the public sector. Our analysis indicates that one of the critical organisational challenges facing public organisations adopting GenAI is resistance among civil servants and IT professionals. Several reasons are attributed to this resistance. For instance, the commonly cited reason stems from fears of job displacement and concerns about AI governance [28, 34, 35]. Frisch-Aviram et al. [36] also found that organisational culture plays a significant role in whether GenAI is successfully adopted or not. Furthermore, integrating GenAI into public sector workflows might be challenging because it requires effective change management strategies and reskilling public servants using the technology. It is also worth noting that employees using GenAI solutions might resist its adoption because of the fear of more work. Paradoxically, several studies [34–36] found that GenAI could create additional work rather than reduce the load. One explanation is that AI-generated outputs at the initial stage require human oversight, corrections, and validation, potentially adding cognitive load to civil servants.

3.3   Strategies for Successful GenAI Adoption in the Public Sector

Prior studies have identified several challenges that prevented public organisations from successfully realising the benefits of GenAI adoption. Our literature review indicates that various strategic interventions can be employed to mitigate these hurdles while maximising the potential benefits of AI-driven public service delivery. However, addressing these challenges requires a multi-dimensional approach encompassing regulatory oversight, misinformation mitigation, workforce readiness, interoperability enhancement, and ethical AI development.

Strengthening regulatory frameworks and AI governance structures: Previous studies have reiterated that the rapidly evolving nature of GenAI and the constantly changing legal landscape call for a robust AI governance structure in the public sector. According to our analysis, a robust legal and regulatory framework is necessary to ensure that GenAI adoption aligns with ethical standards, data protection regulations, and public accountability. For instance, studies found that [8, 32] comprehensive AI governance policies emphasising data privacy, algorithmic fairness, and explainability are invaluable to maintaining public trust. To this end, establishing legal guidelines that mandate bias audits, accountability structures, and GenAI certification processes can prevent potential misuse or unintended consequences of technology use in public administration operations. This is consistent with the principles of responsible AI stipulated by the OECD [37], which emphasise human-centric design, fairness, transparency, and accountability. Furthermore, Persson and Zhang [18] highlight the importance of public engagement and transparency mechanisms to enhance citizen trust in the use of GenAI in public administration. Thus, public organisations should adopt participatory GenAI policy-making that includes stakeholder consultations, ethical review boards, and AI regulatory sandboxes to assess and refine policies before full-scale deployment. Such participatory approaches are gaining traction, with examples like the City of Amsterdam's AI register [37] providing a transparent overview of AI systems used by the city and enabling citizen feedback. At the macro level, it is in the best interest of governments to work towards cross-border AI regulatory frameworks to ensure alignment with international AI governance standards. For instance, this is particularly important for regions governed by the European AI Act [33] and similar global initiatives. By harmonising national AI regulations with international guidelines, policymakers can facilitate the responsible deployment of GenAI across the public sector.

Mitigating inaccurate information, AI hallucination, and data privacy risks: Given the risk of GenAI-generated misinformation and AI hallucinations, organisations in the public sector should resort to multifaceted strategies to ensure that the use of GenAI results in outcomes based on accurate information. The extant literature provides a list of propositions, including fact-checking capabilities, content verification mechanisms, and real-time validation processes. For instance, the findings of studies [21, 28, 29] suggest the integration of explainable AI (XAI) models that allow users to trace AI decision-making processes and verify GenAI-generated outputs for accuracy. XAI techniques, such as LIME (Local Interpretable Model-agnostic Explanations) and SHAP (SHapley Additive exPlanations), can provide insights into the decision-making processes of AI models, making them more transparent and understandable [39, 40]. Additionally, real-time misinformation detection algorithms should be developed to monitor AI-generated content, particularly in legal documentation, public policy drafts, and citizen information portals. GenAI-driven content moderation, supported by human oversight, can ensure that erroneous or misleading outputs are identified and corrected before dissemination [21, 29].

On the other hand, to enhance data privacy and prevent AI models from inadvertently exposing sensitive information, researchers [22, 25] propose ***privacy-preserving AI architectures***, including blockchain-enabled data encryption, differential privacy techniques, and secure federated learning models. These suggestions resonate with the findings of prior studies [41, 42] suggesting various technological solutions to ensure that citizen data remains protected while still allowing AI models to be trained on aggregated and anonymised datasets. Moreover, Beltran et al. [24] and Hernandez Gonzalez [20] argue that implementing strict access controls and AI model auditing is invaluable to preventing unintended leaks of confidential data. Thus, governments should enforce AI compliance audits to ensure that GenAI applications do not compromise national security, personal privacy, or intellectual property.

Enhancing organisational readiness and overcoming workforce resistance: Prior studies have found that the successful implementation of GenAI in the public sector cannot be realised without the will and skillsets of employees. Thus, GenAI adoption requires significant workforce adaptation, training, and digital transformation efforts. Unfortunately, prior empirical studies found that civil servants and IT professionals are concerned about job displacement, AI-generated workload increases, and skill gaps. According to

Mainardi [27] and Knutsen et al. [34], tackling these issues calls for structured change management strategies that include targeted AI literacy programmes, upskilling initiatives, and cross-functional AI training to help employees gain the skills and necessary expertise to integrate GenAI into their workflows. Moreover, Giraldi et al. [35] and Frisch-Aviram et al. [36] highlight the importance of fostering a culture of digital transformation within public organisations. Leadership teams must proactively address employees' concerns about GenAI's impact on their roles, ensuring that AI complements rather than replaces human decision-making. Another crucial strategy for overcoming workforce resistance towards GenAI adoption is the integration of the technology with human oversight. According to Elliott et al. [4] and Papageorgiou et al. [35], hybrid AI-human collaboration models should be established, where AI handles repetitive administrative tasks while humans remain responsible for critical decision-making, validation, and ethical judgment. Furthermore, at the macro level, prior studies suggest that governments should incentivise AI adoption through career development programmes that provide opportunities for civil servants to specialise in AI governance, ethical AI auditing, and AI project management [16, 22].

Improving AI interoperability and cross-sector integration: One of the barriers to GenAI adoption in the public sector is the lack of interoperability between AI systems and existing government digital infrastructure. Both technical and non-technical approaches to tackling this issue have been proposed in the studies we reviewed. For instance, researchers [16, 22, 23] argue for cross-sector collaboration to develop standardised AI architectures that allow different government agencies to integrate AI-driven platforms seamlessly. The argument is that AI interoperability can be improved through, for instance, Application Programming Interfaces (APIs), cloud-based AI service models, and secure data-sharing protocols that enable public organisations to exchange GenAI-driven insights without compromising security. Other researchers propose macro-level solutions to benefit the public sector at large. For instance, Ojo et al. [26] and Yun et al. [19] argue that building AI ecosystems that integrate with existing e-government services and ensuring that AI solutions are embedded into digital governance frameworks rather than functioning as standalone tools goes a long way. Moreover, collaboration between AI developers, policymakers, and civil society organisations can help establish co-designed AI systems that align with the public operations of public service delivery, aligned with the sector's priorities and citizen needs. Mainardi [22] and Hernandez Gonzalez [20] also propose public-private partnerships where AI research institutions, government agencies, and industry leaders collaborate to develop tailored AI solutions for governance.

Addressing AI bias, language-specific limitations, and inclusive AI development: One of the challenges limiting the adoption of AI in the public sector, mainly GenAI, is the potential for algorithmic bias, exclusionary AI models, and language-specific constraints. The study by Yun et al. [19] and Hernandez Gonzalez [20] found that most GenAI models are trained predominantly in English, which has attracted much criticism since this was associated with inequitable access to AI-driven public services for non-English-speaking populations. Thus, to enhance inclusivity, AI training datasets should be diversified to include underrepresented languages, dialects, and cultural contexts. To this end, researchers [18, 23] argue that the multilingual AI models ensure that public sector AI tools are accessible to linguistically diverse communities. Research in multilingual natural language processing (NLP) is advancing rapidly, with models like mBERT [31] and XLM-R [8] demonstrating improved performance across multiple languages. Additionally, synthetic data generation has been identified as a solution to enhancing AI predictive accuracy and mitigating bias. Studies found that the use of synthetic data creates more representative training datasets that improve GenAI's ability to serve diverse populations fairly [20, 22, 43].

4   Concluding Remarks

This study explored the opportunities, challenges, and strategic considerations surrounding the adoption of GenAI within the public sector. The primary aim was to identify and categorise the critical factors influencing the successful integration of GenAI for enhanced public service delivery and to propose future research avenues that could further our understanding and provide actionable insights for practical implementation.

Our review was guided by the research question: What are the anticipated benefits, key challenges, and effective strategies for mitigating these challenges associated with the adoption of generative AI in public organisations?

Through a systematic and rigorous review of the extant literature, this study established that whilst GenAI offers transformative potential for improving efficiency, citizen engagement, and data-driven policy formulation within public administration, its adoption presents numerous technological, ethical, legal, and organisational challenges. The results also indicate that key issues such as AI hallucinations, data privacy concerns, algorithmic bias, regulatory uncertainties, and employee resistance remain significant impediments to its widespread implementation in the sector. However, the study also identified several strategic interventions that can effectively mitigate these challenges and pave the way for the successful deployment of GenAI in the sector. These include *strengthening AI governance frameworks, ensuring regulatory compliance, fostering a culture of digital transformation and AI readiness within the workforce*, and *promoting interdisciplinary collaboration between policymakers, technologists, and ethicists*. By proactively addressing these challenges, public organisations can harness the transformative power of GenAI to enhance public service delivery, improve citizen engagement, and drive innovation in governance.

4.1   Implications for Research and Practice

This study makes contributions to both research and public practice. From a research perspective, it synthesised fragmented literature on GenAI adoption in the public sector, offering a holistic overview of its benefits, challenges, and strategic considerations. By consolidating knowledge from interdisciplinary studies in IS, public administration, and AI governance, this study provides a comprehensive overview that furthers our understanding of GenAI's implications for public sector transformation. Moreover, it highlights the need for further empirical research to delve deeper into the sociotechnical and regulatory dynamics influencing GenAI adoption across diverse contexts within the public sector.

From a practical standpoint, this study offers valuable insights for policymakers, public sector leaders, and GenAI developers. For instance, the findings underscore the necessity of establishing robust AI governance structures, ensuring ethical AI deployment, and fostering public trust through transparency and accountability measures. Furthermore, the study proposes actionable strategies for overcoming resistance among public sector employees, advocating for targeted AI literacy programmes and hybrid human-GenAI collaboration models, where human oversight and ethical judgment remain central to decision-making processes. Given AI's rapidly evolving regulatory landscape, this study also underscores the significance of a roadmap for aligning GenAI adoption with emerging legal frameworks such as the European AI Act and international AI ethics guidelines. By embracing these recommendations, public sector leaders can navigate the complexities of GenAI implementation, harnessing its transformative potential to enhance public services and improve citizens' lives while mitigating potential risks.

4.2 Limitations and Future Research Directions

Despite its contributions, this study has certain limitations that warrant acknowledgement. Firstly, whilst the systematic literature review methodology ensures a structured synthesis of existing research, it inherently relies on the availability and quality of published studies. The rapid advancement of GenAI technologies means that newer insights may emerge, potentially altering or refining the conclusions drawn here. Secondly, the study focuses primarily on English-language publications, which may introduce a bias in the geographical and cultural representation of findings, limiting the generalizability of the conclusions. Future research should address these limitations by conducting empirical studies that explore real-world implementations of GenAI in diverse public sector contexts. Longitudinal case studies could provide deeper insights into the practical challenges and outcomes of GenAI adoption over time, offering valuable data on the long-term impacts and sustainability of GenAI solutions. Additionally, comparative analyses between public and private sector AI implementations could help clarify the unique constraints and opportunities associated with public administration settings, enabling the development of tailored strategies for GenAI adoption in government. Furthermore, there is a pressing need for research on the socio-ethical implications of GenAI, particularly regarding its impact on marginalised communities and the digital divide in access to AI-driven public services. Investigating strategies for mitigating AI bias, promoting data diversity, and enhancing multilingual AI capabilities in government applications would be valuable areas for future inquiry. This will ensure that GenAI serves all members of society equitably, fostering inclusivity and social justice.

In conclusion, while the adoption of GenAI in the public sector presents both opportunities and challenges, strategic planning, ethical considerations, and regulatory alignment will be key to its responsible and effective deployment. Continued research and interdisciplinary collaboration will be essential to ensure that GenAI serves as a force for innovation and positive social impact while upholding the principles of fairness, transparency, and public accountability. Only through such a comprehensive and conscientious approach can we truly harness the transformative potential of GenAI for the benefit of all citizens.

Appendix (Concept Matrix)

Articles	Operational Efficiency and Automation	Citizen Engagement and Accessibility	Data-driven decision and policy Formulation	Privacy and security	Organisational challenges	Ethical and transparent AI	Regulatory and Legal Compliance	Workforce transformation and Resistance	Technological challenges	Bias, inclusion and language Equity	AI Governance and oversight	System interoperability	Cross-sector integration
[4]					x	x		x			x		
[8]						x	x				x		x
[9]	x					x				x	x		
[10]	x												
[15]	x												
[16]	x	x			x			x	x		x	x	x
[17]	x					x							x
[18]		x								x			
[19]		x								x		x	
[20]		x		x						x		x	
[21]			x			x			x		x		
[22]			x	x				x		x		x	x
[23]			x							x		x	x
[24]				x			x						
[25]				x									
[26]	x										x	x	
[27]	x				x	x	x	x					x
[28]									x				
[29]				x					x				
[32]						x	x				x		
[33]							x	x			x		
[34]					x			x					x
[35]					x			x					x
[36]					x			x					
[43]	x	x	x							x			

References

1. Bommasani, R., et al.: On the opportunities and risks of foundation models. arXiv preprint arXiv:2108.07258 (2021)
2. Feuerriegel, S., Hartmann, J., Janiesch, C., Zschech, P.: Generative/AI. Bus. Inf. Syst. Eng. **66**(1), 111–126 (2024)
3. Zhang, J., Mora, L.: Nothing but symbolic: Chinese new authoritarianism, smart government, and the challenge of multi-level governance. Gov. Inf. Q. **40**(4), 101880 (2023)
4. Elliott, M.T.J., DP, Maccarthaigh, M.: Evolving generative AI: entangling the accountability relationship. Digit. Government Res. Pract. **6**(1), 1–13 (2025)
5. Ananny, M., Crawford, K.: Seeing without knowing: limitations of the transparency ideal and its application to algorithmic accountability. New Media Soc. **20**(3), 973–989 (2018)
6. Liu, Y., Zhang, Z., Wu, Y.: Will generative AI create a new social divide? Investigating the impacts of generative AI use on social capital in China. Int. J. Hum. Comput. Interact. 1–17 (2024)
7. Zuiderveen Borgesius, F.J.: Strengthening legal protection against discrimination by algorithms and artificial intelligence. Int. J. Hum. Rights **24**(10), 1572–1593 (2020)
8. Weerts, S.: Generative AI in public administration in light of the regulatory awakening in the US and EU. In: Cambridge Forum on AI: Law and Governance, vol. 1, no. e3, pp. 1–19 (2025)
9. Esposito, M., Tse, T.: Mitigating the risks of generative AI in government through algorithmic governance. In: Proceedings of the 25th Annual International Conference on Digital Government Research, pp. 605–609 (2024)
10. Bhuyan, S.S., et al.: Generative artificial intelligence use in healthcare: opportunities for clinical excellence and administrative efficiency. J. Med. Syst. **49**(1), 10 (2025)
11. Moore, M.H.: Creating Public Value: Strategic Management in Government. Harvard University Press (1997)
12. Swartz, M.K.: Prisma 2020: an update. J. Pediatr. Health Care **35**(4), 351 (2021)
13. Webster, J., Watson, R.T.: Analyzing the past to prepare for the future: writing a literature review. MIS Q. xiii–xxiii (2002)
14. Androniceanu, A.: Generative artificial intelligence, present and perspectives in public administration. Adm. Public Manag. Rev. (43) (2024)
15. Bright, J., Enock, F., Esnaashari, S., Francis, J., Hashem, Y., Morgan, D.: Generative AI is already widespread in the public sector: evidence from a survey of UK public sector professionals. Digit. Gov. Res. Pract. **6**(1), 1–13 (2025)
16. Aryfiyanto, H., Alamsyah, A.: Public service with generative AI: exploring features and applications. In: 2024 7th International Conference of Computer and Informatics Engineering (IC2IE), pp. 1–7. IEEE (2024)
17. Jackson, S., Panteli, N.: Ai-based digital assistants in the workplace: an idiomatic analysis. Commun. Assoc. Inf. Syst. **55**(1), 22 (2024)
18. Persson, P., Zhang, Y.: Openness and transparency by design: crafting an open generative AI platform for the public sector. In: Proceedings of the 58th Hawaii International Conference on System Sciences (HICSS), pp. 1834–1843 (2025)
19. Yun, L., Yun, S., Xue, H.: Improving citizen-government interactions with generative artificial intelligence: Novel human-computer interaction strategies for policy understanding through large language models. PLoS ONE **19**(12), e0311410 (2024)
20. Hernandez Gonzalez, J.A.: Assistance system for judicial awards for the Colombian state legal defence agency through NLP-andje. In: Proceedings of the 2022 5th International Conference on Machine Learning and Natural Language Processing, pp. 258–265 (2022)

21. Hill, G., Waddington, M., Qiu, L.: From pen to algorithm: optimizing legislation for the future with artificial intelligence. AI Soc. 1–12 (2024)
22. Nikiforova, A., Lnenicka, M., Milić, P., Luterek, M., Rodríguez Bolívar, M.P.: From the evolution of public data ecosystems to the evolving horizons of the forward-looking intelligent public data ecosystem empowered by emerging technologies. In: International Conference on Electronic Government, pp. 402–418. Springer (2024)
23. Maragno, G., Tangi, L., Gastaldi, L., Benedetti, M.: The spread of artificial intelligence in the public sector: a worldwide overview. In: Proceedings of the 14th International Conference on Theory and Practice of Electronic Governance, pp. 1–9 (2021)
24. Beltran, M.A., Ruiz Mondragon, M.I., Han, S.H.: Comparative analysis of generative AI risks in the public sector. In: Proceedings of the 25th Annual International Conference on Digital Government Research, pp. 610–617 (2024)
25. Jalali, N.A., Hongsong, C.: Comprehensive framework for implementing blockchain-enabled federated learning and full homomorphic encryption for chatbot security system. Clust. Comput. **27**(8), 10859–10882 (2024)
26. Ojo, A., Mellouli, S., Ahmadi Zeleti, F.: A realist perspective on AI-era public management. In: Proceedings of the 20th Annual International Conference on Digital Government Research, pp. 159–170 (2019)
27. Mainardi, I.: Change management: artificial intelligence (AI) at the service of public administrations. AI Soc. 1–29 (2024)
28. Cantens, T.: How will the state think with ChatGPT? The challenges of generative artificial intelligence for public administrations. AI Soc. 1–12 (2024)
29. van Staalduine, N., Zuiderwijk, A.: Exploring the viability of ChatGPT for personal data anonymization in government: a comprehensive analysis of possibilities, risks, and ethical implications. Digit. Gov. Res. Pract. (2024)
30. Conneau, A., et al.: Unsupervised cross-lingual representation learning at scale. In: Proceedings of the 58th Annual Meeting of the Association for Computational Linguistics, pp. 8440–8451 (2020)
31. Devlin, J., Chang, M.W., Lee, K., Toutanova, K.: Bert: pre-training of deep bidirectional transformers for language understanding. In: Proceedings of the 2019 conference of the North American chapter of the Association for Computational Linguistics: Human Language Technologies, Volume 1 (long and short papers), pp. 4171–4186 (2019)
32. Vainionpää, F., Väyrynen, K., Lanamäki, A., Parmiggiani, E.: Practices of anticipation: how public sector organizations anticipate artificial intelligence and its regulation. In: ECIS 2024 Proceedings, p. 3 (2024)
33. Papageorgiou, G., Sarlis, V., Maragoudakis, M., Tjortjis, C.: Enhancing egovernment services through state-of-the-art, modular, and reproducible architecture over large language models. Appl. Sci. **14**(18), 8259 (2024)
34. Knutsen, L.Z., David Patón-Romero, J., Hannay, J.E., Tanilkan, S.S.: A survey on the perception of opportunities and limitations of generative AI in the public sector. In: World Conference on Information Systems for Business Management, pp. 503–520. Springer (2023)
35. Giraldi, L., Rossi, L., Rudawska, E.: Evaluating public sector employee perceptions towards artificial intelligence and generative artificial intelligence integration. J. Inf. Sci. 01655515241293775 (2024)
36. Frisch-Aviram, N., Spanghero Lotta, G., Jordão de Carvalho, L.: "Chat-up": the role of competition in street-level bureaucrats' willingness to break technological rules and use generative pre-trained transformers (GPTs). Public Adm. Rev. **85**(2), 468–485 (2025)
37. Yeung, K.: Recommendation of the council on artificial intelligence (OECD). Int. Leg. Mater. **59**(1), 27–34 (2020)
38. Högberg, C.: Stabilizing translucencies: governing AI transparency by standardization. Big Data Soc. **11**(1), 20539517241234296 (2024)

39. Ribeiro, M.T., Singh, S., Guestrin, C.: "Why should I trust you?" Explaining the predictions of any classifier. In: Proceedings of the 22nd ACM SIGKDD International Conference on Knowledge Discovery and Data Mining, pp. 1135–1144 (2016)
40. Lundberg, S.M., Lee, S.I.: A unified approach to interpreting model predictions. In: Proceedings of the 31st Conference on Neural Information Processing Systems (NIPS 2017), pp. 1–10 (2017)
41. Dwork, C., Roth, A., et al.: The algorithmic foundations of differential privacy. Found. Trends Theor. Comput. Sci. 9(3–4), 211–407 (2014)
42. Yang, Z., Dai, Z., Yang, Y., Carbonell, J., Salakhutdinov, R.R., Le, Q.V.: Xlnet: generalized autoregressive pretraining for language understanding. In: Advances in Neural Information Processing Systems, vol. 32 (2019)
43. Pandey, J.K.: Unlocking the power and future potential of generative AI in government transformation. Transforming Gov. People Process Policy (2024)

A Deliberation Knowledge Graph: Bridging Institutional and Civic Democratic Discourse

Simone Vagnoni[1,2](✉)(iD) and Víctor Rodríguez-Doncel[2](iD)

[1] LAST-JD, University of Bologna, Bologna, Italy
`simone.vagnoni3@unibo.it`
[2] OEG, Universidad Politécnica de Madrid, Madrid, Spain
`vrodriguez@fi.upm.es`

Abstract. Democratic deliberation is taking place nowadays in the digital sphere: discussions in the social media, in the new eDemocracy platforms and in the official parliamentary sessions that create digital data. These deliberation data hold immense potential for analysis and insight, and the interest grows when diverse sources are interconnected. This paper introduces the Deliberation Knowledge Graph, a technological solution to integrate deliberation processes, arguments and participants across different institutional and civic spheres. First, the Deliberation Ontology is presented, a joint data model. Then, the systematic integration of deliberation data from European Parliament proceedings, civic participation platforms, and public forums is described. As an example of application that can have this new technology, the paper describes how this knowledge graph particularly enhances the capacity to examine argument quality, identify reasoning patterns, and trace the evolution of policy positions across different deliberative spaces. Potential applications and problems are discussed.

Keywords: knowledge graph · deliberation · semantic web · ontology · parliamentary debates · civic participation

1 Introduction

Public deliberation refers to the process through which citizens, elected representatives, and other stakeholders engage in reasoned discussion to shape collective decisions. As highlighted by the OECD [1], public deliberation is a core component of democratic innovation, enabling informed, inclusive, and reflective input into policymaking. Public deliberation occurs in institutional settings such as parliaments, in civic participation platforms, and increasingly through informal channels like social media, where public arguments and opinions contribute to forging the democratic discourse.

In recent years, civic participation platforms such as Decidim[1], Consul[2], and other digital democracy tools have proliferated, offering digital spaces for engage-

---

[1] https://decidim.org.
[2] https://consuldemocracy.org/.

© The Author(s), under exclusive license to Springer Nature Switzerland AG 2026
A. Kő et al. (Eds.): EGOVIS 2025, LNCS 16049, pp. 122–136, 2026.
https://doi.org/10.1007/978-3-032-02225-7_9

ment. At the same time, institutional deliberative forums, such as parliaments, have also begun leaving digital traces of their discussions. Together, these diverse deliberative spaces generate rich datasets that capture arguments, positions, and decision-making processes. This data can be used to analyze public discourse, track policy evolution, identify key arguments, and assess the impact of deliberation on decision-making. It also enables the development of AI-driven tools for summarization, sentiment analysis, and trend detection, enhancing transparency and civic engagement.

The immense potential of these datasets could be even greater if they were analyzed together. However, their heterogeneous formats pose a technical challenge. This paper presents the proof-of-concept of a technical solution to unlock the full potential of integrated deliberative data: the Deliberation Knowledge Graph (DKG)[3] and the underlying Deliberation Ontology (DEL).

A Knowledge Graph is a structured representation of real-world facts, entities, and their relationships, typically organised as a network of nodes and edges. Knowledge Graphs have been published in the last few years in many contexts –from the general Google Knowledge Graph to domain-specific ones. Entities in a knowledge graph on deliberations include indeed 'arguments', 'participants' or 'topics'. Relations include the membership to a 'political party', or the connection between an 'argument' and some 'evidences'.

Knowledge graphs are connected to external datasets, meaning that the exploration of the information can extend beyond the limits of the graph itself. For example, deliberations can be connected to the legislation (which is also digitally published), members of the parliaments can be connected to their activity elsewhere, data can be connected to Wikidata facts. The possibilities are unlimited –the more the connections, the more broader the applications– and this is the principle behind the idea of Semantic Web linked data [2]. The integration of data from heterogeneous sources requires, however a core model. Knowledge graphs are anchored to core models, usually defined by means of *computer ontologies*.

The remainder of this paper is organized as follows: Sect. 2 presents the background, including motivation and a very clear statement on the work limitations. Section 3 presents the Deliberation Ontology, including its conceptual model and key components. Section 4 describes the data integration process for connecting diverse deliberation datasets and the technical implementation details of the Deliberation Knowledge Graph. Section 6 reviews related work before Sect. 7 concludes the paper discussing future work.

2 Background

2.1 Motivation

Computers have analyzed many aspects of human life, improving processes, detecting errors, and driving innovation. If it's data, it can be analysed. However, the analysis of deliberation data remains underexploited (at least publicly).

---

[3] https://stocastico96.github.io/Deliberation-Knowledge-Graph/.

Two conditions make our effort timely: on the one hand, only now deliberation data is from institutional sources being made widely available online; on the other hand, natural language processing technologies have only recently reached a level of performance that makes large-scale analysis feasible.

Having data that is connected, readily accessible from a single point, and structured according to a common model is a precondition for meaningful exploitation. The Deliberation Knowledge Graph addresses these needs by integrating data from institutional deliberation (such as parliamentary proceedings), citizen deliberation (on civic participation platforms), and potentially even informal argumentation on social media. By doing so, our effort enables:

- *Integration of institutional and civic democratic discourses*, e.g., deliberation taking place at the European Parliament sessions[4] can be connected with the public discussion in internet forums, social networks, and other eParticipation platforms such as 'Have Your Say'[5] or Decidim.
- *Analysis of deliberative processes across different contexts.* A Deliberation Knowledge Graph would be valuable for a wide range of applications, including journalism, historical research, political science, and comparative studies.
- *Standardised representation of argument structures for fallacy detection.* Deliberation that leads to the adoption of key norms—often with far-reaching societal impacts—should be subject to rigorous scrutiny. We launch rockets with millimetric precision, yet the arguments behind norms that affect billions may pass without any structured validation.
- *Cross-dataset queries.* The graph can uncover inconsistencies in party positions, track the evolution of individual viewpoints, or identify mutual influences between different institutions and actors.
- *Semantic enrichment of deliberation data.* Named entity recognition algorithms can annotate deliberative content and link it to external knowledge bases (such as Wikidata[6]), enhancing its interpretability and discoverability.
- *Build epistemic democracy.* The graph empowers citizens with knowledge by integrating diverse deliberative sources –a form of epistemic democracy, where citizens gain access to enhanced information for democratic decision-making. The very distributed and open nature of the Semantic Web –and knowledge graphs are their ultimate expression– makes possible for every citizen to build on this stone. Epistemic democracy based on these networked structures are well explored in the book Linked Democracy [3].
- *Build a pluralistic digital infrastructure* The DKG aligns with the vision of digital plurality articulated by Tang, Weyl, and the Plurality community [4], creating connections between formal institutions and civic spheres. By bridging these traditionally separate deliberative spaces, the DKG enables accountability across contexts and supports what Tang describes as *rough consensus* in digital deliberation.

---

[4] https://data.europarl.europa.eu/.

[5] https://ec.europa.eu/info/law/better-regulation/have-your-say_en.

[6] https://www.wikidata.org/.

2.2 Limitations

Designing an ontology requires a considerable effort, populating a Knowledge Graph with significant amounts of data even more. The exploratory ambitions of this work are however limited: the ontology model is minimal and the amount of data in the graph modest –this is enough for developing a proof-of-concept knowledge graph that evidences the possibilities and limitations of the approach. But beyond the limitations derived from the limited size of the graph, there is a number of fundamental problems that can be advanced from the very beginning.

Lack of Pragmatics. The Deliberation Knowledge Graph is an embodiment of the Semantic Web's ideals –structured data, formal semantics, and machine-readable meaning [5]. In linguistics, *syntax* concerns the structural relationships between linguistic forms—the rules that govern well-formed sequences; *semantics* addresses the relationships between those forms and the entities they refer to in the world; *pragmatics* studies how linguistic forms relate to their users — their intentions, assumptions, and the context of communication. The Semantic Web is, at best, Semantic. It overlooks the user, the context, the deliberation participant intentions, the play of ambiguity and irony, the social dynamics of communication –in short, everything that gives language its human meaning. While detecting fallacies and inaccuracies is useful, it is less significant compared to the broader context often omitted: the pragmatic dimension matters far more. Arguments do not exist in a vacuum; they are offered, contested, ignored, or strategically reframed by participants with intentions, beliefs, and stakes. What is not said –what is implied, presupposed, or withheld—often carries more weight than what is explicitly stated. The DKG captures the surface of deliberation – the who-said-what– and how it connects, but the deeper currents of meaning flow beneath, in what remains unsaid, in context, in silence.

Representing the deliberation participants' needs and contexts to facilitate the automated interactive and collective management of knowledge –the *pragmatic turn*, as it has been called [6], would mitigate the problems, but making progress is costful and not much effective. Building a *Pragmatic Web* as 'a set of pragmatic contexts of semantic resources' [7] is quixotic, and the partial efforts not really useful: Bonacin proposed a communication act ontology that links acts, agents and behaviour patterns [8], but the number of those is unlimited. In their book, Sperber and Wilson claim that relevance is seen as the key to human communication and cognition [9], but attempts to model relevance show the difficulties, even in well-defined contexts [10].

Privacy and Contextual Integrity. The DKG's cross-platform integration enables new forms of participant profiling by linking contributions across different contexts and time periods, potentially revealing political evolution and social networks beyond participants' original intent. This creates risks of political targeting or reputational harm through *contextual integrity* violations [11], where formal argument structures may be instrumentalized outside their original deliberative context. The knowledge graph may be repurposed in ways that ignore the context-sensitivity of deliberation –reframing participants' contributions out of context, instrumentalising argument structures for unintended goals (e.g., surveillance), or creating an illusion of objectivity and neutrality where in fact norms and intentions were essential. In this light, the very strength of the DKG –its formalism and reusability– become a liability when contextual integrity is not respected.

Hypersuasion. Additionally, as Floridi argues, increased connectivity could potentially enable more sophisticated forms of persuasive influence or *hypersuasion* [12]. Hypersuasion uses the capacity of artificial intelligence to influence individuals' beliefs and behaviors through personalized, data-driven strategies. The entire deliberative process becomes compromised if human autonomy is undermined by manipulative machines. In other words, if deliberation becomes data, deliberation can be controlled. Is digitizing deliberation a good idea at all?

AI-optimised software realizes Wiener's vision in his book *The Human use of Human Beings* [13] –the title says it all. Cybernetics and feedback loops make it possible to optimise environments, and in this case, the consensus within a particular forum. In this subtle form of warfare, power is unevenly distributed: those with greater computational resources –or more crucially, with more personal data– will possess stronger AIs capable of imposing their manufactured consent.

Having acknowledged its limitations –and, more troublingly, its potential for misuse– it is now time to turn to the modest yet constructive contributions of this work.

3   Deliberation Ontology

3.1   Rationale

One of the most quoted definitions of computer ontology is the one by Studer: "a formal, explicit specification of a shared conceptualization" [14]. If different data sources are to be integrated, having an explicit conceptualization to pivot on is key. The ontology serves as the formalised data model that structures and represents knowledge in a manner intelligible to both machines and humans.

Ontologies were born to formalise domain-expert consensus on a certain matter, but with the years, they have proved to be excellent data models in computer applications as well –in particular, ontologies serve as the best defined data models for knowledge graphs.

Parliaments, civic participation platforms and social networks host, in a way, different sorts of democratic deliberation. If they are to publish data, they will speak about 'members the parliament', 'citizens' or 'users' respectively to those participating in the debates. These debates will be called, perhaps, 'sessions', 'issues' and 'threads'. Yet, they refer essentially to the same ideas, at least in relation to the deliberation that is taking place. A computer ontology can define core concepts, and entities from each of the data sources can be linked to it. Ontologies provide a standardized vocabulary and a hierarchical framework, specifying, for instance, that "MPs" (members of parliament) belong to "political parties," which in turn are types of "organizations". This structured representation enhances the interoperability of data across systems, supports advanced querying, and facilitates semantic reasoning.

Ontologies have been defined for all the conceivable domains. Here and there ontologies have flourished, big and small, complex and simple, with a computing purpose or even without it. Because the mere formalization of a consensus is of great interest.

In the design of computer ontologies, a joint effort is made by ontologists and domain experts. Creating ontologies in some technical domains is relatively straightforward. For instance, in the domain of transportation, experts may define concepts like 'vehicle', 'road', 'traffic light', and 'driver', along with their relationships—such as 'a vehicle travels on a road' or 'a driver operates a vehicle'. These relationships are clear, and consensus is often easy to reach. However, the domain of democratic deliberation is much more sensitive. It involves complex, subjective concepts like 'argument', 'consensus', 'disagreement', and 'public opinion', which may have different interpretations depending on cultural, political, or legal contexts. Reaching a consensus on these terms is a challenging task, as it requires aligning diverse perspectives on how deliberative processes should be represented and understood. Therefore, in order to build the ontology to serve as the basis for the DKG, a minimal commitment has been ambitioned. Moreover, its design has been led by the technical operations intended to be made on the data.

3.2   Requirements

The creation of an ontology is a process that can be engineered, i.e. there are standard methodologies to be followed and quality assurance mechanisms that grant some minimum quality levels. In particular, the Deliberation Ontology was developed following the LOT methodology [15], guided by an Ontology Requirements Specification Document (ORSD) that defines its purpose, scope, and requirements. The ORSD for the Deliberation Ontology specifies both functional and non-functional requirements and is also online[7]. The functional requirements are expressed as competency questions (i.e., "What contributions were made in a specific deliberation?") grouped into six categories:

1. *Deliberation Process Structure:* Questions about the stages, timeline and organization of the deliberation processes.
2. *Participant Information:* Questions about the individuals and organizations involved in deliberations.
3. *Contributions and Arguments:* Questions about the content, structure and relationships of the deliberative contributions.
4. *Information Resources:* Questions about the documents, legal sources, and other information referenced in the deliberations.

---

[7] https://github.com/Stocastico96/Deliberation-Knowledge-Graph.

5. *Fallacy Detection:* Questions about the identification and classification of logical fallacies in arguments.
6. *Cross-Dataset Integration:* Questions about the standardization and mapping of deliberation data across different platforms.

The nonfunctional requirements include compatibility with existing platforms, extensibility, reuse of existing ontologies, multilingual support, and consistency across data sources.

3.3   Ontology Description

The Deliberation ontology (DEL) is organized around three core models:

1. *Process Model*: Represents deliberation processes, their stages, timelines, and organizational context.
2. *Participant Model*: Represents individuals, groups, and organizations involved in deliberations, along with their roles and relationships.
3. *Argument Model*: Represents arguments, positions, and other contributions made during deliberations, including their structure and relationships.

The OWL ontology is publicly available online[8], along with its documentation[9].

In Fig. 1, the key entities in the Deliberation Ontology are represented. The Ontology contains three main models: Process, Participant and Argument, representing the three ingredients relevant to every public deliberation process. The Knowledge Graph is populated in two different forms. First, harvesting from public sources will create data related to the process and the participation. Second, an analysis of this objective data will create the data on the arguments. In the diagram, the dotted red line divides the Data Layer, obtained directly from the sources, from the Analysis Layer, which is obtained after processing the first one.

The Deliberation ontology reuses and aligns with several existing ontologies:

- *FOAF (Friend of a Friend):* For representing people and their relationships.
- *Dublin Core:* For metadata about resources.
- *SIOC (Semantically Interlinked Online Communities):* For online discussion structures.
- *AMO (Argument Model Ontology):* For argument structures.
- *SKOS (Simple Knowledge Organization System):* For concept schemes and taxonomies.
- *Time Ontology:* For temporal aspects of deliberation processes.
- *Organization Ontology:* For organizational structures and roles.

---

[8] https://w3id.org/deliberation.
[9] https://w3id.org/deliberation/ontology.

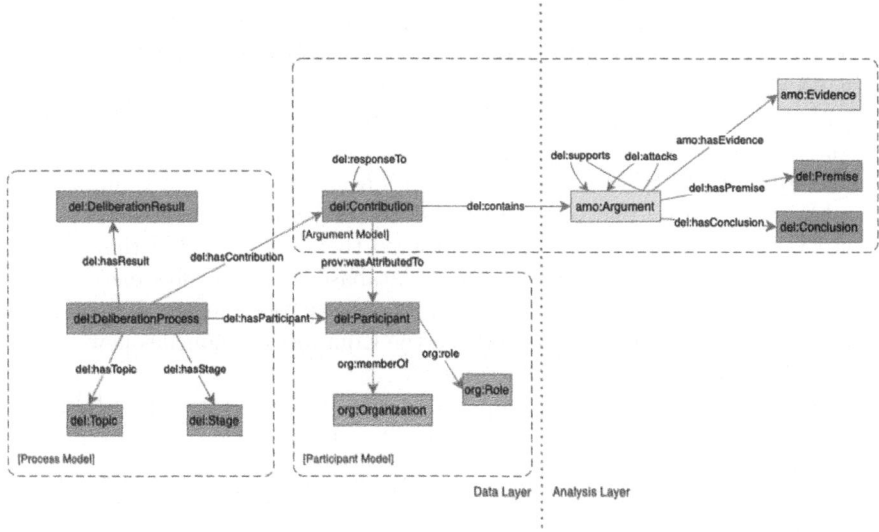

Fig. 1. Representation of the key entities in the Deliberation Ontology and the relationships between data layers.

4 The Deliberation Knowledge Graph

4.1 Data Sources

Choosing the right sources for a knowledge graph is not a trivial issue, and a systematic procedure should be followed [16]. However, at this stage, where a proof-of-concept is sufficient, we have selected several deliberation datasets based on their availability and their ability to represent the different types of deliberative processes:

- **European Parliament Debates:** This dataset consists of verbatim reports of plenary sessions from the European Parliament, published in HTML format and updated daily, as open government data. The data represents formal institutional deliberation at the European level, with structured transcripts of speeches, debates, and procedural elements.
  Alignment: The dataset maps to our model with Speaker → del:Participant (including role and political group affiliation), Speech → del:Contribution, Debate → del:DeliberationProcess, and Topic → del:Topic. The temporal structure of debates is captured through del:startDate and del:endDate.
- **Decide Madrid:** This dataset is sourced from Madrid's official citizen participation platform, containing proposals, debates, and comments submitted by citizens. Available as Open Data, it includes structured CSV files of citizen proposals and associated comments, with fields capturing user information, proposal content, voting data, and discussion threads. The platform generates new data continuously as citizens engage with municipal issues.

Alignment: The dataset maps to our ontology with author_name → del:Participant, Proposal/Comment → del:Contribution, and Debate → del:DeliberationProcess. The support/voting mechanism is captured through del:supports relationships, while the threaded nature of discussions is represented through del:responseTo properties.

- **EU Have Your Say:** This dataset comes from the European Commission's public consultation platform, which collects citizen and stakeholder feedback on EU initiatives and policies. We gathered them using an API that permits the download of CSV files and a SQLite database containing feedback submissions, initiative descriptions, and metadata about contributors. The platform continuously accumulates new data as the Commission launches new consultations and stakeholders provide input.
Alignment: The dataset maps to our model with Feedback → del:Contribution, Initiative → del:DeliberationProcess, Contributor → del:Participant, and Policy Area → del:Topic. The formal structure of EU consultations is represented through del:Stage entities, while the relationship between feedback and initiatives is captured through del:hasContribution properties.

- **DeliData:** [17] This research dataset focuses on deliberation in multi-party problem solving, created by Karadzhov et al.. It contains structured records of group deliberations with detailed annotations of message types, deliberation patterns, performance metrics and multi-level deliberation annotations.
Alignment: The dataset maps to our ontology with Participant → del:Participant, Message → del:Contribution, Group Chat → del:DeliberationProcess, and Annotation Types → del:ArgumentStructure.

- **Habermas Machine:** [18] This dataset derives from a deliberative democracy experiment by Google DeepMind labs. Stored in Parquet format, it contains pairwise comparisons, preference rankings, position statement ratings, and survey responses from structured deliberation exercises. The dataset captures how participant preferences evolve through deliberative processes.
Alignment: The dataset maps to our model with Participant → del:Participant, Position Statement → del:Position, Comparison → del:Argument, and Deliberation Round → del:Stage within a broader del:DeliberationProcess. The preference rankings provide data for del:supports relationships, while the structured nature of the experiment maps clearly to the stage-based process model in our ontology.

- **US Supreme Court Arguments:** This dataset contains, in CSV format, transcripts of oral arguments before the United States Supreme Court from 2017–2021. Available as public domain government works, it provides verbatim accounts of legal deliberation at the highest judicial level, including questions from justices, responses from attorneys, and the complete flow of legal argumentation. Each transcript includes case metadata, speaker identification, and the full text of exchanges.
Alignment: The dataset maps to our ontology with Justice/Attorney → del:Participant (with appropriate del:Role), Statement → del:Contribution, Case → del:DeliberationProcess, and Legal Question → del:Topic. The adver-

sarial nature of legal argumentation is captured through del:supports and del:attacks relationships, while references to precedents and statutes are represented through del:references connections to del:LegalSource entities.

– **Decidim Barcelona:** This dataset comes from Barcelona's implementation of the Decidim open-source participation platform, representing digital deliberation at the municipal level. Available under CC-BY licence in CSV format, it contains structured data on proposals, debates, participatory processes, assemblies, consultations, and user interactions. The platform generates continuous data on citizen engagement with urban governance, capturing both formal and informal deliberative processes.

   Alignment: The dataset maps to our model with User → del:Participant, Proposal/Comment
   → del:Contribution, Participatory Process → del:DeliberationProcess. The platform's multi-level participation structure is represented through nested del:Stage entities, while the various forms of user engagement are captured through specialized subtypes of del:Contribution.

These mappings enable the transformation of heterogeneous data into a unified representation based on the Deliberation ontology.

4.2   Harvesting and Conversion

We developed data conversion pipelines for each dataset to transform the original data into RDF format aligned with the Deliberation ontology. The general process includes:

1. **Data Extraction:** Extracting data from the original source (HTML, CSV, JSON, etc.).
2. **Data Cleaning:** Cleaning and normalizing the data to ensure consistency.
3. **Entity Identification:** Identifying key entities (participants, contributions, topics, etc.).
4. **Relationship Extraction:** Identifying relationships between entities.
5. **RDF Conversion:** Converting the data to RDF format aligned with the Deliberation ontology.

For each dataset, we created specific conversion scripts tailored to its structure and content.

These tools are implemented in Python using libraries such as BeautifulSoup for HTML parsing and RDFLib for RDF manipulation. The tools are designed to be modular and extensible, allowing for the addition of new data sources and formats. The code is available in a Github repository.[10]

---

[10] https://github.com/Stocastico96/Deliberation-Knowledge-Graph.

4.3   Data Storage and Publication

The integrated RDF data will be stored in a triple store (Virtuoso Open Source) that provides SPARQL query capabilities. The triple store will be exposed through a SPARQL endpoint that allows for complex queries across the integrated datasets. The data will also available as downloadable RDF dumps for offline analysis.

We developed a web-based query interface that allows users to explore the integrated deliberation data through predefined queries and visualizations. The interface will provide:

- Basic search functionality for finding deliberation processes, participants, and contributions.
- Advanced query capabilities using SPARQL for complex analysis.
- Visualizations of deliberation structures, participant networks, and argument flows.
- Export options for query results in various formats (CSV, JSON, RDF).

Figure 2 illustrates the complete pipeline architecture.

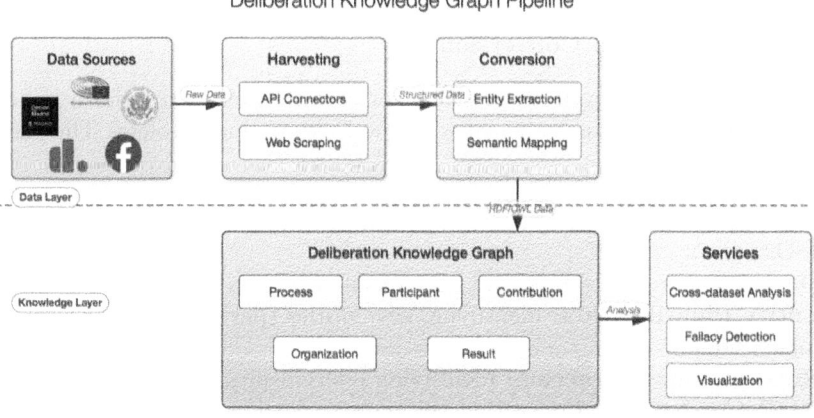

Fig. 2. Represents the pipeline for the creation of the Deliberation Knowledge Graph. It shows the different sources from which data is harvested, the preprocessing and the mapping to the Deliberation Ontology, upon which several services can be built.

4.4   Technical Implementation

The technical implementation of the DKG includes the ontology implementation, data conversion tools, and a query interface.

The Deliberation ontology is implemented in OWL 2 (Web Ontology Language). The three models are implemented as a single file and published with a persistent URI: http://w3id.org/deliberation/.

4.5   Proof-of-Concept Validation

This work demonstrates the technical feasibility of integrating heterogeneous deliberation datasets through our unified ontological framework. The successful data conversion validates the ontology's cross-platform mapping capabilities. Detailed SPARQL query examples and the ORSD are available online[11]. Future work will explore hybrid NLP pipelines combining discourse marker detection, BERT-based classification, and LLM-assisted population of the Analysis Layer with argument structures. While comprehensive evaluation remains future work, this establishes the foundation for integrated deliberation analysis across institutional and civic contexts.

5   Related Work

Several ontologies have been developed to represent aspects of deliberation and argumentation. However, each has limitations that the DKG aims to address.

5.1   Existing Deliberation Ontologies

- **DELIB Ontology** The DELIB Ontology [19] models e-participation deliberation processes with social media integration. It explicitly supports dual e-participation (government and citizen-led) and connects deliberation with social media content. However, it focuses primarily on electronic participation and lacks detailed representation of legal frameworks. It is not maintained or available.
- **Deliberation Ontology** The Deliberation Ontology by Panagiotopoulos et al. [20] supports public decision-making in policy deliberations with a strong focus on legal information integration. However, it adopts a government-centric approach with limited participant modeling and does not account for informal deliberation spaces. It is not maintained as well.
- **Argument Representation Ontologies** The Argument Interchange Format [21] Ontology provides a sophisticated model for argument structure and relations, capturing support/attack relationships with a strong theoretical foundation. Also the Argument Model Ontology (AMO)[12] has been developed for the same goal. However, they focuses only on argumentation, not broader deliberation processes, and has limited integration with other aspects of deliberation.
- **Related Domain Ontologies** The Semantically Interlinked Online Communities (SIOC) ontology [22] describes online discussion information structure and is widely used in social media applications. However, it is not specifically designed for deliberation and lacks political and legal conceptualization.
  The Legal Knowledge Interchange Format (LKIF) [23] facilitates communication between legal knowledge systems with comprehensive legal information

---

[11] https://github.com/Stocastico96/Deliberation-Knowledge-Graph.

[12] https://sparontologies.github.io/amo/current/amo.html.

modeling. However, it is highly specialized for the legal domain and lacks direct connection to civic participation concepts.

- **PAKT Framework** The PAKT (Perspectivized Argumentation Knowledge Graph) by Plenz et al. [24] represents arguments with premises and conclusions while connecting them to author perspectives, values, and frames. Although not formally an ontology, it demonstrates how knowledge graphs can reveal patterns in deliberative discourse. However, PAKT focuses on analyzing existing debates rather than standardizing deliberation across platforms.

5.2   Comparative Analysis of Existing Approaches

Table 1 compares existing ontologies with our approach across key deliberation dimensions:

Table 1. Comparison of deliberation-related ontologies across key dimensions

Ontology	Institutional	Civic	Arguments	Cross-Platform	Maintained
DELIB (Porwol)	Limited	✓	Limited	✓	No
Panagiotopoulos	✓	Limited	Limited	No	No
AIF	N/A	N/A	✓	Limited	Yes
AMO	N/A	N/A	✓	No	Yes
SIOC	No	✓	No	✓	Yes
LKIF	✓	No	Limited	No	Yes
PAKT	Limited	Limited	✓	Limited	Yes
DEL	✓	✓	✓	✓	Yes

The DKG, based on DEL ontology, addresses critical gaps as the first maintained framework that comprehensively integrates institutional deliberation, civic participation, structured argument representation, and cross-platform standardization in a unified model. While existing ontologies excel in specific areas—AIF and AMO for argument structures, SIOC for online communities, LKIF for legal knowledge—none provides the comprehensive coverage necessary for analyzing deliberation across both formal and informal democratic contexts.

6   Conclusion and Future Work

The digitalisation of public deliberation processes presents a major opportunity to enhance democratic engagement. By integrating currently fragmented sources of deliberative information and bridging the divide between institutional debates and civic participation, a wide range of new applications becomes possible. This paper has proposed a technical solution to address this challenge and discussed its benefits and limitations.

The main contributions are the Deliberation Ontology –a model that captures deliberative processes across institutional and civic contexts– and the Deliberation Knowledge Graph, a dataset connecting information from various open data sources. To support this, data conversion pipelines have been developed to integrate heterogeneous datasets, and semantic querying capabilities allow for cross-context analysis.

Acknowledgment. This work has been partially funded by the project HARNESS, which has received funding from the EU's Horizon 2020 research and innovation programme under grant agreement no. 101169409, see https://www.harness-network.eu in the framework of the research training projects "Territorio: Transizione tecnologica, culturale, economica e sociale verso la sostenibilità" (PR. FSE + 2021/2027DGR n. 509 del 03/04/2023) - CUPJ33C23000610006 and with the support of the EU Commission funds within ERC HyperModeLex. Grant agreement ID: 101055185.

We gratefully acknowledge Monica Palmirani for her technical assistance and insightful suggestions.

References

1. OECD, Innovative Citizen Participation and New Democratic Institutions: Catching the Deliberative Wave. Paris: OECD Publishing, (2020). https://doi.org/10.1787/339306da-en
2. Bizer, C., Heath, T., Idehen, K., Berners-Lee, T.: Linked data on the web (LDOW2008). In: Proceedings of the 17th International Conference on World Wide Web, pp. 1265–1266 (2008)
3. Poblet, M., Casanovas, P., Rodríguez-Doncel, V.: Linked Democracy: Foundations, Tools, and Applications. Springer, Cham (2019)
4. Weyl, E.G., Tang, A.: The Plurality Community. (2023) Plurality: The future of collaborative technology and democracy. https://github.com/pluralitybook/plurality/blob/main/contents/english
5. Berners-Lee, T., Hendler, J., Lassila, O.: The semantic web. Sci. Am. **284**(5), 34–43 (2001)
6. Casanovas, P., Rodríguez-Doncel, V., González-Conejero, J.: The role of pragmatics in the web of data. In: Poggi , F., Capone, A. (eds.) Pragmatics and Law. Practical and Theoretical Approaches, Berlin, Heidelberg: Springer Verlag (2016). https://ssrn.com/abstract=2697832
7. De Moor, A.: Patterns for the pragmatic web. In: International Conference on Conceptual Structures
8. Bonacin, R., Dos Reis, J.C., Hornung, H., Baranauskas, M.C.C.: An ontological model for supporting intention-based information sharing on collaborative problem solving. Int. J. Collaborative Enterp. **3**(2/3)
9. Sperber, D., Wilson, D.: Relevance: Communication and Cognition, 2nd edn. Basil Blackwell, Oxford (1995)
10. Santos, C., Doncel, V., Casanovas, P., Robaldo, L., van der Torre, L.: An approach for modelling relevance in legal ontologies. In: Proceedings of the VII Workshop on Artificial Intelligence and the Complexity of Legal Systems (AICOL), Nice, France, (2016)

11. Nissenbaum, H.: Privacy in Context: Technology, Policy, and the Integrity of Social Life. Stanford University Press, Stanford (2010)
12. Floridi, L.: Hypersuasion – on AI's persuasive power and how to deal with it. Philos. Technol. (2024) forthcoming. https://ssrn.com/abstract=4815890
13. Wiener, N.: The Human Use of Human Beings: Cybernetics and Society, 2nd edn. Doubleday Anchor, New York (1954)
14. Studer, R., Benjamins, V.R., Fensel, D.: Knowledge engineering: Principles and methods. Data Knowl. Eng. **25**(1–2) (1998)
15. Poveda-Villalón, M., Fernández-Izquierdo, A., Fernández-López, M., García-Castro, R.: Lot: An industrial oriented ontology engineering framework. Eng. Appl. Artif. Intell. **111**, 104755 (2022). https://www.sciencedirect.com/science/article/pii/S0952197622000392
16. Tamašauskaitė, G., Groth, P.: Defining a knowledge graph development process through a systematic review. ACM Trans. Softw. Eng. Methodol. **32**(1), 1–40 (2023)
17. Karadzhov, G., Stafford, T., Vlachos, A.: Delidata: a dataset for deliberation in multi-party problem solving. arXiv preprint arXiv:2108.05271 (2023). https://arxiv.org/abs/2108.05271
18. Tessler, M.H., et al.: AI can help humans find common ground in democratic deliberation. Science **386**(6719), eadq2852 (2024). https://www.science.org/doi/abs/10.1126/science.adq2852
19. Porwol, L., Ojo, A., Breslin, J.G.: An ontology for next generation e-participation initiatives. Gov. Inf. Quart. **33**(4), 819–832 (2016). https://doi.org/10.1016/j.giq.2016.01.007
20. Panagiotopoulos, P., Gionis, G., Psarras, J., Askounis, D.: Supporting public decision making in policy deliberations: an ontological approach. Oper. Res. Int. J. **11**(3), 281–298 (2011). https://doi.org/10.1007/s12351-010-0081-3
21. Chesnevar, C.I., McGinnis, J., Modgil, S., et al.: Towards an argument interchange format. Knowl. Eng. Rev. **21**(4), 293–316 (2006)
22. Passant, A., Bojārs, U., Breslin, J.G., Decker, S.: The SIOC project: semantically-interlinked online communities, from humans to machines. In: Padget, J., Artikis, A., Vasconcelos, W., Stathis, K., da Silva, V.T., Matson, E., Polleres, A. (eds.) COIN -2009. LNCS (LNAI), vol. 6069, pp. 179–194. Springer, Heidelberg (2010). https://doi.org/10.1007/978-3-642-14962-7_12
23. Hoekstra, R., Breuker, J., Di Bello, M., Boer, A.: The LKIF core ontology of basic legal concepts. In: Workshop on Legal Ontologies and Artificial Intelligence Techniques, pp. 43–63 (2007)
24. Plenz, M., Heinisch, P., Frank, A., Cimiano, P.: Pakt: Perspectivized argumentation knowledge graph and tool for deliberation analysis. arXiv preprint:2404.10570 (2024). https://arxiv.org/abs/2404.10570

Customizing Investment Recommendations Using Investor's Financial Situation in Digital Banking and E-Government

Asefeh Asemi[1], Adeleh Asemi[2], and Andrea Ko[1(✉)]

[1] Corvinus University of Budapest, Budapest 1093, Hungary
{asemi.asefeh,andrea.ko}@uni-corvinus.hu
[2] Universiti Malaya, 50603 Kuala Lumpur, Malaysia
adeleh@um.edu.my

Abstract. This study proposes an ANFIS-based investment recommendation system for digital banking and e-government financial services, enhancing decision-making through artificial intelligence and machine learning. The system personalizes investment suggestions based on a customer's financial situation, risk tolerance, and investment goals, aligning with the broader digital transformation of e-government and smart financial governance. Clustering techniques are utilized to categorize customers with similar financial behaviors, improving personalization and efficiency in automated financial advisory services. The system was tested using a dataset of 1542 potential investors, demonstrating its capability to classify customers accurately and offer tailored investment recommendations. By integrating AI-driven decision-making into e-government frameworks, this research highlights the potential for intelligent automation in public financial services. Future research directions include refining AI models for enhanced accuracy and aligning with digital governance policies. Overall, the proposed system represents a significant advancement in personalized digital banking, supporting smart governance and automated financial services in the era of digital transformation.

Keywords: ANFIS · digital banking · e-government · investment recommendation · financial technology · artificial intelligence · machine learning · clustering · smart governance

1 Introduction

Investment recommendation systems have become increasingly important in the retail banking sector as they provide a personalized approach to financial planning for potential investors. The use of advanced data analysis techniques and machine learning algorithms has enabled these systems to analyze and predict the investment preferences of potential investors based on their financial situation. Among these techniques, Adaptive Neuro-Fuzzy Inference System (ANFIS) has emerged as a powerful tool for modeling and predicting investment decisions. ANFIS is a hybrid system that combines the capabilities of both artificial neural networks and fuzzy logic systems, allowing for accurate

A. Kő et al. (Eds.): EGOVIS 2025, LNCS 16049, pp. 137–162, 2026.
https://doi.org/10.1007/978-3-032-02225-7_10

predictions in uncertain and dynamic environments. In recent years, various studies have used ANFIS for investment recommendations in the retail banking sector. For example, a study proposed by Davies et al. [1] fuzzy logic-based prediction system for stock market forecasting, while another study by Jain et al. [2] applied a fuzzy analytic hierarchy process to personalize investment for individual investors. These studies demonstrate the potential of ANFIS in providing accurate and personalized investment recommendations in retail banking. Here are the differences between the proposed system and existing systems:

- The proposed system uses ANFIS, which is well-suited for investment recommendations where the market is constantly changing, and the risk tolerance of potential investors can vary greatly. This is different from existing systems that only use traditional machine-learning methods like decision trees, logistic regression, and random forests [3].
- The proposed system incorporates expert knowledge and investor feedback, which helps to personalize recommendations for each individual potential investor. This is different from existing systems that only use historical data to make recommendations [4].
- The proposed system uses clustering techniques to group potential investors with similar financial situations and investment goals, which further enhances the personalization of the recommendations. This is different from existing systems that do not use clustering techniques [5–10].
- The proposed system uses multiple inputs such as current savings, monthly expenses, financial situation, and spending plan for savings. This is different from existing systems that only use one or two inputs to make recommendations [11].

This research aims to propose a model for an investment recommender system using ANFIS based on the potential investors' financial situation in retail banking. The proposed model will analyze the financial situation of potential investors and provide customized investment recommendations based on their risk tolerance and investment goals. The results of this research will contribute to the development of more accurate and personalized investment recommendation systems in retail banking.

2 Literature Review

Investment recommendations play a crucial role in digital banking and e-government financial services by assisting investors in making informed financial decisions. The integration of data analysis, machine learning, and AI-driven automation has led to more personalized financial services tailored to individual risk profiles and investment goals. One of the most effective techniques in this domain is the ANFIS, which merges artificial neural networks (ANNs) with fuzzy logic systems to enhance predictive accuracy in complex financial environments [12–14]. ANNs, inspired by neural processes in the human brain, enable efficient pattern recognition for financial forecasting, while fuzzy logic handles uncertainty, making ANFIS a highly adaptable tool for investment recommendations. Several studies highlight the effectiveness of ANFIS in digital financial applications. Lin et al. [15] demonstrated its superiority in stock market forecasting using historical data and technical indicators. Asemi et al. [7] applied ANFIS to personalize investment recommendations based on user demographics and financial behavior, achieving enhanced customization. Furthermore, D'lima and Khan [16] developed an ANFIS-driven foreign exchange investment model, incorporating clustering techniques to refine accuracy. Similarly, Wei et al. [17] explored the classification of mutual fund investors through clustering and machine learning, reinforcing the role of ANFIS in financial prediction. Personalization in financial recommendations is further improved through clustering techniques, which segment investors based on financial behavior patterns, leading to more tailored recommendations [18]. For instance, Thompson et al. [5] analyzed financial transactions via clustering to predict investor behavior, while Asemi et al. [7] developed an AI-powered business recommender model incorporating real-time investor feedback. Szafranko et al. [19] further validated the adaptability of ANFIS-based financial models through expert-driven investment predictions. The proposed ANFIS model integrates multiple variables, including savings, expenses, and financial stability, to generate adaptive investment recommendations. By incorporating expert knowledge and real-time investor feedback, the system enhances accuracy and adaptability, making it particularly relevant to digital banking and e-government frameworks [20]. However, certain limitations exist. The model primarily relies on historical data, which may not fully capture real-time market dynamics, and does not yet incorporate real-time financial updates. Future research should focus on expanding datasets, integrating additional investment products, and improving real-time analytics for enhanced recommendation precision [21]. Additionally, implementing ANFIS-based systems in real-world financial services necessitates addressing data privacy, security, and interoperability concerns, particularly within e-government infrastructures [22]. In conclusion, ANFIS-based financial advisory systems present a promising direction for digital banking and e-government financial strategies, leveraging AI, clustering, and fuzzy logic to optimize investor decision-making and financial planning [23]. Overall, the literature suggests that ANFIS, when combined with clustering techniques and AI-driven decision-making, has the potential to revolutionize digital investment advisory systems. By integrating these technologies into digital banking and e-government services, financial institutions and policymakers can enhance accessibility, efficiency, and personalization in financial decision-making.

3 Methodology

The methodology used in this research is a combined method, which refers to the use of multiple research methods in a single study. The proposed model for the investment recommendation system is based on the use of ANFIS and the clustering of data related to the types of investments used by potential investors. Table 1 shows the methodology in different steps of the research.

The first step in the methodology is to import the data into MATLAB and JMP software. The data used in the research is collected from a questionnaire that includes four questions related to the type of investment. The answers given by the potential investors are coded and converted into numerical data, which can then be analyzed in MATLAB and JMP software. The second step is to prepare the data to be clustered

Table 1. Methodology in different steps of the research

Steps	Method	Tools	Data
1	Data Import	MATLAB and JMP	Investment-type data from potential investor surveys
2	Data preparation for clustering	K-Means technique in MATLAB and JMP	Investment-type data from potential investor surveys
3	Clustering of investment types	K-Means technique in MATLAB and JMP	Investment-type data from potential investor surveys
4	Comparison of clusters	MATLAB and JMP	Clustered investment-type data from potential investor surveys
5	Finalizing clusters	Expert knowledge and investor feedback analysis	Clustered investment-type data from potential investor surveys
6	ANFIS Inputs	MATLAB	Financial situation data from potential investor surveys
7	ANFIS Output	ANFIS algorithm in MATLAB	Clustered investment-type data from potential investor surveys and financial situation data from potential investor surveys

using the K-Means technique in MATLAB and JMP. The K-Means technique is a popular method for clustering data and is used to group similar data points together. The third step is to cluster the types of investments into three clusters using the K-Means technique. The K-Means technique is used to group the data into three clusters based on the similarity of the data points. The fourth step is to compare the clusters of MATLAB and JMP. The clusters generated by MATLAB and JMP are compared to ensure that the results are consistent and to identify any potential discrepancies. The final step is to finalize the clusters. The final clusters are used as the inputs for the ANFIS model, which is used to determine the investment-type recommendations for investors based on the scoring of each cluster. ANFIS utilizes two types of rules for prediction: those based on data training and those based on investor feedback analysis and expert knowledge. To implement the ANFIS, MATLAB software is used. This software is widely used in data analysis, and its use ensures the validity of the results. The proposed model will analyze the financial situation of potential investors and provide customized investment recommendations based on their risk tolerance and investment goals.

4 The Proposed Model

In this research, we propose a model for an investment recommendation system using ANFIS based on the potential investors' financial situation in retail banking. The proposed model aims to analyze the financial situation of potential investors and provide customized investment recommendations based on their risk tolerance and investment goals.

4.1 Model Structure

The proposed investment recommendation system consists of multiple interconnected layers, ensuring efficient data processing and accurate investment suggestions.

- Data Acquisition Layer: This layer collects investment-related data from potential investors via surveys, financial statements, and market data. It ensures compliance with privacy regulations such as GDPR and HIPAA while maintaining data accuracy and scalability [14, 20].
- Data Storage Layer: The acquired data is securely stored in structured formats compatible with machine learning tools. This layer emphasizes scalability, security, and real-time data updates for effective data management [24].
- Machine Learning Layer: The system utilizes K-Means clustering to segment investors based on their financial behavior. This clustering enhances recommendation accuracy by identifying investment patterns and aligning them with investor goals. The model undergoes fine-tuning and evaluation using key performance metrics [25]–[29].
- ANFIS Layer: The ANFIS refines investment recommendations by incorporating expert insights and investor feedback. The model uses Gaussian Membership Functions to process investor traits and generate tailored investment suggestions [26, 30]–[33].
- Application Layer: The final layer presents recommendations to users via a web or mobile platform. It offers interactive features such as real-time financial tracking and expert consultations while maintaining compliance with data security standards [6]–[8, 21, 34, 35]

This structured approach ensures a comprehensive and adaptable recommendation system that personalizes investment strategies based on investor profiles and financial trends.

5 Experiments and Results

This section outlines the methodology for clustering investment types, analyzing investor financial situations, and implementing the ANFIS-based recommendation model.

5.1 Clustering Investment Types (ANFIS Output)

To categorize investment preferences, the study employs MATLAB and JMP, two widely used software for data analysis and clustering. Both platforms utilize the K-Means algorithm, a popular clustering method for grouping similar data points. MATLAB offers extensive analytical tools, including the Statistics and Machine Learning Toolbox, whereas JMP provides an interactive interface for data visualization and statistical analysis. While both software uses the same clustering technique, variations in dataset structure, the number of clusters, and implementation methods may lead to different outcomes. The clustering process follows four key steps:

Data Import: Investment-related data is collected from investor surveys and transformed into numerical format for analysis. The dataset includes investment types such as mutual funds, voluntary pension funds, and government securities.

Data Preparation: Preprocessing and handling missing values using imputation techniques (mean/median replacement).

Clustering Execution: The K-Means algorithm is applied in MATLAB and JMP, generating three distinct clusters. In JMP, the first cluster contains 592 items, the second 406, and the third 340.

Result Visualization: Scatter plots and statistical comparisons help assess the clustering validity and differences across platforms.

By leveraging ANFIS-based clustering, the study enhances investment personalization, ensuring that recommendations align with investors' financial situations and preferences (Fig. 1).

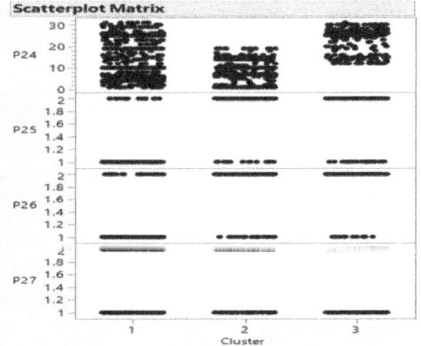

Fig. 1. Scatterplot for the investment type's clusters in JMP

Table 2 provides a summary of the characteristics of each cluster, including the number of respondents, the investment types, and the investment habits and behaviors of the respondents. It also includes Investment in Stock Market (Last 3 Years), Monitoring of Stock Performance, and Investment in Government Bonds (Table 2).

In MATLAB, K-means when using the k-means function indicates that some of the rows in our data matrix (X) contain missing values. k-means algorithm is sensitive to missing data, it will ignore the rows with missing data when computing the cluster assignments. This can result in a loss of information and affect the accuracy of the clustering results. To handle missing data, we remove rows with missing data by using "rmmissing" function before passing the data to the k-means function. Also, the missing data can be imputed with a suitable value, such as the mean or median of the feature. It's important to handle missing data properly because missing data can affect the accuracy of the clustering results. The results showed that the clusters contain a similar number of items to clusters in JMP. Figure 2 shows the "histfit" plot for the investment type clusters in JMP.

Table 2. A general overview of the output clusters in JMP

Cluster	Number of Respondents	Investment Types	Investment in Stock Market (Last 3 Years)	Monitoring of Stock Performance	Investment in Government Bonds
1	592	Stocks/Shares, Mutual Funds, Government Securities	No	No	No
2	406	Stocks/Shares, Mutual Funds, Voluntary Pension Funds, Government Securities	Yes	Yes	Yes
3	340	Stocks/Shares, Voluntary Pension Funds, Government Securities	Yes	Yes	No

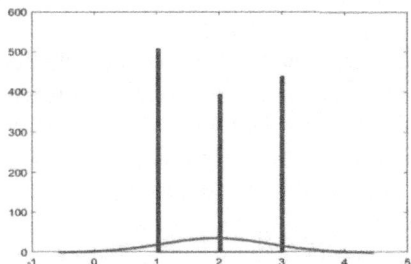

Fig. 2. Histfit plot for the investment type's clusters in MATLAB

d. Comparing and combining the clusters generated in MATLAB and JMP to ensure consistency of the results and identify any potential discrepancies and finalize the clusters. Multiple methods are used to evaluate and compare the results of clustering in MATLAB and JMP to ensure the validity of the findings:

Visual Comparison: One way to compare the results is to visually compare the visualized of the clusters generated by each software. It can be done by creating scatter plots of the clusters in JMP and tree plots in MATLAB. The scatter function will require 2 columns of data, our data has more columns than 2, then it needs to use different columns for x and y values. In this way, we can compare the distribution and similarity of the data points in each cluster.

Combine the results: A third way to compare the results is to combine them. For example, if the clustering results in MATLAB and JMP are similar, then the clusters can be combined to create a final set of clusters. If the clustering results are different, then the clusters can be merged based on the similarity of the data points in each cluster.

Expert knowledge: Another way to combine the results is to use expert knowledge, for example, if the researcher has knowledge of the data set and the type of investments, they can use their experience to validate the results and combine the clusters.

The investment types' clusters are a way to group similar respondents based on their investment habits and behaviours. The interpretation of the clusters depends on the specific characteristics of each cluster and what they represent. The final clusters are used to determine the investment-type recommendations for investors based on the scoring of each cluster. The results show, the first cluster is composed of individuals who were not invested in the stock market in the last 3 years and did not regularly monitor stock performance. Suitable investment products for this cluster included stocks/shares in the stock market, mutual funds, and government securities, with most not investing in government bonds. This cluster represents individuals who are not currently invested in the stock market and have not been monitoring stock performance. The second cluster is composed of individuals who had invested in the stock market in the last 3 years and regularly monitored stock performance. Suitable investment products for this cluster included stocks/shares on the stock exchange, mutual funds, voluntary pension funds, and government securities, with many having investments in government bonds. This cluster represents individuals who are currently invested in the stock market, regularly monitor stock performance, and have investments in government bonds. The third cluster is composed of individuals who had been investing in the stock market for the last 3 years and regularly monitored stock performance. Suitable investment products for this cluster included stocks/shares, voluntary pension funds, and government securities, with many not investing in government bonds. This cluster represents individuals who are currently invested in the stock market, and regularly monitor stock performance, but do not have investments in government bonds. In general, investment type clusters show that the first cluster represents individuals who are not currently invested in the stock market, the second cluster represents individuals who are currently invested in the stock market and have investments in government bonds, and the third cluster represents individuals who are currently invested in the stock market but do not have investments in government bonds.

5.2 Financial Situation (ANFIS Inputs)

Some questions in the questionnaire were designed to measure the financial situation of potential investors. Four questions (inputs 1–4) were asked of the respondents about their current savings, monthly expenses, overall financial situation, and spending plans for their savings. This information is crucial in understanding the potential investors' financial capabilities and risk tolerance, which can help to gauge how well they can handle unexpected events or major expenses. It helps in providing personalized investment recommendations based on their individual needs and preferences. This research uses four inputs to determine the investment-type recommendations for investors based on their financial situation (Table 3).

Input 1, current savings, is related to the amount of savings that potential investors currently have. It includes 6 membership functions (MFs) with different options for

Table 3. A general overview of the inputs and membership functions

Inputs	Membership Function	Description
1	MF1, MF2, MF3, MF4, MF5, MF6	Current savings
2	MF1, MF2, MF3, MF4, MF5, MF6	Monthly expenses
3	MF1, MF2, MF3, MF4, MF5	Financial situation
4	MF1, MF2, MF3, MF4	Spending plan for savings

potential investors to choose from. Option 1, "I could buy a new car," is considered for MF1, option 2, "I could buy a 4–5-year-old car," is considered for MF2, option 3, "I could buy a property from my savings," is considered for MF3, option 4, "I could pay for a foreign vacation," is considered for MF4, option 5, "I can buy a mid-range smartphone anytime," is considered for MF5, and option 6, "There are no," is considered for MF6. These options reflect the potential investors' current financial status and their spending plan for their savings (Table 4).

Table 4. Potential Investors' Statement to Have Savings

Options	f	(%)
MF1: I could buy a new car for myself	410	26.6
MF2: I could buy a 4–5-year-old car for myself	345	22.4
MF3: I could buy a property from my savings	396	25.7
MF4: I could pay for a foreign vacation	276	18.0
MF5: I can buy a mid-range smartphone anytime	83	5.4
MF6: There are no	29	1.9

Input 2, monthly expenses, is related to the statement of the potential investors for their household in terms of average monthly living expenses. It also includes 6 MFs with different options for potential investors to choose from. Option 1, "We can regularly set aside savings," is considered for MF1, option 2, "In addition to our regular spending (entertainment, shopping), we can set you aside for the holidays," is considered for MF2, option 3, "We're just getting out, a little every month to buy new clothes for fun," is considered for MF3, option 4, "We can spend regularly on entertainment and shopping," is considered for MF4, option 5, "Our monthly income provides our basic livelihood (housing, food)," is considered for MF5, and option 6, "We do not come out of our monthly revenue," is considered for MF6. These options reflect the potential investors' ability to manage their monthly expenses and their financial priorities (Table 5). Input 3, financial situation, is related to the description of the current financial statement by the potential investors. It includes 5 MFs with different options for potential investors to choose from. Option 1, "I have no daily problems but in the long run," is considered for MF1, option 2, "Everything's okay," is considered for MF2, option 3, "I'm calm about myself, but the future of the children is uncertain," is considered for MF3, option 4, "It's hard, but I live," is considered for MF4, and option 5, "hopeless," is considered for MF5. These options reflect the potential investors' current financial situation and their level of comfort with their financial status (Table 6).

Table 5. Average Monthly Living Expenses of the Potential Investors

Options	f	(%)
MF1: We can regularly set aside savings	1086	70.5
MF2: In addition to our regular spending (entertainment, shopping), we can set you aside for the holidays	244	15.8
MF3: We're just getting out, a little every month to buy new clothes for fun	90	5.8
MF4: We can spend regularly on entertainment and shopping	104	6.8
MF5: Our monthly income provides our basic livelihood (housing, food)	13	0.8
MF6: We do not come out of our monthly revenue	4	0.3

Table 6. Description of the Current Financial Statement by the Potential Investors

Options	f	(%)
MF1: I have no daily problems but in the long run	471	30.5
MF2: Everything's okay	573	37.1
MF3: I'm calm about myself, but the future of the children is uncertain	470	30.4
MF4: It's hard, but I live	23	1.5
MF5: Hopeless	5	0.3

Input 4, spending plan for savings, is related to the expected or planned spending of savings by the potential investors. It includes 4 MFs with different options for potential investors to choose from. Option 1, "I plan to use my savings in one or two weeks or one month," is considered for MF1, option 2, "Within one year or 2–3 years," is considered for MF2, option 3, "Within 4–5 years or 5–8 years," is considered for MF3, and option 4, "Over 8 years or I do not plan to use my savings," is considered for MF4. These options reflect the potential investors' plans for their savings and their investment horizon (Table 7).

In summary, the inputs in this study are four questions (inputs 1–4) that were asked of the respondents about their current savings and financial situation. These inputs provide information about the potential investors' current financial situation, which can be used to gauge how difficult an unexpected event or major release is for them. Based on the data presented in the table, it can be seen that the majority of potential investors have stated

Table 7. Expectation to Spend Savings by the Potential Investors

Options	f	(%)
MF1: I plan to use my savings in one or two weeks or one month	38	2.5
MF2: Within one year or 2–3 years	240	15.5
MF3: Within 4–5 years or 5–8 years	143	9.3
MF4: Over 8 years or I do not plan to use my savings	1119	72.7

that they have savings (MF1: 27%, MF2: 22%, MF3: 25%, MF4: 18%, MF5: 5%, MF6: 2%) and plan to use them within 1–2 years or 4–5 years (MF2: 16%, MF3: 9%) or do not plan to use them (MF4: 73%). Most potential investors also stated that they can regularly set aside savings for living expenses (MF1: 70%) and have a stable financial situation (MF2: 37%, MF1: 31%, MF3: 30%). These results indicate that most potential investors have some level of financial stability and savings that they plan to use for specific purposes soon and are suitable for investment recommendations based on their financial situation and investment goals. Input 1 (current savings) measures the amount of savings that the potential investors have available to them and how they plan to use them. Input 2 (monthly expenses) measures the financial situation of the potential investors in terms of their monthly expenses and how they are managing their expenses. Input 3 (financial situation) measures the financial situation of the potential investors in terms of their current financial statement. Input 4 (spending plan for savings) measures the potential investors' plans for spending their savings and how soon they expect to use them. These inputs provide a comprehensive understanding of the potential investors' current financial situation, including their savings, expenses, financial statements, and plans for spending their savings. This information can be used to make personalized investment recommendations that are tailored to the individual needs and goals of each potential investor. Overall, these inputs provide a comprehensive understanding of the potential investors' financial situation and their investment goals, which allows for personalized investment recommendations based on their individual needs and preferences.

5.3 Proposition FinancialANFIS Model

The FinancialANFIS model utilizes two types of rules for prediction: those based on data training and those based on investor feedback analysis and expert knowledge. The ANFIS is a type of fuzzy logic system that utilizes "IF_THEN" rules based on input membership functions (MFs). The FIS architecture consists of three components: fuzzy rules, membership functions, and a reasoning mechanism to generate output. In this case, the FinancialANFIS system has four inputs and one output, with three membership functions per input. The membership functions used are Gaussian Membership Function (gaussmf), which range from a minimum of zero to a maximum of one. To create the FinancialANFIS, a fuzzy logic toolbox in MATLAB was utilized, following six steps: importing data, designing the FIS, loading data, generating the FIS, training the FIS, and testing the FIS.

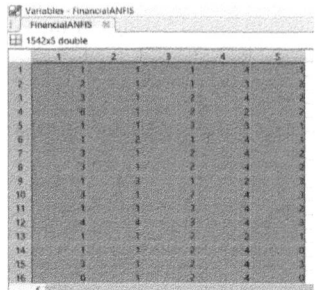

Fig. 3. FinancialANFIS Variables

Figure 3 shows the FinancialANFIS variables. It consists of four inputs including the current savings, monthly expenses, financial situation, and spending plan for savings (Fig. 4).

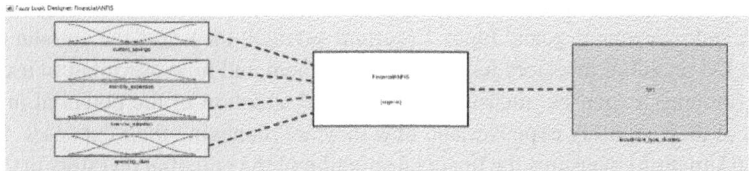

Fig. 4. FinancialANFIS Sugeno: 4 inputs and 1 output

Figure 5 shows loaded data for the next steps of data training and data testing in FinancialANFIS. To train data for the new FIS, a grid partition was considered, and optimization of the method was hybrid with error tolerance 0 and epochs 3. Then the FinancialANFIS was generated as a new FIS.

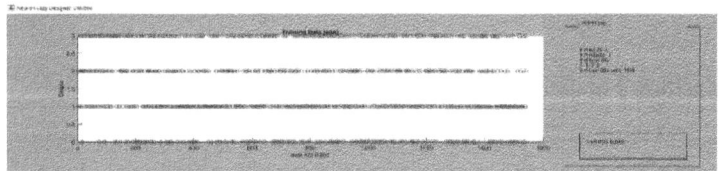

Fig. 5. Prepared data in the FinancialANFIS

Figure 6 shows generated a new FIS named FinancialANFIS. This system included 4 inputs and 1 output. The data set index included 1542 on the x-axis and the y-axis shows the distribution of output based on the investment-type clusters.

In Fig. 7, the trained FinancialANFIS network is shown with four input variables and one output for investment-type clusters. The training process used a hybrid method with three epochs. The error for each epoch was around 0.89. The FinancialANFIS network contained 1489 nodes, 720 linear parameters, 42 nonlinear parameters, and a total of 762

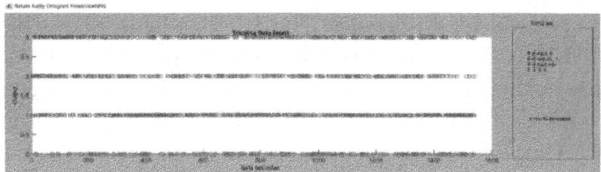

Fig. 6. The generated FinancialANFIS

parameters. It was trained using 1542 data pairs and had 720 fuzzy rules. The minimal training Root Mean Squared Error (RMSE) was 0.7888411.

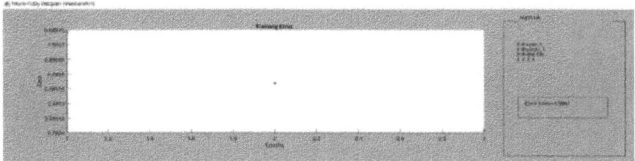

Fig. 7. The trained FinancialANFIS

Figure 8 shows the tested FinancialANFIS. The average testing error is 0.88826. Two thousand and seven hundred rules are generated by the FinancialANFIS.

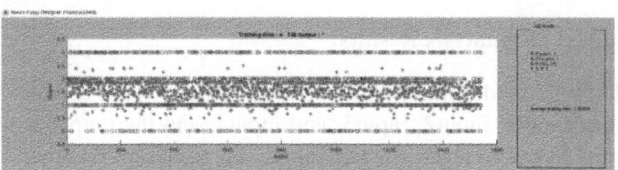

Fig. 8. Tested FinancialANFIS

Figure 9 shows a part of the generated rules in the proposed FinancialANFIS in verbose format. It is possible to add, change, or delete the rules based on the experts' viewpoints and investors' feedback.

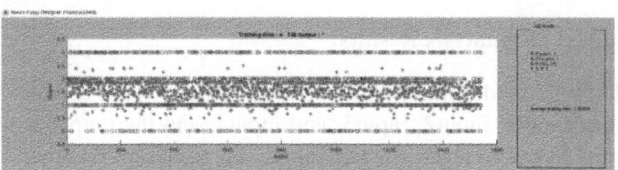

Fig. 9. A part of the generated rules in the FinancialANFIS

A part of the rule viewer is shown in Fig. 10. This figure shows the open system of the FinancialANFIS. There are 2700 rules with 101 plot points. It includes the system's name, type, version, number of inputs, outputs, and rules, as well as the methods used for fuzzy logic operations such as "and," "or," "implication," "aggregation," and "defuzzification." The table also provides information on the input and output variables, including their ranges and the number and type of membership functions used for each input and output.

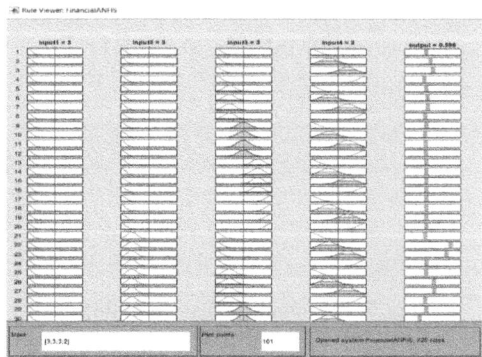

Fig. 10. A part of the rule viewer in the FinancialANFIS

5.4 FinancialANFIS Analysis Results

The FinancialANFIS model has 4 inputs and 1 output, with 720 rules in total. The inputs are named input1, input2, input3, and input4, and the output is named output. The membership functions used for the inputs are Gaussian membership functions, and the output has 720 constant membership functions. The rules provided are part of the Fuzzy Inference System (FIS) that is used in the ANFISIRS. The FIS uses fuzzy logic to make decisions based on input variables, in this case, the financial situation of potential investors. Here are presented FinancialANFIS Configuration which includes the system's properties and the properties of the input and output:

```
[System]
Name='FinancialANFIS Ruls'
Type='sugeno'
Version=2.0
NumInputs=4
NumOutputs=1
NumRules=720
AndMethod='prod'
OrMethod='probor'
ImpMethod='prod'
AggMethod='sum'
DefuzzMethod='wtaver'
 [Input1]
Name='input1'
Range=[0 6]
NumMFs=6
MF1='in1mf1':'gaussmf',[0.505924599435783 -0.00189439683556451]
MF2='in1mf2':'gaussmf',[0.50428216819331 1.19648451071156]
MF3='in1mf3':'gaussmf',[0.50365659837494 2.39255827828617]
MF4='in1mf4':'gaussmf',[0.512200648939718 3.58800496023208]
MF5='in1mf5':'gaussmf',[0.52941473878969 4.78640770722068]
MF6='in1mf6':'gaussmf',[0.513668815314422 5.9978167195858]
[Input2]
Name='input2'
Range=[0 6]
NumMFs=6
MF1='in2mf1':'gaussmf',[0.509630866505576 1.97976824547824e-05]
MF2='in2mf2':'gaussmf',[0.509606393516228 1.20001404785888]
MF3='in2mf3':'gaussmf',[0.509578643022572 2.4000005252814]
MF4='in2mf4':'gaussmf',[0.509583852803805 3.59997953441616]
MF5='in2mf5':'gaussmf',[0.509636419631854 4.79996463518774]
MF6='in2mf6':'gaussmf',[0.50964076741018 5.99997512062908]
[Input3]
Name='input3'
Range=[1 5]
NumMFs=5
MF1='in3mf1':'gaussmf',[0.424659313579378 0.999999328009502]
MF2='in3mf2':'gaussmf',[0.424633377799767 2.00000656309624]
MF3='in3mf3':'gaussmf',[0.424659188130285 3.00000070153398]
MF4='in3mf4':'gaussmf',[0.424653712042049 4.0000030314382]
MF5='in3mf5':'gaussmf',[0.424660803292909 5.00000003952626]
[Input4]
Name='input4'
Range=[0 4]
NumMFs=4
MF1='in4mf1':'gaussmf',[0.566259232288328 2.64744897299502e-05]
MF2='in4mf2':'gaussmf',[0.566216490513653 1.33335137308839]
MF3='in4mf3':'gaussmf',[0.566192952572373 2.66667649845446]
MF4='in4mf4':'gaussmf',[0.566192779653757 4.00001216833845]
[Output1]
Name='output'
Range=[0 3]
NumMFs=720
MF1='out1mf1':'constant',[-0.300947361897584]
MF2='out1mf2':'constant',[8.58980967060902]
MF3='out1mf3':'constant',[14.4668350456806]
MF4='out1mf4':'constant',[-4.33740584053419]
MF5='out1mf5':'constant',[-0.0107450728819144]
MF715='out1mf715':'constant',[0.0853000145425462]
MF716='out1mf716':'constant',[0.00160308743909113]
MF717='out1mf717':'constant',[0.00447802743339785]
MF718='out1mf718':'constant',[0.43374694221604]
MF719='out1mf719':'constant',[0.422574494651317]
MF720='out1mf720':'constant',[0.00164952657818109]
```

For example, the first rule is for input1 which, has a range of [0 6] and six membership functions (MF1-MF6). Each membership function represents a range of values for the input variable and is defined using a Gaussian membership function, which is a bell-shaped curve. For example, MF1 has a center value of 0.505924599435783 and a spread of -0.00189439683556451. This means that input1 values near 0.505924599435783 will have a high membership value in MF1, while values further away will have a lower membership value.

```
[Rules]
1 1 1 1, 1 (1) : 1
1 1 1 2, 2 (1) : 1
1 1 1 3, 3 (1) : 1
1 1 1 4, 4 (1) : 1
1 1 2 1, 5 (1) : 1

6 6 4 3, 715 (1) : 1
6 6 4 4, 716 (1) : 1
6 6 5 1, 717 (1) : 1
6 6 5 2, 718 (1) : 1
6 6 5 3, 719 (1) : 1
6 6 5 4, 720 (1) : 1
```

For example, the rule "1 1 1 1, 1 (1): 1" suggests that when the input criteria for current savings, monthly expenses, financial situation, and spending plan for savings all fall within the first membership function of each input, the recommended investment type cluster is also the first cluster. This means that the system has determined that individuals with this specific set of input criteria (savings available, managing expenses well, positive current financial statement, and short-term plans for spending savings) are not currently invested in the stock market and do not regularly monitor stock performance. Therefore, the recommended investment products for these individuals would include stocks/shares in the stock market, mutual funds, and government securities, with most not investing in government bonds. Table 8 shows the rule numbers, inputs, output, and description of 5 samples of the generated rules.

Table 8. Description of the five possible generated rules

Rule Number	Input 1	Input 2	Input 3	Input 4	Output	Description
1	1	1	1	1	1	This rule represents individuals who have a significant amount of savings available to them, have a good financial situation in terms of their monthly expenses, have a stable financial statement, and have long-term plans for spending their savings. These individuals are likely to be suitable for investment products such as stocks/shares in the stock market, mutual funds, and government securities
2	2	2	3	2	2	This rule represents individuals who have some savings available to them, have a moderate financial situation in terms of their monthly expenses, have a stable financial statement, and have medium-term plans for spending their savings. These individuals are likely to be suitable for investment products such as stocks/shares on the stock exchange, mutual funds, and voluntary pension funds

(continued)

Table 8. (*continued*)

Rule Number	Input 1	Input 2	Input 3	Input 4	Output	Description
3	3	3	1	4	3	This rule represents individuals who have a limited amount of savings available to them, have a poor financial situation in terms of their monthly expenses, have a stable financial statement, and have long-term plans for spending their savings. These individuals may not be suitable for investment products such as stocks/shares or mutual funds and may be more suitable for government securities
4	4	4	2	3	1	This rule represents individuals who have a significant amount of savings available to them, have a poor financial situation in terms of their monthly expenses, have a stable financial statement, and have medium-term plans for spending their savings. These individuals may not be suitable for investment products such as stocks/shares or mutual funds and may be more suitable for government securities

(*continued*)

Table 8. (continued)

Rule Number	Input 1	Input 2	Input 3	Input 4	Output	Description
5	5	5	3	2	2	This rule represents individuals who have a limited amount of savings available to them, have a poor financial situation in terms of their monthly expenses, have an uncertain financial statement, and have medium-term plans for spending their savings

The FinancialANFIS training results show that the model is able to achieve a minimal training root mean squared error of 0.888411, with 1489 nodes, 720 linear parameters, 42 nonlinear parameters, and 762 total parameters. The model was trained using 1542 data pairs, with no data pairs reserved for checking. The number of fuzzy rules used in the model is 720, indicating that the model can effectively classify, and group potential investors based on their financial situation and investment goals. These results demonstrate the effectiveness of the proposed ANFISIRS in providing personalized investment recommendations for retail banking potential investors. For example:

1. *Rule 1: Input 1 (current savings) is in the range of 0-1, Input 2 (monthly expenses) is in the range of 0-1, Input 3 (financial situation) is in the range of 1-2, and Input 4 (spending plan for savings) is in the range of 0-1. The output for this rule is cluster 1 (individuals who are not currently invested in the stock market and have not been monitoring stock performance). This rule suggests that individuals with a low amount of current savings, low monthly expenses, a poor financial situation, and a short-term plan for spending their savings are more likely to be part of cluster 1.*
2. *Rule 2: Input 1 (current savings) is in the range of 0-1, Input 2 (monthly expenses) is in the range of 0-1, Input 3 (financial situation) is in the range of 1-2, and Input 4 (spending plan for savings) is in the range of 1-2. The output for this rule is also cluster 1 (individuals who are not currently invested in the stock market and have not been monitoring stock performance). This rule suggests that individuals with a low amount of current savings, low monthly expenses, a poor financial situation, and a medium-term plan for spending their savings are also more likely to be part of cluster 1.*
3. *Rule 3: Input 1 (current savings) is in the range of 0-1, Input 2 (monthly expenses) is in the range of 0-1, Input 3 (financial situation) is in the range of 2-3, and Input 4 (spending plan for savings) is in the range of 0-1. The output for this rule is also cluster 1 (individuals who are not currently invested in the stock market and have not been monitoring stock performance). This rule suggests that individuals with a low amount of current savings, low monthly expenses, an average financial situation, and a short-term plan for spending their savings are also more likely to be part of cluster 1.*

The proposed FinancialANFIS system aims to investigate the relationship between financial situation and investment type. The three-dimensional graphs in Figs. 11a, 11b, 11c and 11d) illustrate the impact of certain pair inputs on investment type. These graphs, which are nonlinear and monolithic, display recommendations for investment type based on the given inputs.

Figure 11a is a 3D plot with the x-axis representing the value of Input 1 (current savings), the y-axis representing the value of Input 4 (spending plan for savings), and the z-axis representing the value of output (investment type clusters). The plot shows a surface representing the rule, where the red area represents the first cluster (individuals who were not invested in the stock market in the last 3 years and did not regularly monitor stock performance), the blue area represents the second cluster (individuals who had invested in the stock market in the last 3 years and regularly monitored stock

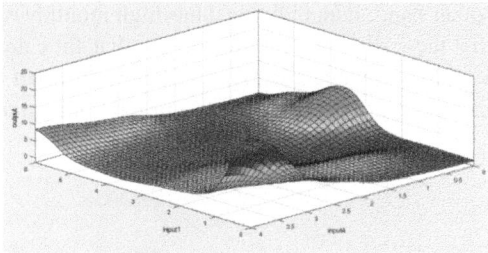

Fig. 11a. Effectiveness of the relations of pair inputs 1&4 of financial situation on investment type

performance), and the green area represents the third cluster (individuals who had been investing in the stock market for the last 3 years and regularly monitored stock performance). The plot shows that as the value of current savings increases and the value of the spending plan for savings decreases, the likelihood of the individual belonging to the first cluster (not currently invested in the stock market) also increases. On the other hand, as the value of current savings increases and the value of the spending plan for savings increases, the likelihood of the individual belonging to the second or third cluster (currently invested in the stock market) also increases.

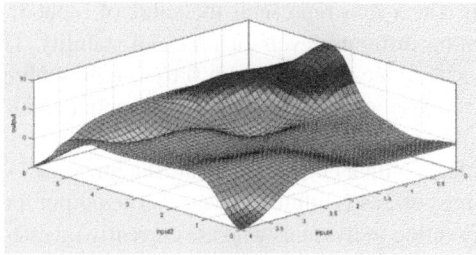

Fig. 11b. Effectiveness of the relations of pair inputs 2&4 of financial situation on investment type

Figure 11b represents the relationship between Input 2 (monthly expenses), Input 4 (spending plan for savings), and the output (investment type clusters). The surface of the plot shows the different regions where certain values of Input 2 and Input 4 result in a specific investment type cluster as the output. The x-axis represents the different levels of monthly expenses, with lower values on the left and higher values on the right. The y-axis represents the different spending plans for savings, with shorter timeframes on the bottom and longer timeframes on the top. The z-axis represents the investment-type clusters, with Cluster 1 at the bottom, Cluster 2 in the middle, and Cluster 3 at the top. This plot allows us to see the relationship between the different inputs and the output and how they impact the final investment type cluster recommendation. For example, if an individual has low monthly expenses and a short-term spending plan for their savings, the plot shows that they are likely to fall into Cluster 1, which represents individuals who are not currently invested in the stock market and have not been monitoring stock performance. On the other hand, if an individual has high monthly expenses and a long-term spending plan for their savings, the plot shows that they are likely to fall into Cluster 3, which represents individuals who are currently invested in the stock market and regularly monitor stock performance but do not have investments in government bonds.

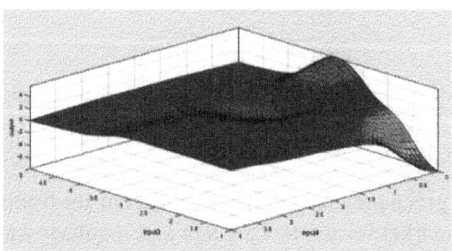

Fig. 11c. Effectiveness of the relations of pair inputs 3&4 of financial situation on investment type

Figure 11c shows the relationship between Input 3 (current financial statement), Input 4 (spending plan for savings), and the output (investment type clusters) for a specific rule. The surface represents the regions where the rule is most active or has the highest firing strength. The x-axis represents the value of Input 3, with values ranging from 1 to 5, representing different levels of financial stability. The y-axis represents the value of Input 4, with values ranging from 0 to 4, representing different plans for spending savings. The z-axis represents the value of the output, with values ranging from 0 to 3, representing different investment-type clusters. This figure shows that the rule is most active for individuals with a current financial statement of 1–3 (less stable) and a spending plan for savings of 2–4 (within 1–5 years). The output for this rule is likely to be cluster 2 or 3, representing individuals who are currently invested in the stock market and regularly monitor stock performance.

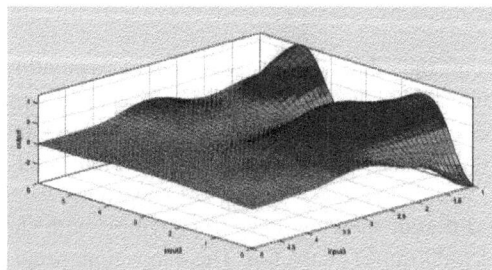

Fig. 11d. Effectiveness of the relations of pair inputs 2&3 of financial situation on investment type

The surface in Fig. 11d represents the rule that is associated with a specific combination of values for Input 3 (current financial statement), Input 2 (Monthly Living

Expenses), and output (investment type clusters). The plot shows how changes in the values of Input 3 and Input 2 can affect the output, and how different regions on the plot correspond to different investment type clusters. For example, in the plot, we can see that when the value of Input 3 is low and the value of Input 2 is high, the output is likely to be in the first cluster, representing individuals who are not currently invested in the stock market and have not been monitoring stock performance. On the other hand, when the value of Input 3 is high and the value of Input 2 is low, the output is likely to be in the second or third clusters, representing individuals who are currently invested in the stock market and regularly monitor stock performance. The plot can help us to understand how the input values relate to the output and how the system makes its recommendation for the investment type clusters.

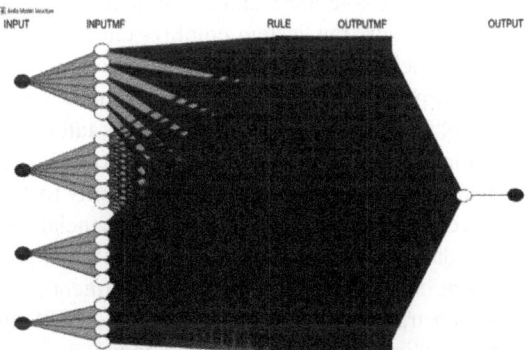

Fig. 12. FinancialANFIS Model Structure

Figure 12 shows the FinancialANFIS Model Structure. The model of the investment recommendation system would consist of the following components:

- Input Layer: The input layer takes in the financial information of the potential investors, such as their current savings, monthly expenses, financial statement, and spending plans for their savings.
- Fuzzification Layer: The fuzzification layer converts the crisp input values into fuzzy sets, which are used to represent the degree of membership of the input values to different linguistic terms.
- Rule Base: The rule base consists of a set of fuzzy if-then rules that are used to make decisions based on the input values. These rules are generated using expert knowledge and investor feedback.
- Inference Engine: The inference engine uses the fuzzy input values and the fuzzy rules to infer the degree of membership of the output value to different linguistic terms.
- Defuzzification Layer: The defuzzification layer converts the fuzzy output values into crisp values, which represent the final decision made by the system.
- Output Layer: The output layer provides the personalized investment recommendations to the potential investors based on their financial situation and investment

goals. The system uses clustering techniques to group customers with similar financial situations and investment goals, which further enhances the personalization of the recommendations.

- Training and Testing: The model is trained and tested using a dataset of potential investors' financial information and investment behavior, to evaluate the performance of the system.To run a chatbot for this investment recommendation system, several steps would need to be taken.

6 Discussion

This study introduces an ANFIS-based investment recommendation system (ANFISIRS) for digital banking and e-government financial services, personalizing recommendations based on financial situations, risk tolerance, and investment goals. By integrating expert knowledge and investor feedback, the system employs clustering techniques to group customers with similar financial attributes, enhancing recommendation accuracy [36, 37]. Key innovations of the proposed system include personalization through clustering investors using demographic and investment behavior data, tailoring recommendations accordingly [20]. Additionally, the system integrates expert knowledge and investor feedback to refine recommendation accuracy, ensuring adaptability to market changes [38]. By utilizing clustering techniques, investors with similar financial goals are grouped for more relevant recommendations [18], and the hybrid ANFIS model effectively handles uncertainty, learning from data patterns to optimize investment suggestions [39]. The results of this study demonstrate the effectiveness of using ANFIS and clustering techniques in providing personalized investment recommendations in digital banking and e-government financial ecosystems. The proposed system accurately classifies potential investors into different groups based on their financial situation and investment behavior, providing personalized recommendations aligned with their risk tolerance and investment goals. By analyzing current savings, monthly expenses, financial statements, and spending plans, the system gains deeper insights into investors' financial capabilities. For instance, high-savings investors with short-term usage plans may receive stock or mutual fund recommendations, whereas long-term planners may be directed toward government bonds or pension funds. Additionally, risk tolerance is considered—conservative investments for those with lower financial stability and higher-risk opportunities for confident investors with strong financial statements. Several studies align with these findings. These studies support the efficacy of ANFIS and clustering techniques in investment advisory systems across different financial sectors, including foreign exchange, stock markets, and digital banking. A major strength of the proposed system is its ability to integrate expert knowledge and investor feedback, allowing continuous improvement and market adaptability. The clustering techniques used further personalize investment suggestions by grouping similar investors. Additionally, FinancialANFIS combines the strengths of fuzzy systems and neural networks, handling data uncertainty and dynamically adjusting to changing market trends. Despite its advantages, the study identifies several limitations. The limited dataset restricts generalizability, and expanding the sample size would improve the model's robustness. Furthermore, incorporating a broader range of investment products and real-time data analytics would enhance recommendation accuracy. A comprehensive evaluation comparing the system with models like

Random Forest and SVM is needed to benchmark its performance. Additionally, the absence of user acceptance testing limits insights into practical usability, and security measures must be reinforced to protect investor data privacy.

7   Conclusion

The ANFISIRS model can be seamlessly integrated into digital banking and e-government financial infrastructures to improve customer service and enhance financial policymaking. Furthermore, the model helps identify high-risk investors, supporting more effective credit risk management in public financial services. Future studies should focus on expanding datasets, incorporating real-time data, and conducting case studies to validate the system's practical effectiveness. Additionally, implementing chatbot-based recommendation systems using NLP and machine learning could enhance citizen interactions with government financial services. Security enhancements must also be prioritized to safeguard user data privacy. In conclusion, ANFISIRS presents a promising approach to personalized investment recommendations in digital banking and e-government services, leveraging machine learning and clustering techniques to refine decision-making. By addressing existing limitations, future research can further enhance the system's effectiveness and adoption in real-world applications. Additionally, integrating the system with open government data initiatives and digital identity (eID) frameworks could further enhance transparency, security, and accessibility in financial decision-making.

References

1. Davies, H.L., Blyth, A.J.C.: Determining the value of information security investments: a decision support system. In: KMIS 2014 - Proceedings of the International Conference on Knowledge Management and Information Sharing, INSTICC Press, pp. 426–433 (2014). https://doi.org/10.5220/0005170704260433
2. Jain, J., Walia, N., Gupta, S.: Evaluation of behavioral biases affecting investment decision making of individual equity investors by fuzzy analytic hierarchy process. Rev. Behav. Finan. **12**(3), 297–314 (2019). https://doi.org/10.1108/RBF-03-2019-0044
3. Abraham, R., et al.: Forecasting a stock trend using genetic algorithm and random forest. J. Risk Finan. Manage. **15**(5), 5 (2022). https://doi.org/10.3390/jrfm15050188
4. Janková, Z., Dostál, P.: Type-2 fuzzy expert system approach for decision-making of financial assets and investing under different uncertainty. Math. Probl. Eng. **2021**, e3839071 (2021). https://doi.org/10.1155/2021/3839071
5. Thompson, J.R., Feng, L., Reesor, R.M., Grace, C.: Know your clients' behaviours: a cluster analysis of financial transactions. J. Risk Finan. Manage. **14**(2), 2 (2021). https://doi.org/10.3390/jrfm14020050
6. Asemi, A., Asemi, A., Ko, A.: Investment recommender system model based on the potential investors' key decision factors. BIG DATA (2023). https://doi.org/10.1089/big.2022.0302
7. Asemi, A., Asemi, A., Ko, A.: Adaptive neuro-fuzzy inference system for customizing investment type based on the potential investors' demographics and feedback. J. Big Data **10**, 1 (2023). https://doi.org/10.1186/s40537-023-00784-7
8. Asemi, A., Asemi, A., Ko, A.: Unveiling the impact of managerial traits on investor decision prediction: ANFIS approach. Soft. Comput. (2023). https://doi.org/10.1007/s00500-023-08102-2

9. Asemi, A., Asemi, A., Ko, A.: Adaptive neuro-fuzzy inference system for customizing investment type based on the potential investors' demographics and feedback. J. Big Data **10**(1), 87 (2023). https://doi.org/10.1186/s40537-023-00784-7

10. Asemi, A., Ko, A.: A novel combined business recommender system model using customer investment service feedback. In: 34th Bled eConference Digital Support from Crisis to Progressive Change: Conference Proceedings, University of Maribor Press, pp. 223–237 (2021). https://doi.org/10.18690/978-961-286-485-9.17

11. Wang, J., Yang, L., Yang, J.: How sustainable environment is influenced by the foreign direct investment, financial development, economic growth, globalization, innovation, and urbanization in China. Environ. Sci. Pollut. Res. (2023). https://doi.org/10.1007/s11356-023-25634-0

12. Jang, J.S.R.: ANFIS: adaptive-network-based fuzzy inference system. IEEE Trans. Syst. Man Cybern. **23**(3), 665–685 (1993). https://doi.org/10.1109/21.256541

13. Mishra, K.C., Metilda, M.J.: A study on the impact of investment experience, gender, and level of education on overconfidence and self-attribution bias. IIMB Manage. Rev. **27**(4), 4 (2015). https://doi.org/10.1016/j.iimb.2015.09.001

14. Asemi, A.: Behavioral insights of investors using generative AI & ML: A case study based on survey data & predictive modeling. key speaker. In: Presented at the 5th ACM International Conference on AI in Finance, ICIAF 2024, USA: New York, University of New York, Nov. (2024). https://sites.google.com/view/ml-for-financial-wellness/program?authuser=0

15. Lin, S.-Y., et al.: Fog computing based hybrid deep learning framework in effective inspection system for smart manufacturing. Comput. Commun. **160**, 636–642 (2020). https://doi.org/10.1016/j.comcom.2020.05.044

16. N. D'lima and S. Khan, "FOREX rate prediction using ANN and ANFIS Conference," 2016. Accessed: Jan. 19, 2023. [Online]. Available: https://www.semanticscholar.org/paper/FOREX-rate-prediction-using-ANN-and-ANFIS-D%27lima-Khan/6817d1cc9f7ac35cf28404f0e17e358b54fa16d1

17. Wei, L.-Y., Cheng, C.-H., Wu, H.-H.: A hybrid ANFIS based on n-period moving average model to forecast TAIEX stock. Appl. Soft Comput. J. **19**, 86–92 (2014). https://doi.org/10.1016/j.asoc.2014.01.022

18. T. Kovács, A. Ko, and A. Asemi, "Exploration of the investment patterns of potential retail banking customers using two-stage cluster analysis," *Journal of Big Data*, vol. 8, no. 1, 2021, https://doi.org/10.1186/s40537-021-00529-4

19. Szafranko, E., Srokosz, P.E., Jurczak, M., Śmieja, M.: Application of ANFIS in the preparation of expert opinions and evaluation of building design variants in the context of processing large amounts of data. Autom. Constr. **133**, 104045 (2022). https://doi.org/10.1016/j.autcon.2021.104045

20. Benkraiem, R., Gaaya, S., Lakhal, F., Lakhal, N.: Economic policy uncertainty, investor protection, and the value of excess cash: a cross-country comparison. Financ. Res. Lett. **52**, 103572 (2023). https://doi.org/10.1016/j.frl.2022.103572

21. Asemi, A., Asemi, A., Ko, A.: A model for investment type recommender system based on the potential investors based on investors and experts feedback using ANFIS and MNN. J. Big Data **11**, 128, https://doi.org/10.1186/s40537-024-00965-y

22. Chatterjee, A., Geaumont, B., DeSutter, T., Hopkins, D., Rakkar, M.: Rapid shifts in soil organic carbon mineralization within sodic landscapes. Arid Land Res. Manage. **29**(2), 255–263 (2015). https://doi.org/10.1080/15324982.2014.944958

23. Pinter, R., Racskó, P., Rab, Á.S.: Openness to robot financial investment recommendation systems, among users of a Hungarian financial portal. J. Appl. Sci, **22**(6) (2025). https://doi.org/10.12700/APH.22.6.2025.6.4

24. Aksar, M., Hassan, S., Kayani, M., Khan, S., Ahmed, T.: Cash holding and investment efficiency nexus for financially distressed firms: the moderating role of corporate governance. 12(1), 67–74 (2022). https://doi.org/10.5267/j.msl.2021.7.001

25. Asemi, A., Asemi, A., Ko, A.: A systematic review and propose an ANFIS-based investment type recommender system using investors' demographic. In: A Hybrid Conference 8th International Congress on Information and Communication Technology ICICT 2023, London, UK, 20–23 (2023). https://www.researchgate.net/publication/369019468_System atic_Review_and_Propose_an_ANFIS-Based_Investment_Type_Recommender_System_ using_Investors'_Demographic. Accessed 03 Jul 2023

26. Birim, Ş.Ö., Sönmez, F.E., Liman, Y.S.: Estimating return rate of blockchain financial product by ANFIS-PSO method. In: Kahraman, C., Tolga, A.C., Cevik Onar, S., Cebi, S., Oztaysi, B., Sari, I.U. (eds.) LNNS, vol. 504 LNNS, pp. 802–809 (2022). https://doi.org/10.1007/978-3-031-09173-5_92

27. Jankova, Z.: Application of artificial neural networks and fuzzy logic in stock trading. In: Soliman, K.S. (ed.,) Education Excellence and Innovation Management Through Vision 2020, Norristown: International Business Information Management Assoc-Ibima, pp. 2610–2619 (2019). https://www.webofscience.com/wos/woscc/full-record/WOS:000503 988804022. Accessed 03 Mar 2024

28. Jiang, H., Guo, G. and Sabetzadeh, F.: Opinion mining and DENFIS approaches for modelling variational consumer preferences based on online comments. In: Nakamatsu, K., Kountchev, R., Patnaik, S., Abe, J.M., Tyugashev, A. (eds.) Advanced intelligent technologies for industry in smart innovation, systems and technologies, pp. 229–238. Springer Nature, Singapore (2022). https://doi.org/10.1007/978-981-16-9735-7_21

29. SheidaeiNarmigi, A.L.I., Rahnamay Roodposhti, F., Radfar, R.: Optimization of network-based matrix investment portfolio and comparison with fuzzy neural combination pattern and genetic algorithm (ANFIS). J. Invest. Knowl. 9(36), 293–315 (2020). http://www.jik-ifea.ir/article_16818_en.html. Accessed 27 Mar 2024

30. Zhao, H., Wang, X.: Study on real estate project investment decision-making based on principal component analysis and adaptive network-based fuzzy inference system. In: 2010 International Conference on Biomedical Engineering and Computer Science, pp. 1–4 (2010). https://doi.org/10.1109/ICBECS.2010.5462375

31. Oduro-Gyimah, F.K., Boateng, K.O.: Application of canfis model in the prediction of multiple-input telecommunication network traffic. ITU J. ICT Discoveries 2, 9 (2018)

32. Mottahedi, A., Sereshki, F., Ataei, M.: Overbreak prediction in underground excavations using hybrid ANFIS-PSO model. Tunn. Undergr. Space Technol. 80, 1–9 (2018). https://doi.org/10.1016/j.tust.2018.05.023

33. Seputra, Y.E.A.: Analysis of investment and export of economic growth using neural network computing ANFIS. KSS KnE Soc. Sci. 3(11), 1050 (2018)

34. Asemi, A.: Data for A model for the investment recommender system using ANFIS based on the Potential Investors' Decision Key Factors (PIDKFs)" - Mendeley Data (2023). https://data.mendeley.com/drafts/j9y7snrbpm. Accessed 10 Mar 2023

35. Azamathulla, H.M., Chang, C.K., Ghani, A.A., Ariffin, J., Zakaria, N.A., Hasan, Z.A.: An ANFIS-based approach for predicting the bed load for moderately sized rivers. In: Journal of Hydro-environ. Res. 3(1), 35–44 (2009). https://doi.org/10.1016/j.jher.2008.10.003

36. Asemi, A., Asemi, A., Ko, A.: Systematic review and propose an investment type recommender system using investor's demographic using ANFIS. In: Yang, X.-S., Sherratt, R.S., Dey, N., Joshi, A. (eds.) Proceedings of Eighth International Congress on Information and Communication Technology, pp. 241–260. Springer Nature, Singapore (2023). https://doi.org/10.1007/978-981-99-3243-6_20

37. Wang, Y., Mei, S., Zhong, W.: Advertising or recommender systems? A game-theoretic analysis of online retailer platforms' decision-making. Manag. Decis. Econ. **43**(6), 2119–2132 (2022). https://doi.org/10.1002/mde.3513

38. Sharma, M., Pant, B., Singh, V.: Demographic profile building for cold start in recommender system: a social media fusion approach. Mater. Today Proc., 11208–11212 (2021). https://doi.org/10.1016/j.matpr.2021.02.428

39. Mishra, K.C., Metilda, M.J.: A study on the impact of investment experience, gender, and level of education on overconfidence and self-attribution bias. IIMB Manag. Rev. **27**(4), 228–239 (2015). https://doi.org/10.1016/j.iimb.2015.09.001

Navigating AI Integration in Public Healthcare: The Role of Dynamic Capabilities in Transforming Service Delivery and Strategic Adaptation

Dóra Horváth[✉], Krisztina Erdős, and Noémi Szilvia Lőrincz

Department of Strategic Management, Corvinus University of Budapest, Fővám Sqr. 8, Budapest 1093, Hungary
horvath.dora@uni-corvinus.hu

Abstract. This study examines the integration of artificial intelligence (AI) in public healthcare organizations in Hungary, focusing on the strategic direction and dynamic capabilities needed to adapt effectively to technological change. Using a qualitative methodology, the research conducts semi-structured interviews with healthcare professionals and industry experts, using thematic coding for analysis. Preliminary findings highlight AI's potential to enhance efficiency and alleviate workforce shortages through automation and improved resource allocation. However, challenges including data quality, ethical considerations, and financial constraints are also examined. The study underscores the critical role of dynamic capabilities in enabling institutions to navigate these complexities and deliver a more resilient, efficient, and patient-centered healthcare system, providing valuable insights for stakeholders.

Keywords: public healthcare · artificial intelligence · dynamic capability · AI-driven diagnostics · decision support

1 Introduction

The development of artificial intelligence (AI) has the potential to bring profound changes to many dimensions of healthcare, promising a future characterized by higher levels of personalization, accuracy, and predictability [1]. The integration of artificial intelligence has the potential to enhance healthcare delivery by optimizing the efficiency and quality of specific services, thereby facilitating an increase in the volume of care [2]. Public healthcare institutions, which are vital for ensuring equitable and accessible care, are increasingly compelled to explore and integrate AI in order to navigate this evolving terrain [3]. Nevertheless, the successful and ethical integration of AI presents complex challenges that extend beyond mere operational implementation, engendering a complex ethical and legal environment, particularly when determining responsibility in the case of errors or unfavourable outcomes [4].

A. Kő et al. (Eds.): EGOVIS 2025, LNCS 16049, pp. 163–172, 2026.
https://doi.org/10.1007/978-3-032-02225-7_11

It is imperative for public healthcare institutions to cultivate and leverage dynamic capabilities, defined as the capacity to sense, seize, and adapt to evolving circumstances. These capabilities empower institutions to proactively adapt to technological advancements, shifting patient demographics, and evolving regulatory frameworks, ensuring their continued agility and responsiveness to change [5]. The integration of AI into public healthcare is predicated on the successful implementation of these dynamic capabilities, which enable healthcare organisations to adapt to technological disruptions, anticipate future needs and opportunities, and optimise resource allocation, operational efficiency, and service delivery quality. In an era characterised by escalating costs, workforce shortages, and the increasing demand for personalized care [6], dynamic capabilities become particularly crucial in enabling public healthcare institutions to address these challenges and improve service delivery. Dynamic capabilities enable healthcare institutions to respond effectively to rapid digital transformation and increasing systemic pressures. While these capabilities have traditionally been associated with competitive industries, they have also become essential in the healthcare sector. Yale New Haven Health System serves as a pertinent example, having developed the capacity to simultaneously reduce costs and enhance care quality - illustrating the strategic value of dynamic capabilities in advancing sustainable, value-based healthcare delivery [7]. In terms of these capabilities, *Sensing* facilitates the identification of changes in the environment, technology and organisation, as well as the needs of patients, funders and employees. *Seizing* capability integrates new knowledge into operational operations and helps reconfigure internal capabilities. *Transforming* involves the adaptive reorganization of institutional structures, processes and resources for long-term adaptation to a changing environment. The integrated presence of these capabilities allows healthcare institutions to not only respond to the challenges posed by artificial intelligence, but also to strategically exploit its transformative potential [8].

Furthermore, integrating AI into healthcare necessitates a balanced approach, combining short-term problem-solving with long-term strategic planning. In the short term, organisations should target urgent challenges that AI can address efficiently (e.g., automating administrative tasks). Long-term efforts should focus on transforming care delivery through scalable, evolving technologies (e.g. predictive analytics for population health or personalised treatment planning). Successful implementation also depends on the presence of strong leadership, interdisciplinary teams, and a culture that supports innovation. Collaboration with external partners is also essential to ensure responsible and effective AI integration [9]. Moreover, clinical champions play a pivotal role in promoting adoption and attracting essential expertise. This initiative serves as a catalyst for attracting not only clinical and technical expertise, but also prominent industry figures in the field. To guarantee a sustainable and effective AI strategy, it is also vital to ensure clear communication and coordinated action among all stakeholders [10].

It is evident that the healthcare sector is undergoing a substantial transformation due to technological advancements and the mounting emphasis on patient-centred care. The (AI) can be omitted here because the abbreviation for artificial intelligence was defined at the beginning of the article. The investigation focuses on the manner in which these institutions cultivate and deploy dynamic capabilities to navigate the technological evolution of the sector. Specifically, it seeks to explore how AI influences workforce management, financial sustainability, and operational processes, with the goal of uncovering AI's transformative potential. The study's objective is to provide comprehensive insights into the practical and strategic considerations necessary for creating a more resilient, efficient, and effective healthcare system, one that is better equipped to meet the needs of the future. The research employs a qualitative methodology, conducting semi-structured interviews with healthcare professionals and industry experts, and uses thematic coding for the analysis. This article presents the preliminary findings of the research, based on 11 expert interviews. However, the research aims to conduct additional interviews, which are currently underway. These forthcoming interviews will allow for a substantial revision and expansion of the findings, ultimately providing valuable practices and insights for individual actors and stakeholders, including policy makers, healthcare professionals and other key industry participants.

2   Methodology

The present research aims to investigate the multifaceted integration of artificial intelligence within public healthcare institutions in Hungary, exploring not only its operational implementation but also its strategic alignment. Specifically, it seeks to understand how these institutions develop dynamic capabilities - the ability to sense, seize, and reconfigure resources - to effectively adapt to the rapidly evolving healthcare landscape driven by technological advancements. The study also examines the impact of AI adoption on critical aspects of public health, including workforce management, analysing how AI is changing roles, requiring new skills and potentially alleviating staff shortages. It also assesses the impact on financial sustainability, including how AI optimizes resource allocation, reduces costs and enhances revenue streams. Finally, the research assesses the impact on operational efficiency, focusing on how AI streamlines processes, improves patient outcomes and enhances overall service delivery.

In order to achieve this objective, a qualitative research design is employed, incorporating semi-structured interviews with key industry stakeholders, including healthcare administrators, clinicians, technology experts, and policymakers. Participants were selected through purposive sampling, with an emphasis on ensuring a diverse sample in terms of professional background and experience. To capture a wide range of perspectives, concerted efforts were made to ensure variation in the professional roles, sectors and levels of seniority of the participants. The interviews generally lasted between 45 and 60 min. With the aim of enhancing the reliability and trustworthiness of the research and to reduce potential bias, interviewees were assured of anonymity and that their responses would not be attributed to them in any identifiable manner. Throughout the process, ethical considerations were prioritised, thereby fostering an open and honest dialogue.

With regard to the analysis of interview data, thematic coding is employed to systematically analyse patterns and insights by coding the interviews with NVivo software. In order to assess the current landscape and identify key themes, 11 preliminary interviews have already been conducted as part of the research process. The participants' positions and work experience are outlined in Table 1, offering context for their perspectives on AI integration in public healthcare. As data collection progresses, additional interviews will be conducted to refine and expand the findings.

Table 1. List of interviewees

ID	Position	Work experience
1	CEO, Medical Futurologist	• 14 years of experience in medical futures research • 7 years of teaching experience at a medical university
2	CEO, Co-founder	• 5 years of experience in a digital health solutions company • 4 years of experience in a consulting firm
3	Business consultant, health and AI expert	• Has been working as an AI and data science expert for 8 months • Has been working as a healthcare machine learning consultant for 3 years • Taught at a medical university for 7 years
4	PhD student	• Currently pursuing a doctoral degree in pathology/experimental pathology at a medical university • Previously obtained a bachelor's and master's degree in chemical engineering
5	Director of the Emergency Department	• Has been serving as an emergency department director for 3 years • Has been the president of a healthcare committee for 13 years • Served as the head of an emergency department for 16 years
6	Senior Manager	• 6 years of experience in the health and public sector within a consultancy firm • 7 years of teaching experience at a medical university
7	Head of Competence Centre for the Public Sector & Healthcare / IT Management & Transformation	• Over 26 years of experience in management and consulting, with a strong focus on public healthcare
8	Managing Director & Partner	• 15 years of professional experience in consulting for healthcare institutions and governments across multiple continents
9	Senior Manager	• More than 10 years of management, legal and IT consulting experience in the field of public healthcare

(continued)

Table 1. (*continued*)

ID	Position	Work experience
10	Data Science Manager	• Over 5 years of data scientist experience in the fields of artificial intelligence and machine learning
11	Legal Firm Associate	• 7 years of legal experience, with a special focus on information technology law

3 Preliminary Results

The results chapter is intended to present the preliminary findings from the interviews in the form of a short paper. As the data collection progresses, it is expected that this section will be expanded and extensively revised to incorporate additional insights from the ongoing interviews. Section 3.1 provides a concise overview of the potential applications and benefits, while Sect. 3.2 addresses the challenges, focusing on operational, ethical, financial, and strategic issues. Section 3.3 highlights the importance of dynamic capabilities within public healthcare institutions.

3.1 Opportunities and Benefits: AI for Comprehensive Operational Efficiency and Workload Reduction in the Face of Persistent Workforce Shortages

In the context of persistent and escalating shortages in the healthcare workforce, with a particular emphasis on the field of healthcare professionals (e.g. nurses, assistants), artificial intelligence emerges as a pivotal tool for achieving comprehensive operational efficiency within public clinics. Beyond its established role in medical decision support, AI's potential to automate a wide array of operational and clinical processes directly alleviates the workload burden on increasingly strained healthcare professionals. The automation of routine administrative tasks, such as patient registration, electronic health record management, appointment scheduling, and insurance claims processing, has the potential to reduce the time spent on non-clinical activities, allowing clinicians and support staff to focus on direct patient care. Furthermore, the utilisation of AI-driven diagnostic tools, including advanced image analysis for dermatology, radiology and pathology, preliminary symptom assessment through AI-powered chatbots, and predictive analytics for disease progression, has the capacity to streamline diagnostic workflows, enabling faster and more accurate identification of patient needs. An illustration of an AI-supported diagnostic application is evident in the teledermatology service operated by the Department of Dermatology at Semmelweis University in Budapest in collaboration with a private company. This service utilises image analysis assisted by artificial intelligence. Furthermore, Semmelweis University is a participant in the National Laboratory for Artificial Intelligence, contributing to research projects such as the AI-based analysis of mammographic images.

Furthermore, the utilisation of AI powered systems for patient triage, predicated on the analysis of symptoms and medical history, ensures the expeditious direction of patients to the most suitable level of care, thereby optimising resource allocation and reducing wait times. This multifaceted approach to automation, encompassing both back-office and front-line operations, serves not only to reduce immediate workloads but also to mitigate the long-term impact of workforce shortages by maximising the productivity of existing staff, improving resource allocation, and reducing the necessity for excessive overtime. Furthermore, the analysis of large datasets for epidemiological studies, public health monitoring, and resource planning can be facilitated by AI, optimising the efficiency of public health systems.

The reallocation of time facilitated by AI directly translates to fostering enhanced patient-centred care, ensuring that healthcare professionals can devote more time and personalised attention to individual patient needs, by reducing the administrative and diagnostic burden, AI empowers clinicians to focus on building stronger patient relationships, providing comprehensive consultations, and delivering holistic care. This transition towards a patient-centric model is pivotal in addressing the mounting demand for quality healthcare while operating within a constrained workforce, and it contributes to enhanced patient satisfaction and outcomes. Furthermore, the integration of AI has the potential to enhance the professional satisfaction and well-being of healthcare workers by reducing stress associated with administrative overload, thereby enabling them to practice medicine at the pinnacle of their abilities and focus on the aspects of their work they find most rewarding. This enhanced work environment is a key factor in workforce retention, which is critical in mitigating the impact of shortages and ensuring the continuity of care. Consequently, with comprehensive training, ongoing technical support, and ethical guidelines, AI empowers healthcare professionals to concentrate on delivering high-quality, patient-centred care, effectively addressing workforce shortages while simultaneously enhancing the overall efficiency and sustainability of public healthcare delivery systems. It is also important to note that the use of AI has been shown to reduce the incidence of burnout in healthcare workers, which is a key factor in the current shortage of personnel. By automating repetitive tasks, AI reduces the cognitive load on healthcare professionals, allowing them to better manage their workload and maintain a healthy work-life balance. This, in turn, contributes to a more resilient and sustainable healthcare workforce.

3.2 Challenges in the Implementation of AI in Public Healthcare

Core Operational and Ethical Challenges to AI Integration in Public Healthcare
The integration of artificial intelligence into public healthcare has been identified as a potential catalyst for transformative benefits. However, this integration is accompanied by significant challenges, primarily concerning core operational processes and ethical considerations. A primary obstacle lies in the pervasive issue of unstructured healthcare data. Despite the extensive nature of public electronic health records, vital information such as clinical notes and diagnostic reports is often stored in unstructured formats like PDFs, hindering the training of robust AI algorithms, particularly in natural language processing. This data heterogeneity, in conjunction with concerns about data quality and representativeness, directly impacts the accuracy and reliability of AI systems. Another

area requiring central development is the semantically unified management and interpretation of data across healthcare institutions, which can be considered a critical foundation for AI-based advancements.

Furthermore, ethical considerations, particularly regarding algorithmic decision support and the clear delineation of responsibility among healthcare providers, remain paramount. The suggestion-based nature of AI systems, as opposed to definitive medical decision-making, necessitates careful consideration of liability and patient safety. Concurrently, concerns regarding the transparency of algorithms and the potential for job displacement, stemming from professional and patient scepticism, act as significant impediments to AI adoption. These issues are further compounded by technical challenges, including the integration of AI systems with existing infrastructure and the design of user-friendly interfaces catering to diverse user groups.

It is also crucial to emphasise that, in the case of centrally provided public services, the development of technological infrastructure and the expansion of computing capacity are pivotal, as they form the backbone for effective AI integration and the delivery of advanced services. The state plays a significant role in ensuring the equitable distribution of these resources, setting regulatory standards, and fostering collaboration between public institutions, technology providers, and research entities. It is therefore vital to recognize that without adequate infrastructure and computing power, the full potential of AI to enhance service delivery, improve decision-making, and streamline operations cannot be realized.

Financial and Strategic Implementation Challenges of AI in Public Healthcare

The successful implementation of AI in public healthcare is significantly constrained by financial and strategic challenges. Public healthcare institutions, often operating within tightly constrained budgets, face substantial upfront costs associated with AI acquisition, implementation, and maintenance. Notably, the high operational expenses stemming from the necessary computing capacity for data processing, storage, and algorithm execution are a primary concern. Beyond technology acquisition, strategic investments in infrastructure upgrades, specialised personnel, and ongoing software development are essential. Healthcare administrators must possess a deep understanding of the financial landscape, evaluating both immediate expenditures and potential long-term cost savings. While AI has the potential to enhance efficiency through administrative automation, optimisation of resources, and reduction of unnecessary testing, these benefits may not immediately offset the initial investment. Moreover, the budgetary structures of public healthcare institutions, which are often reliant on performance-based models and patient-group-specific funding, present challenges for long-term innovative investments. In contexts like Hungary, where financial flexibility is limited, careful consideration of cost recovery timelines and the broader impact on healthcare quality and efficiency is crucial. Successful integration of AI necessitates a strategic approach that aligns with the specific financial realities of public healthcare, ensuring sustainable and impactful implementation and overcoming the limitations that public funding imposes.

3.3 Dynamic Capabilities for AI Integration in Public Healthcare Institutions

In the context of public healthcare, the concept of dynamic capabilities refers to the ability of healthcare organisations to discern, adapt, and recalibrate their resources in response to a rapidly changing environment, especially as it pertains to the implementation of artificial intelligence. As AI technologies continue to advance, healthcare institutions must develop the dynamic capabilities necessary to effectively integrate AI into their operations, addressing technological advancements, evolving patient needs, and changing regulatory frameworks. The possession of these capabilities is vital for healthcare organisations to maintain agility, adaptability, and proactivity in leveraging AI innovations to enhance healthcare delivery.

A pivotal element in the implementation of AI in healthcare is the cultivation of a data-driven approach that permeates the entirety of the organisation. It is incumbent upon healthcare managers to cultivate a data-oriented culture and to establish the requisite data capabilities, encompassing accurate data entry, analysis, and interpretation. With a robust data infrastructure, healthcare organisations can make well-informed decisions, monitor operations in real-time, and optimise resource allocation. The integration of AI-enabled solutions into core workflows is a key strategy for healthcare managers, as it enhances operational efficiency, improves patient outcomes, and ensures a more responsive healthcare system. A data-driven approach also empowers managers to identify emerging opportunities for innovation, ensuring their institutions stay ahead of industry trends and meet evolving healthcare demands.

The role of managers in public healthcare institutions is pivotal in overseeing the successful implementation of AI technologies. It is the responsibility of managers to ensure that AI systems are aligned with organisational goals, regulatory requirements, and the needs of the patient population. Furthermore, they are required to spearhead initiatives that foster a culture of collaboration, adaptability, and continuous learning within the workforce. This is critical for overcoming potential resistance to AI adoption, as some staff may fear job displacement or disruption of established practices. The provision of effective communication, training and support is therefore paramount to ensure that employees feel confident in their ability to adopt and utilise AI technologies. By prioritising these efforts, managers can ensure that their organisations remain responsive to the dynamic changes brought about by AI, creating a more efficient, patient-centred healthcare system.

4 Summary

This research highlights the transformative potential of artificial intelligence in public healthcare institutions in Hungary, with a specific focus on how these organisations can cultivate dynamic capabilities to adapt to the rapidly evolving technological landscape. As healthcare systems across the globe face increasing pressures due to workforce shortages, escalating costs, and the demand for personalised care, AI presents a critical opportunity to address these challenges while improving patient outcomes and operational efficiency. The integration of AI into fundamental operational processes enables the optimisation of resource allocation, the alleviation of administrative burdens, and the creation of greater time for patient-centred care. This, in turn, addresses workforce shortages and improves overall service delivery.

The study emphasises the importance of dynamic capabilities, such as the ability to sense, seize, and reconfigure resources, for healthcare institutions to maintain agility and responsiveness in this rapidly changing environment. A data-driven approach is instrumental in this process, serving as both a foundation for AI development and a means to anticipate future needs, optimise resources, and enhance decision-making. By leveraging AI-driven insights, healthcare institutions can enhance efficiency, streamline workflows, and ensure more effective workforce management. The integration of AI within healthcare settings holds the potential to transform the landscape of workforce management. This is since it can enhance decision-making processes, alleviate administrative burdens, and promote a more efficient utilisation of clinical staff. Consequently, healthcare professionals can allocate their time and efforts towards more meaningful, patient-centred interactions. Moreover, the capacity of AI to mitigate clinician burnout and enhance workforce retention further underscores its importance in ensuring a robust and sustainable healthcare system.

However, the integration of AI into public healthcare is not without its challenges, including operational and ethical concerns, such as data quality, algorithmic transparency, and responsibility for AI-driven decisions. It is essential to ensure that AI systems are deployed in ways that align with ethical standards and safeguard patient safety. Financial constraints also remain a significant barrier, as the initial costs of AI implementation, along with the need for infrastructure upgrades and specialised training, require strategic planning to ensure long-term sustainability.

In conclusion, while the integration of AI into public healthcare holds considerable promise, its successful implementation depends on a multifaceted approach that includes developing dynamic capabilities, addressing ethical and operational challenges, and ensuring the strategic alignment of AI with financial realities. By adopting these measures, public healthcare institutions can foster the creation of a more resilient, efficient, and patient-centred system, better equipped to address the demands of the future. This research provides a foundation for further study, offering valuable insights into the strategic and practical considerations that will shape the future of AI adoption in public healthcare and contribute to the development of more effective and sustainable healthcare systems.

Acknowledgments. This statement applies only to Dora Horvath, PhD: The project identified by EKOP-CORVINUS-24-4 was realized with the support of the National Research, Development, and Innovation Fund provided by the Ministry of Culture and Innovation, as part of the University Research Scholarship Program announced for the 2024/2025 academic year.

Disclosure of Interests. The authors have no competing interests to declare that are relevant to the content of this article.

References

1. Bajwa, J., Munir, U., Nori, A. and Williams, B.: Artificial intelligence in healthcare: transforming the practice of medicine. Future Healthc. J. **8**, e188–e194 (2021). https://doi.org/10.7861/fhj.2021-0095
2. Hazarika, I.: Artificial intelligence: opportunities and implications for the health workforce. Int. Health **12**, 241–245 (2020). https://doi.org/10.1093/INTHEALTH/IHAA007

3. Olawade, D.B., David-Olawade, A.C., Wada, O.Z., Asaolu, A.J., Adereni, T., Ling, J.: Artificial intelligence in healthcare delivery: prospects and pitfalls. J. Med. Surgery Public Health **3**, 100108 (2024). https://doi.org/10.1016/j.glmedi.2024.100108

4. Ahmed, M.I., Spooner, B., Isherwood, J., Lane, M., Orrock, E., Dennison, A.: A Systematic Review of the Barriers to the Implementation of Artificial Intelligence in Healthcare. Springer Science and Business Media LLC, Cureus (2023). https://doi.org/10.7759/cureus.46454

5. Agwunobi, A., Osborne, P.: Dynamic capabilities and healthcare: a framework for enhancing the competitive advantage of hospitals. California Manage. Rev. **58** (2016). https://doi.org/10.1525/cmr.2016.58.4.1

6. Sarker, M.: Assessing the integration of AI technologies in enhancing patient care delivery in U.S. hospitals. J. Knowl. Learn. Sci. Technol. ISSN: 2959-6386, 338–351 (2023). https://doi.org/10.60087/jklst.vol2.n2.p351

7. Agwunobi, A., Osborne, P.: Dynamic capabilities and healthcare: a framework for enhancing the competitive advantage of hospitals. Calif. Manage. Rev. **58**, 141–161 (2016)

8. Al-Amin, M., Sullivan, E., Szalay, N.E.: An exploratory study of dynamic capabilities and performance improvement in hospitals. J. Healthc. Manage. **69**., 335–349 (2024). https://doi.org/10.1097/JHM-D-23-00144

9. Chen, M., Decary, M.: Artificial intelligence in healthcare: an essential guide for health leaders. In: Healthcare Management Forum, vol. 33, pp. 10–18. SAGE Publications Inc. (2020). https://doi.org/10.1177/0840470419873123

10. Alami, H., Lehoux, P., Papoutsi, C. et al.: Understanding the integration of artificial intelligence in healthcare organisations and systems through the NASSS framework: a qualitative study in a leading Canadian academic centre. BMC Health Services Research 24. BioMed Central Ltd. (2024). https://doi.org/10.1186/s12913-024-11112-x

E-Government Cases

From Dashboards to Do-Boards: A Data-Driven Architecture for Policy Support Systems

Apurva Kulkarni$^{(\boxtimes)}$ (ID), Pooja Bassin (ID), and Srinath Srinivasa (ID)

International Institute of Information Technology Bangalore, 26/C, Electronics City Phase 1, Bengaluru, Karnataka, India
{apurva.kulkarni,pooja.bassin,sri}@iiitb.ac.in

Abstract. Policy Support Systems (PSS) enable transforming data into actionable, evidence-based governance recommendations to aid policymakers. Aligning decisions with the 2030 Sustainable Development Agenda makes the implementation of PSS even more complex, as the Sustainable Development Goals (SDGs) encompass a broad and interconnected set of goals and targets. This necessitates careful consideration of multiple dimensions and the synergies and trade-offs that exist across them. Building on the vast availability of Open Government Data (OGD), we propose a novel data-driven PSS architecture that provides an end-to-end solution for policymakers by transforming raw data into actionable insights through prescriptive dashboards, which we term as *do-boards*. The proposed architecture integrates SDG-based contextual mapping, semantic data retrieval, correlation-based intervention modelling, and prescriptive analysis. Drawing on structured semantic data pipelines, the system generates targeted policy prescriptions mapped to relevant government schemes. The proposed architecture facilitates granular decision-making at the state, district, taluka, and village levels. The manuscript presents an execution workflow that utilizes *do-boards* to address the case study of *student dropout rates* in the Indian state of Karnataka, aligning with SDG 4: Quality Education. The proposed research highlights the potential of *do-boards* in bridging the gap between data analysis and actionable insights. This enables evidence-based policymaking and contributes to sustainable development.

Keywords: PSS · SDG Semantic Mapping · Intervention Modelling · Policy Mapping · Sustainability

1 Introduction

In the digital governance era, it is essential to analyze complex data to facilitate the effective formulation and implementation of policies. As the data continues to grow, policymakers face numerous challenges in formulating, implementing, and evaluating effective policies. The need for a Policy Support System (PSS) stems from the requirement for data-driven decision-making over real-time data that aids in actionable insights. The Sustainable Development Goals (SDGs) provide a comprehensive framework for understanding how policies influence a nation's performance across key domains such as healthcare, education, employment, etc. In designing a system that supports data-driven policy decisions, a core challenge lies in identifying relevant data and determining actionable outputs.

The UN Deputy Secretary-General opened the 2024 High-level Political Forum[1], urging bold policies and investments to accelerate progress on SDGs. The Forum underscores the necessity of integrating the SDGs into policymaking to catalyze action and investment. With a focus on reducing poverty, enhancing food security, combating climate change, and fostering inclusive societies, it highlights the urgency of formulating well-structured, evidence-based policies. This emphasizes the need for a robust policy support system that aligns with SDG strategies, data-driven decision-making, evaluates the impact of policy choices, and provides actionable insights that help implement the decisions.

In this paper, we propose a data-driven architecture for a PSS that delivers a comprehensive end-to-end pipeline. This system is designed to understand administrative needs, map them to relevant SDGs, and identify key data points based on the required time frame and administrative region (state, district, taluka, village, etc.). It further analyses these data points to determine correlations essential for intervention modelling, provides prescriptive guidelines, and highlights existing policies that can facilitate the implementation of the suggested interventions.

This paper presents a proof-of-concept[2,3] developed using five years of data from the Government of Karnataka (GoK). Over time, the architecture has evolved from a data management framework [3,5,15] into a comprehensive end-to-end solution for a PSS. This implementation has been designed to address the specific requirements of government administrators in the Indian state of Karnataka, providing them with actionable insights. A key innovation of this system is the introduction of *do-boards* (prescriptive modelling), which assist administrators in identifying relevant policies (prescriptions to policy mapping) based on the current status, enabling informed decision-making for sustainable development.

Research Contributions

In this paper, we present the following key research contributions:

- **SGD-based pipeline:** The problem statement is semantically mapped to relevant sustainable development goals, targets, and indicators.
- **Semantic data retrieval:** Based on the problem statement, the context-aware data points are used for the analysis.

---

[1] https://news.un.org/en/story/2024/07/1151861.
[2] https://sadrusha.iiitb.ac.in/.
[3] https://kdl.iiitb.ac.in/.

- **Intervention modelling:** The retrieved data points are analysed to understand the correlation, and the ones with a high correlation indicating a strong relationship are considered for further analysis and modelling.
- **Prescriptive analysis through *do-boards*:** The proposed PSS offers a prescriptive analysis, recommending a set of targeted interventions for effective implementation to achieve desired objectives.
- **Prescriptions to policy mapping for implementation:** The PSS identifies relevant policies influencing the actions that are suggested in the prescriptive analysis.
- **Scalable granularity:** The proposed architecture is designed to support administrative granularity across various levels. Every stage of the system-including decision-making, data analysis, prescriptive analysis, and the generation of actionable insights through *do-boards* can operate effectively at different administrative levels.

Section 2 reviews various existing PSS and highlights how our approach differs. Section 3 presents details of the proposed architecture structured across multiple layers, followed by a description of the full execution flow. Section 5 demonstrates the application of the proposed architecture using a case study from SDG 4: Quality Education.

2   Related Literature

The concept of PSS has evolved over the years along with advancements in technology, governance, data analytics, and decision-making frameworks. The PSS stems from the two fundamental research areas, Systems Theory and Policy Sciences. Systems Theory proposed by Bertalanffy in 1968 facilitates understanding of complex concepts by developing theoretical frameworks and conceptual models that represent real-world situations [33]. Policy Science, as discussed by Lasswell in 1951, emphasizes understanding the systematic approach of the policy process [20]. In 1970, the term Decision Support System was introduced by Keen, focusing on analysis-based decision making for more insightful strategic choices [14]. With the availability of computational models and Geographic Information System (GIS), the decision systems for policies were enhanced by leveraging spatial data and data-driven analysis [7]. In 2000, the technology shift supporting Big Data Analytics and E-Government initiatives shifted PSS to the digital space supporting real-world decision-making capability [12,21]. Current-day PSS leverages Artificial Intelligence (AI) [25], Machine Learning (ML), and advanced models for decision-making [11]. Many modern PSS focus on sustainability-based frameworks, which aid in making decisions aligned with the SDGs [8].

PSS helps governments and organizations make informed decisions in governance, climate, energy, and economic development. Global initiatives like the United Nation's Voluntary National Reviews (VNRs) and the Organization for Economic Co-operation and Development (OECD)'s Policy Coherence for Sustainable Development (PCSD) assess policy effectiveness [30], while the

World Bank's Country Policy and Institutional Assessment (CPIA) evaluates governance quality [10]. As digital technology transforms policymaking, tools like the GovTech Maturity Index[4] and OECD Digital Government Index [24] track AI and open data adoption. Climate policies rely on frameworks such as the United Nations Framework Convention on Climate Change (UNFCCC)'s National (NDC) Registry and the Climate Policy Initiative (CPI) to drive sustainability [28], while energy strategies are shaped by the International Energy Agency (IEA)'s Clean Energy Transitions Programme. Economic and social policies benefit from reports like the World Economic Forum's Global Competitiveness Report and the International Labour Organization's Decent Work Programmes. At the national level, India's National Institution for Transforming India[5] (NITI Aayog) SDG Index, the USA's Evidence-Based Policymaking Act [9], and China's Five-Year Plans guide [26] local policy decisions.

Since 2003, researchers at King's College London have collaboratively developed these web-based policy support systems to make scientific knowledge more actionable[6]. Co\$ting Nature, in collaboration with UNEP-WCMC, provides a web-based PSS supporting natural capital accounting and analysing ecosystem services[7]. WaterWorld provides policy support for water resources and hydrological ecosystem services at local to national scales [22]. There are other projects like Eco: Actuary (climate risk) [23], AguAAndes & CompAndes (hydrological policy) [23], MENARA (global SWOT analysis), DESURVEY (land degradation), and FIESTA-FOGINT (fog interception) that support environmental policy and sustainable development. These tools provide data-driven insights for conservation, climate resilience, and resource management.

While many well-designed PSS architectures effectively aid in decision-making, the traditional decision support systems often fall short in governmental policymaking as they do not fully address the complexities of structured and unstructured decision-making. To develop more effective policy support systems, a broader approach that integrates both systematic frameworks and flexible decision-making perspectives is needed [31]. In modern AI/ML-driven policy support systems, a major challenge is support deficiency, where the available data fails to cover all possible actions, resulting in partial or complete failures [29].

Regardless of whether a PSS follows a traditional approach or leverages modern technology, challenges often arise during the implementation phase [13]. For a PSS to be successful, the implementation phase must effectively address two critical tasks: first, identifying the key data points necessary for intervention and understanding their variability across different geographic regions and current conditions; and second, determining the policies that can influence these data points to drive meaningful change.

In this research, we present a novel data-driven architecture for PSS designed to support policy decision-making that bridges the gap between data analysis

---

[4] https://www.worldbank.org/en/programs/govtech/gtmi.
[5] https://niti.gov.in/.
[6] https://www.policysupport.org/home.
[7] https://www.policysupport.org/costingnature.

and actionable insights by providing prescriptive analysis and policy recommendations that support decision implementation.

3   Proposed Architecture

The proposed PSS architecture is depicted in Fig. 1. It demonstrates an end-to-end pipeline for data-driven decision-making considering the SDG perspective. The SDGs act as an anchor to the entire architecture. The architecture incorporates a large volume of Open Government Data (OGD) and aligns it semantically with the SDGs. The SDG-aligned data is ingested into the data store that facilitates seamless retrieval of relevant data points based on the problem statement. The input (problem statement) given by the user (e.g., government administrator) is interpreted through the SDG lens, and subsequently, relevant data points are retrieved. These data points are analysed, and prescriptions are suggested to the user. The proposed PSS goes a step further and suggests relevant policies that can help implement the suggested prescriptions. The proposed architecture is composed of three layers- *Data Processing and Modelling Layer*, *Query Processing and Analytics Layer*, and *Data-Driven Decision Processing Layer*.

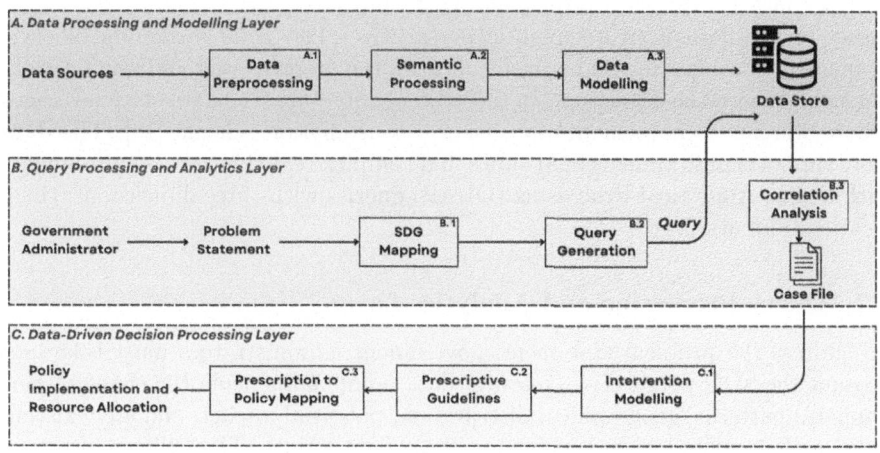

Fig. 1. Architecture for Policy Support System.

3.1   Data Processing and Modelling Layer

The PSS leverages OGD to build the data store. The primary challenge here is to integrate heterogeneous data sources and structure the data sources [18]. The current implementation is built over the Karnataka At a Glance (KAG)[8]

---
[8] https://kgis.ksrsac.in/kag/.

dataset. This is a yearly report generated by the GoK capturing various data points across departments like agriculture, healthcare, education, transportation, infrastructure, etc. The report is made available over the web in PDF format. The initial step converts an unstructured format (PDF) into a structured (tabular) format. The converted structured data points are validated with a basic data cleaning and pre-processing pipeline, including handling outliers and missing values.

The key element in the data-driven decision-making process is identifying data points relevant to the problem statement and aiding in SDG-aligned prescriptions. Traditional keyword-based approaches are not capable of identifying context-dependent nuances in data. The PSS uses a *Semantic Processing* module indicated in Fig. 1, Block A.2, that builds the semantic layer over the data, enabling the retrieval of the data that are inherently related to the SDGs and the problem statement aiming to intervene [17]. For example, the data file capturing the status of functional and non-functional electronic devices in Karnataka - 'Details of electronic devices in school in Karnataka 2023' is ingested. The data points will be tagged with location: Karnataka, time frame: 2023, SDG: SDG 4, Target: 4.1, Indicator 4.1.2: Average annual dropout rate at secondary level, Context: Education, Students, Schools, Electronics devices, etc. The tagging of data helps in indexing and faster retrieval during the query execution phase. The primary challenge is implementing a data store that facilitates seamless access to the data from a semantic perspective. The *Data modelling* block is responsible for ingesting and transforming all the preprocessed and semantically tagged data into the data store. In this PSS architecture, the data store leverages a data warehouse implementation using a constellation schema [19]. The data store supports multidimensional cubes and complex real-time data environments with Online Analytical Processing (OLAP) queries with three dimensions: time, location, and attributes.

3.2   Query Processing and Analytics Layer

To address the problem statement, government administrators must take into account the SDG perspective, relevant data points influencing the change, their temporal patterns, geographical distribution, potential impact, and any existing policies that may already be shaping these data points. The PSS architecture proposes a query processing layer dedicated to handling the input problem statement and converting it into a query that is responsible for retrieving the data from the data store.

The query is interpreted as a tuple having three components: relevant SDGs, administrative regions (location), and the context for the problem statement *'Reduce student dropout rate in Karnataka'*. In the process of tuple formation, the first step is to identify the SDGs influenced by the input. A semantic pipeline, which uses pre-trained GloVe embeddings and the KeyBERT package to convert SDG keywords into vectors and assess similarity with the query descriptions using cosine similarity [1, 16]. A similar semantic pipeline is used to identify the data points relevant to context [17]. The second step involves identifying the time frame and geographical entity (state, county, taluka, village, etc.). The underlying data store enables data retrieval based on these tags. The current implementation utilizes spatial data, including shape files of Karnataka State[9] in India, along with district, taluk, and village-level data within Karnataka for efficient data retrieval. Finally, the *Query Generation* module converts these data points into a complex SQL query [19] and fetches the relevant data from the data store. The retrieved data is further analysed by the *Correlation Analysis* block for understanding the influence and correlation among the data points.

The *Correlation Analysis* module uses the Pearson correlation coefficient to understand the correlations among the data points. The data points that exhibit a statistically significant correlation (p-value < 0.05) are retained for further analysis [4]. These positively and negatively correlated attributes are then further analysed using information-theoretic measures. The current implementation uses Mutual Information and Conditional Entropy to identify strong correlations [6, 32]. The refined set of data points from this analysis forms a narrower set of options for intervention modelling, prescriptive analysis, and visualization on the dashboard, ensuring meaningful insights. The set of most relevant attributes, referred to as a *case file*, is forwarded to the next layer for decision processing. For the problem statement *'Reduce student dropout rate in Karnataka'*, the identified indicator, I, is - SDG 4.1.2: average annual dropout rate at secondary level, and a case file that includes the correlated attributes (later referred to as factors $(f_1, f_2, .., f_k)$) influencing the indicator is generated. Subsection 3.3 discusses the detailed process of the case file processing for intervention modelling.

3.3   Data-Driven Decision Processing Layer

The *case file* from the Query Processing Layer can serve multiple tasks. For our purposes, we use it for *Intervention Modelling* [27] that facilitates policymakers with data-driven decision making to implement SDG-based policies [2]. It is critical to analyze the varied impact across regions when a factor affecting the SDG indicator is changed based on a given policy. Hence, for a given geographical unit a, various factors from the case file ($F = f_1, f_2, ..., f_k$) that are associated with the SDG indicator, I, are assessed based on a multivariate linear regression model [4] as given in Eq. 1 below:

$$\hat{I}^a = \hat{\beta}_0 + \hat{\beta}_1 f_1^a + \hat{\beta}_2 f_2^a + ... + \hat{\beta}_k f_k^a \tag{1}$$

where, $\hat{\beta}_j$ is the estimated regression model coefficient for factor f_j^a. If we change the factor f_j^a by $x\%$, the differential impact on the indicator will be,

$$\Delta I^a = (\frac{x}{100}) \times \hat{\beta}_j \times f_j^a \tag{2}$$

Equation 2 helps us in identifying a predicted change in the indicator across various regions. This forms the first block of this layer.

---

[9] https://kgis.ksrsac.in/kgis/downloads.aspx.

Another essential feature of this layer is to provide prescriptive guidelines to policymakers when they need to mitigate an issue or improve an indicator. Thus, by recognizing the key areas of concern, they can implement targeted interventions to advance the SDGs. We do this by taking a prescriptive modelling approach to attain a given target, I_{tar}. The new value of the factor, $^{new}f_j^a$ is calculated in Eq. 3:

$$^{new}f_j^a = {}^{old}f_j^a + \alpha_j * \left[\frac{(I_{tar} - I_{curr})}{\hat{\beta}_j} \right] \tag{3}$$

where,

$$\hat{\beta}_j = \frac{\partial I^a}{\partial f_j} \tag{4}$$

$^{old}f_j^a$ is the current value of the factor, I_{curr} is the original aggregated value of the indicator, and α_j is the sensitivity associated with f_j^a that can be overridden by the policymaker based on the present significance of the factor to the indicator. This concludes the second block, C.2, of this layer.

The new values determined by Eq. 3 for all of the factors associated with I^a produce a prescriptive guideline for the policymakers. This supports recommendations for evaluating the impact and suitability of interventions for a given region. Based on these recommendations and the factors linked to the indicator, appropriate policies are identified, and budget allocations are determined for each policy. Thus, the amount, A, allocated for a given scheme will be,

$$A_{f_j} = \frac{\alpha_j * \frac{1}{|\hat{\beta}_j|}}{\sum_{i=1}^{k} \alpha_i * \frac{1}{|\hat{\beta}_i|}} \times A \tag{5}$$

Section 5 further elaborates the process using a case study from SDG 4.

4   Execution Workflow

The concept of a PSS represents a comprehensive approach to policy-making and implementation, leveraging real-world data for informed decision-making. This section explores the proposed architecture's intricate workflow, encompassing data ingestion and data-driven decision-making stages that facilitate the interaction between data-driven analysis and real-world scenarios.

Figure 2 illustrates the process of execution of the proposed PSS architecture. The execution workflow comprises two stages: the data ingestion process and the data-driven decision-making process.

Data Ingestion Process: In this process, the data from various open data sources is first converted into a structured form, and a basic cleaning operation is performed. The data is tagged with relevant SDGs, administrative regions, time frames, and contexts and stored in a data warehouse [19]. The ingestion process is a bulk operation that runs initially to incorporate all available data sources

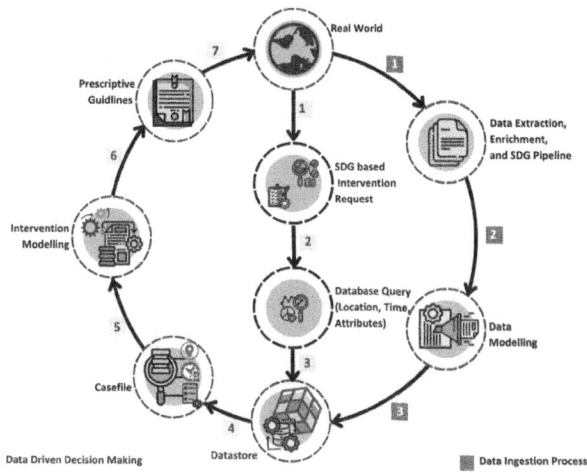

Fig. 2. Execution Workflow: Data-driven Architecture for Policy Support System.

and is subsequently triggered for any new data ingestion. Each new dataset undergoes this process to ensure its accessibility within the PSS architecture.

Data-Driven Decision-Making Process: This is an interactive process in which policymakers analyze real-world issues, formulate policies and regulations, evaluate the potential impact and efficacy of proposed policies, and implement them in practice. The dynamic process is initiated when the government administrator inputs a problem statement. For example, *"Decrease student dropout rate in Karnataka by 30%"*. The PSS reflects the relevant SDGs (SDG 4: Quality Education, Indicator 4.1.2: average annual dropout rate at secondary level). As discussed in the Subsect. 3.2, the input is used to query the data store and retrieve the relevant data.

In the above problem statement, the data points related to student dropout rate like number of teachers trained in computer, count of people deprived of housing, number of schools without functional laptops/notebooks/desktops/PCs, number of schools without an English teacher, drinking water facility, school infrastructure, distance to school etc., for all the districts of Karnataka are retrieved. After the correlation analysis, the data points with strong correlation are presented to the domain expert for selection. The selected data points are used for generating the intervention modelling and prescriptive analysis. The dashboards allow user to pick and try multiple data points, analyse their influence on the problem statement, and understand their impact. The *do-boards* allow users to pick a data point and analyse the possible policies that can be used to intervene on that data point. For example, the user chooses to increase the "drinking water facility" factor. The proposed PSS provides a district-wise analysis of the selected data points while also displaying relevant policies such as Jal Jeevan Mission (JJM)[10], Swachh Bharat Mission (SBM)[11], Smart Cities Mission[12], and Pradhan Mantri Krishi Sinchayee Yojana (PMKSY)[13] to offer actionable insights.

Factor	Description
Number of teachers trained in computer (f_1)	The total count of teachers who have received formal training in computer skills, which may impact digital learning opportunities.
Count of people deprived of housing (f_2)	The number of individuals lacking stable and adequate housing, potentially influencing school attendance rates.
Number of schools without functional laptops/notebooks/desktops/PCs (f_3)	The count of educational institutions that do not have any working computing devices, limiting digital education resources.
Number of schools without an English teacher (f_4)	The number of schools that lack a dedicated English teacher, potentially affecting language proficiency and academic performance.

Geographical Unit (a)	SDG Indicator (i)	f_1	f_2	f_3	f_4	...	f_n
a_1	val_1	val_1	val_1	val_1	val_1	~	val_1
a_2	val_2	val_2	val_2	val_2	val_2	~	val_2
a_3	val_3	val_3	val_3	val_3	val_3	~	val_3
a_4	val_4	val_4	val_4	val_4	val_4	~	val_4
.	.	.	.	.	.	.	.
a_n	val_n	val_n	val_n	val_n	val_n	~	val_n

(a) Correlated Attributes contributing to the case file of the Indicator SDG 4.1.2: Average annual dropout rate at secondary level

(b) General organisation of the case file capturing datapoints across geographical unit, SDG indicator, and the correlated factors

Fig. 3. (a) Correlated attributes contributing to the SDG indicator: *Student dropout rate.* (b) General organisation of the case file

5   Case Study on SDG 4: Quality Education

In this section, we focus on demonstrating the PSS implementation and intermediate results using a case study focusing on a problem statement focusing on SDG 4-Quality Education in India. On 16 June 2023, the Deccan Herald reported, *'School dropout rate is worrying- Govt must address issue to ensure every child enrols and completes education '*[14]. The article discussed the high school dropout rates in several states, including Karnataka (14.6%) in 2020–21, which are concerning, as also reported by the Ministry of Education. The government, through the National Education Policy (NEP 2020)[15], aims to address the issue by training faculties, providing adequate resources, improving infrastructure, and tracking student progress.

To understand the end-to-end execution of the PSS architecture, let's consider a problem statement - *'Reduce student dropout rate in Karnataka'.* As discussed in the Subsect. 4, based on the problem statement, the SDG Indicator 4.1.2: average annual dropout rate at secondary level and the attributes- number

---

[10] https://jaljeevanmission.gov.in/.
[11] https://swachhbharatmission.ddws.gov.in/.
[12] https://smartcities.gov.in/.
[13] https://pmksy.gov.in/.
[14] https://www.deccanherald.com/opinion/editorial/school-dropout-rate-is-worrying-1228180.html.
[15] https://www.education.gov.in/nep/about-nep.

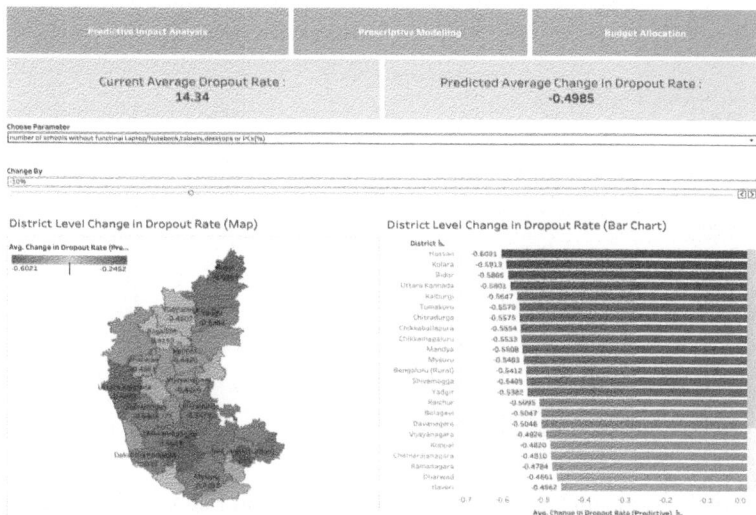

Fig. 4. Differential impact is seen across various districts of the Indian state of Karnataka when there is a 10% decrease in the number of schools that do not have functional electronic devices such as laptops, desktops, or PCs.

of teachers trained in computer, count of people deprived of housing, number of schools without functional laptops/notebooks/desktops/PCs, number of schools without an English teacher, drinking water facility, school infrastructure, distance travel to school etc. are retrieved from the data store. These attributes are analysed by the *Correlation Analysis* block discussed in the layer 3.2. The layer identifies strongly correlated attributes listed in the Fig. 3 and generates the case file.

Using this *case file* on *student drop-out rate*, we perform intervention modelling on the 31 districts of the Indian state of Karnataka as described in Subsect. 3.3. Figure 4 displays an integrated intervention dashboard for the *Data-driven Decision Processing* layer. Under the *Predictive Impact Analysis* dashboard, we see the differential impact across various districts of Karnataka when one of the factors, *number of schools that do not have functional electronic pieces of equipment*, is reduced by 10%. *Hassan* district, followed by *Kolar, Bidar*, and *Uttar Kannada* show high sensitivity towards this change in the factor.

Figure 5 illustrates that the *student drop-out rate* needs to be reduced from the current average of 14.34 to the target value of 10. The sensitivity of the factor, *number of schools with an English teacher*, is set to 0.8, leading to an increase in its value based on the new values calculated using Eq. 3. In contrast, the sensitivities of the other three factors have been lowered, resulting in a decrease in their respective values. Based on this, the highest impact of this combination of interventions is observed in the district of *Ramanagara*, followed by *Raichur*, and *Vijayanagara*. This indicates that these interventions are best suited for these high-ranking districts, while their impact in the low-ranking districts remains

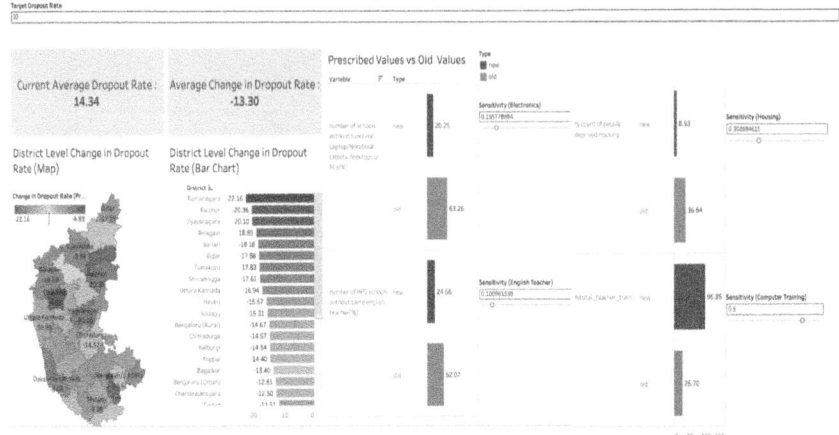

Fig. 5. Prescriptive modelling dashboard for SDG indicator *student drop-out rate*. The target *drop-out* is set to 10.

minimal. Hence, we refer to such dashboards as *do-boards*, which assist the policymakers with a *'what-to-do'* analysis going beyond the conventional *'what-if'* analysis.

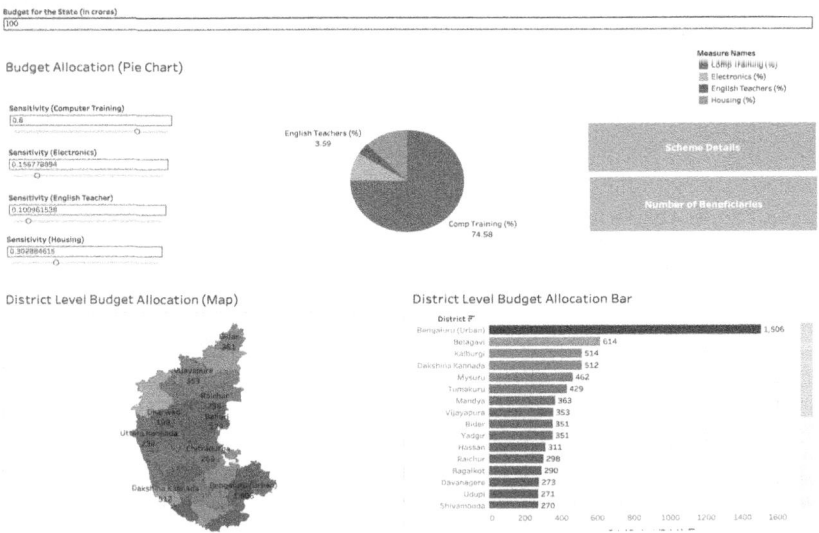

Fig. 6. Budget Allocation Dashboard for the districts of Karnataka.

Based on the strengths and sensitivities of each factor, the budget is allo-cated across corresponding policies such as DIKSHA[16], Samagra Shiksha[17], and Basava Vasati Yojana[18] as shown in Fig. 6. With a high sensitivity for *computer training*, the largest share of the budget is allocated to the *computer teacher training* policy. *Bengaluru (Urban)* district receives the highest allocation, as it is one of the most populous cities in the state.

6 Conclusions and Future Work

The proposed research introduces a data-driven PSS that aids in evidence-based decision-making and actionable insights. The key contribution is the *do-boards*, which extend the traditional dashboards by providing prescriptive analysis and actionable policy recommendations to support effective decision implementa-tion. The proposed research discusses the systematic layered architecture ded-icated to data ingestion and modelling, query processing and analytics, and data-driven decision processing. The research discusses the execution workflow through a case study that analyses student dropout rates in the Indian state of Karnataka. The detailed walk-through illustrated through visualizations, dash-boards, and *do-boards* highlights how the proposed architecture translates raw data into actionable policy recommendations. Future work will focus on widen-ing the scope of the architecture by accommodating data across different states in India. The proposed approach plays a pivotal role that transforms the data insights into actionable recommendations, which government administrators and decision-makers can leverage to drive sustainable policy outcomes.

Acknowledgements. The authors thank the Planning and Statistics Department, Government of Karnataka, India, and DataWeave (Infoweave Analytics Private Lim-ited, Bangalore, India) for their support.

References

1. Kulkarni, A.,Patidar, R., Srinivasa, S., Patil, S.: Semantic SDG-mapper: browser extension for mapping sustainable development goals to open webpages. In: CODS-COMAD Dec 2024, December 18–21, 2024, Jodhpur, India (2025). ACM ISBN 979-8-4007-1124-4/24/12. https://doi.org/10.1145/3703323.3704269, preprint
2. Bassin, P.: A data-driven approach for supporting policy intervention in sustainable development (2022). https://ic-sd.org/wp-content/uploads/2022/11/submission_357.pdf
3. Bassin, P.: Network learning on open data to aid policy making. In: Link, S., Reinhartz-Berger, I., Zdravkovic, J., Bork, D., Srinivasa, S. (eds.) Proceedings of the ER Forum and PhD Symposium 2022 co-located with 41st International

---

[16] https://ciet.ncert.gov.in/initiative/diksha.
[17] https://samagra.education.gov.in.
[18] https://ashraya.karnataka.gov.in/index.aspx.

Conference on Conceptual Modeling (ER 2022), Virtual Event, Hyderabad, India, October 17, 2022. CEUR Workshop Proceedings, vol. 3211. CEUR-WS.org (2022). http://ceur-ws.org/Vol-3211/CR_098.pdf

4. Bassin, P., AG, K., Srinivasa, S.: Design of a data-driven intervention dashboard for SDG localization. In: Proceedings of the Thirty-Third International Joint Conference on Artificial Intelligence, pp. 8606–8609 (2024). https://doi.org/10.24963/ijcai.2024/990

5. Bassin, P., Parasa, N.S., Srinivasa, S., Mandyam, S.: Big data management for policy support in sustainable development. In: International Conference on Big Data Analytics, pp. 3–15. Springer (2021)

6. Battiti, R.: Using mutual information for selecting features in supervised neural net learning. IEEE Trans. Neural Networks 5(4), 537–550 (1994). https://doi.org/10.1109/72.298224

7. Batty, M., Densham, P.J.: Decision support, GIS, and urban planning (1996)

8. Birner, J., Bornemann, B., Biermann, F.: Policy integration through the sustainable development goals? the case of the German federal government. Sustain. Dev. 32(4), 3877–3889 (2024)

9. Burkhauser, R.V., Burkhauser, S.V.: Policy research institutes' role in the development of evidence for evidence-based policymaking in the united states. J. Policy Anal. Manage. 43(4), 1260–1269 (2024)

10. Edwards, D.B., Jr., Caravaca, A., Rappeport, A., Sperduti, V.R.: World bank influence on policy formation in education: a systematic review of the literature. Rev. Educ. Res. 94(4), 584–622 (2024)

11. Farina, M., Yu, X., Lavazza, A.: Ethical considerations and policy interventions concerning the impact of generative AI tools in the economy and in society. AI Ethics 5(1), 737–745 (2025)

12. Heeks, R.: Understanding and measuring egovernment: international benchmarking studies. In: UNDESA workshop,"E-participation and E-government: Understanding the present and creating the future", Budapest, Hungary, pp. 27–28 (2000)

13. Hudson, B., Hunter, D., Peckham, S.: Policy failure and the policy-implementation gap: can policy support programs help? Policy Des. Pract. 2, 1–14 (2019). https://doi.org/10.1080/25741292.2018.1540378

14. Keen, P.G.: Decision support systems: a research perspective. In: Decision Support Systems: Issues and Challenges: Proceedings of an International Task Force Meeting, pp. 23–44 (1980)

15. Kulkarni, A., Bassin, P., Parasa, N.S., Venugopal, V.E., Srinivasa, S., Ramanathan, C.: Ontology augmented data lake system for policy support. In: International Conference on Big Data Analytics, pp. 3–16. Springer (2022)

16. Kulkarni, A., Ramadurg, I.A.K., Srinivasa, S., Patil, S.: Introspecting policy documents through semantic lenses of sustainable development goals. In: Sachdeva, S., Watanobe, Y., Bhalla, S. (eds.) Big Data Analytics in Astronomy, Science, and Engineering, pp. 95–105. Springer, Cham (2025)

17. Kulkarni, A., Ramanathan, C., Venugopal, V.E.: Cognitive retrieve: Empowering document retrieval with semantics and domain specific knowledge graph. In: EKG-LLM@ CIKM (2023)

18. Kulkarni, A., Ramanathan, C., Venugopal, V.E.: Toward sustainable data practices: integrating open data with SDG-based data lake frameworks. IEEE Technol. Soc. Mag. 43(1), 62–69 (2024). https://doi.org/10.1109/MTS.2024.3365591

19. Kulkarni, A., Srinivasa, S., Patil, S.: Sdg aligned data warehouse implementation over open government data. In: International Conference on Electronic Government and the Information Systems Perspective, pp. 154–167. Springer (2024)

20. Lasswell, H.D.: The emerging conception of the policy sciences. Policy Sci. **1**(1), 3–14 (1970)
21. Mayer-Schönberger, V., Cukier, K.: Big Data: A Revolution that Will Transform How We Live, Work, and Think. Houghton Mifflin Harcourt, Boston (2013)
22. Mulligan, M.: Waterworld: a self-parameterising, physically based model for application in data-poor but problem-rich environments globally. Hydrol. Res. **44**(5), 748–769 (2013)
23. Mulligan, M., Burke, S., Douglas, C., van Soesbergen, A.: Methodologies to assess and map the biophysical effectiveness of nature based solutions. In: Greening Water Risks: Natural Assurance Schemes, pp. 51–65. Springer, Cham (2023)
24. OECD: 2023 OECD digital government index: Results and key findings. OECD Public Governance Policy Papers No. 44, OECD Publishing, Paris (2024). https://doi.org/10.1787/1a89ed5e-en. https://doi.org/10.1787/1a89ed5e-en. Accessed via OECD iLibrary
25. Papadakis, T., Christou, I.T., Ipektsidis, C., Soldatos, J., Amicone, A.: Explainable and transparent artificial intelligence for public policymaking. Data Policy **6**, e10 (2024)
26. Qiang, L.: Report on the work of the government. In: Delivered at the Second Session of the 14th National People's Congress of the People's Republic of China on March, vol. 5, p. 2024 (2024)
27. Rachuri, S.N., Malavalli, A., Parasa, N.S., Bassin, P., Srinivasa, S.: Modeling the impact of policy interventions for sustainable development. In: Proceedings of the Thirty-Second International Joint Conference on Artificial Intelligence, pp. 7167–7170 (2023)
28. Remling, E., Meijer, K.: Conflict considerations in the united nations framework convention on climate change's national adaptation plans. Climate Dev. **17**(1), 37–51 (2025)
29. Sachdeva, N., Su, Y.H., Joachims, T.: Off-policy bandits with deficient support. In: Proceedings of the 26th ACM SIGKDD International Conference on Knowledge Discovery Data Mining (2020). https://doi.org/10.1145/3394486.3403139
30. Sorooshian, S.: The sustainable development goals of the united nations: a comparative midterm research review. J. Cleaner Prod. 142272 (2024)
31. Te'eni, D.: Support systems for high level policy making: what makes them special. Inf. Manag. **19**, 41–50 (1990). https://doi.org/10.1016/0378-7206(90)90013-8
32. Vergara, J.R., Estévez, P.A.: A review of feature selection methods based on mutual information. Neural Comput. Appl. **24**, 175–186 (2014)
33. Von Bertalanffy, L.: Problems of general system theory. Hum. Biol. **23**(4), 302 (1951)

An Agentic Approach to Retrieving and Drafting Legislative Definitions

Leonardo Zilli[iD], Michele Corazza[iD], Monica Palmirani[✉][iD],
and Salvatore Sapienza

CIRSFID-ALMA-AI, University of Bologna, Bologna, Italy
leonardo.zilli@studio.unibo.it,
{michele.corazza2,monica.palmirani,salvatore.sapienza}@unibo.it

Abstract. The complexity, dynamicity over time, and multilingual nature of legislative documents pose significant challenges for the accurate retrieval and reuse of legislative definitions, an essential task in legal drafting. This research introduces an AI-driven system leveraging Large Language Models (LLMs) to assist in the retrieval and generation of legal definitions from a multilingual, multi-jurisdictional dataset of XML-encoded legislative documents. The system functions as a conversational AI agent, enabling natural language queries tailored to different end-user types, such as lawyers, legislators and judges. It employs a hybrid retrieval approach, integrating dense semantic search with sparse keyword-based methods, and incorporates legislation-aware and point-in-time filtering to ensure jurisdictional and temporal accuracy. If no suitable definition is found, the system leverages Retrieval-Augmented Generation (RAG) to generate a novel one that is grounded in and consistent with in-force legislative documents. The system is evaluated using automatic quantitative metrics and qualitative assessments from legal experts, demonstrating strong retrieval capabilities but highlighting limitations in generating legally sound definitions.

Keywords: Large language models (LLMs) · Retrieval-augmented generation (RAG) · Legal AI · Legislative definitions · Akoma Ntoso

1 Introduction and Motivation

Legislative definitions are a fundamental component of normative documents, providing precise descriptions that clarify the scope and parameters of specific terms within the legislative system, ensuring that the text is clear and understandable to all parties involved. While creating new ad hoc definitions is possible, reusing existing ones can be beneficial for achieving harmonization within and across legal frameworks. The ability to analyze and query existing definitions serves multiple purposes: it helps prevent redundancy, informs drafters about other (possibly divergent) definitions for the same term, and streamlines legal analysis and interpretation. However, the volume and complexity of legal

© The Author(s), under exclusive license to Springer Nature Switzerland AG 2026
A. Kő et al. (Eds.): EGOVIS 2025, LNCS 16049, pp. 190–204, 2026.
https://doi.org/10.1007/978-3-032-02225-7_13

texts, especially in multilingual and multi-jurisdictional contexts, pose significant challenges to this task.

To address this, we propose an agentic AI system designed to assist legal professionals through natural language-driven retrieval of existing legislative definitions, with support for jurisdictional and temporal filtering. The system also enables context-aware generation of new definitions, leveraging the in-context learning capabilities of Large Language Models (LLMs).

2   Legal Informatics Methodology

2.1   Legislative Definitions

A legislative definition consists of two main elements: the *definiendum*, the term being defined, and the *definiens*, the explanation or description of the term being defined. While these two elements are common to all definitions, in practice the structure of definitions can vary significantly. *Static definitions*[1] are the simplest type of definition, following the standard form of *"X means Y"*, where X is the definiendum and Y is the definiens. *Dynamic definitions*[1] are more complex, as they leverage normative references to other existing definitions or concepts to ensure consistency with other legal fragments, either within the same text or in external documents. The reference may correspond to the entirety of the definiens (e.g. *"'Systemic risk' means systemic risk as defined in point (10) of Article 3(1) of Directive 2013/36/EU;"*[2]) or to the specification of the entity that constitutes it (e.g. *"European Semester" means the process set out in Article 2-a of Council Regulation (EC) No 1466/97;*[3]). *Definitions structured as a list* are definitions where the definiens is structured as a list of elements, grouping multiple related definitions under a single definiendum. The different definiens are presented as alternatives, each entry providing a different interpretation of the definiendum and possibly specifying precise conditions such as applicable jurisdictions, timeframes, or contextual constraints.

Additionally, we have different kinds of definitions according to the role played in the normative system. A definition can be: i) a constitutive rule when the definition creates a new legal concept (e.g., mobbing); ii) an exception with respect to a previous definition; iii) a declaration of membership in a group of legal concepts (e.g., stalking is a crime); iv) an interpretation for specific situations; v) an equivalence with another definition; vi) a description of technical phenomena (e.g., a mile is 1825 m).

2.2   Hybrid AI for Legislative Systems

Within the field of Artificial Intelligence, there is a historical division between symbolic and subsymbolic (statistical) approaches. While in recent years the

---

[1] This nomenclature is extracted from the *Joint Practical Guide of the European Parliament* [8].

[2] http://data.europa.eu/eli/reg/2013/575/oj, Article 4, point (11).

[3] http://data.europa.eu/eli/reg/2021/240/oj, Article 2, point (5).

usage of statistical methods has led to the most promising results, they also have some shortcomings, which are particularly problematic in the context of the legal domain. In particular, statistical methods are based on patterns that emerge from the data itself. While this can lead to high accuracy, it can be problematic when analyzing an ever-changing phenomenon such as the legislative corpus. In the legal domain, new laws are constantly being approved, and existing ones amended, meaning that a system relying solely on existing laws may produce biased output when laws change.

In this context, an approach called Hybrid AI is emerging, especially in the legal domain [15]. This Hybrid methodology combines the usage of statistical methods with a more structured representation of the legislative documents. This allows these approaches to leverage temporal and jurisdictional information while retaining the capabilities of state-of-the-art machine learning models.

2.3   LegalXML Annotation with Akoma Ntoso

Akoma Ntoso (AKN) [16,23] is a standard for an XML-based markup language which allows for the representation of parliamentary, legislative, judicial, and soft law documents in an open and machine-readable format. It provides a descriptive and rich vocabulary that enables the representation of the structure, content, and metadata of legal documents in a structured and hierarchical way. The AKN schema also defines a naming convention [22] based on the Functional Requirements for Bibliographic Records [21] model (FRBR), providing an explicit and meaningful solution to identify of different versions, formats and variants of legal texts. Specifically, the schema defines four entity types: a *Work* represents the abstract concept of a legal resource; an *Expression* represents a specific version of the resource whose content is specified and different from others for any reason (language, versions, etc.); a *Manifestation* represents any physical–or electronic–instance of the text, and a *Item* represents the actual physical copy–or file–containing the text.

Another crucial aspect of the AKN XML standard is the standardization of a temporal model for the legislative system. In particular, through the usage of URIs that are based on the FRBR model, the various consolidated versions of a single document can be uniquely identified. This also means that all normative references are part of this temporal model, as referencing the wrong consolidated document can produce inconsistent results. This is crucial for definitions, since many definitions are *dynamic*, meaning that they use normative references to adopt a *definiens* from other legislative documents. Furthermore, the whole timeline of each definition can be traced by examining the various consolidated versions of each definition.

2.4   Hierarchy of Legal Sources and Conflict of Norms

The theory of law is based on the hierarchy of legal sources that defines the rules of validity, superiority between norms, and competencies between different legislative documents. The validity of a law is defined by the legitimacy of the institutions that promulgate high-level norms (e.g., Grundnorm in Kelsen theory, Constitution, basic texts [5]). The other legal sources must be compliant with the validation rules defined by the high-level norm. This is an implicit principle of the legal sources called the "hierarchy of the norms". This fundamental concept defines some important mechanisms that are crucial to include by-design in LegalTech projects to resolve conflicts of norms or to rank the results of the information retrieval task. There are three main issues that we have taken into consideration:

- *lex superior derogat inferiori*: secondary law is overruled by primary law or constitutional law. In European legislation, regulation is immediately effective in the domestic law of each member state; on the contrary, the directive should be harmonized with the domestic law and depends on the national legal system. The different hierarchy of the legal source influences the output system based on Large Language Models (LLM) or in general of information retrieval;
- *lex specialis derogat generali*: the hyper-specification of the legislation for particular domains of application produces a priority principle that the specific law overrides the general regulation;
- *lex posterior derogat priori*: the temporal evolution over time of the legal sources creates a diachronic sequence of normative snapshots during the time [2].

A LegalTech system should take in consideration these principles for better address the end-user to the correct ouput of the elaboration.

2.5 Transparency and Explicability

One of the most important requirements of the AI Act[4] is to guarantee the transparency of the decision of the AI output and the explicability of the results. Articles 13 and 14 of the AI Act (Regulation (EU) 2024/1689) request several parameters to the AI process that provide the necessary documentation on datasets, algorithms, process, training, and testing. For these reasons, our methodology includes by-design these principles.

3 Related Work

The usage of NLP-based techniques in the legal domain in general and in the legislative domain in particular is an ever-increasing trend [10] as it allows researchers to investigate a multitude of different tasks for the legal domain. As observed in most NLP-related fields, the usage of Transformer-based models is now the de facto standard for many tasks [9]. More recently, the capabilities of LLMs have led to their increasing adoption in the legal domain, allowing the generation of text and the zero or few-shot classification of data from the legal

---

[4] http://data.europa.eu/eli/reg/2024/1689/oj.

domain. In this context, Retrieval-Augmented Generation (RAG) [11] is a technique that has been widely applied to mitigate the shortcomings of LLMs in various applications, such as the development of chatbots for conflict resolution [3] and conversational agents for answering legal questions [13,19]. This approach is crucial when dealing with legislative documents, as it allows the model to dynamically access the ever-changing legislative documents that are in force.

In the context of AI systems in support to the legislative-making process, Palmirani et al. [17] integrated AI-driven methodologies into the LEOS web editor, using embedding-based semantic similarity algorithms to suggest legal references and retrieve existing definitions. Specifically addressing legal definition retrieval and generation, Chouhan and Gertz [7] developed *LexDrafter*, a RAG-based framework that retrieves definitions from a collection of EUR-Lex documents. If no exact match is found, the system generates a definition using an LLM, enriching the generation prompt with contextual information. When multiple definitions exist for a term, a ranking strategy based on EuroVoc keywords selects the most relevant one. However, LexDrafter lacks filtering capabilities for retrieved definitions and is implemented as a set of terminal-based scripts, limiting accessibility for non-technical users. The system proposed in this work addresses these limitations by incorporating a more flexible retrieval strategy, filtering capabilities, and a conversational approach.

4   Legislative Definitions Dataset

The definitions used and retrieved by the proposed system are extracted from three XML-encoded datasets stored in an eXist-db database. a) *EurLex*: a dataset of EU Legislation documents in English, extracted from the EUR-Lex portal[5] and converted to the AKN format. 889 of the documents in the dataset have been enriched with definition annotations and metadata using a symbolic AI approach [4]; b) *Normattiva*: a dataset of 3,195 Italian legislative acts extracted from the Normattiva portal[6] and converted to the AKN format; c) *Progetti di Legge (PDL)*: a dataset of 3,709 Italian legislative bills from the 18th and 19th legislatures of the Italian Parliament, extracted from the official website of the Italian Parliament[7] and converted to the AKN format.

Legal definitions are extracted from the documents by iterating over each <definition> element in the metadata of the documents and using their href attributes to retrieve the definiendum and definiens from the body. For each definition entry, we also extract metadata from the source document, including the document's FRBR work and expression URIs, the document ID and the name of the dataset from which the definition was extracted. If the definition body contains external references, we extract the URIs of the referenced documents (i.e. the href attribute of each <ref> element in the definition body) and store them in the metadata of the definition entry. The extracted definitions undergo

---

[5] https://eur-lex.europa.eu/homepage.html.

[6] https://www.normattiva.it/.

[7] https://www.camera.it/.

filtering and formatting operations to ensure consistency. A full version of the definition text is constructed by concatenating the definiendum and definiens, separated by a colon. If the definition contains references, their URIs are resolved by querying the eXist-db database to retrieve the referenced text fragments, which are then appended to the string of the full definition.

The definitions are transformed into vector representations using BGE-M3 [6], a multilingual, multi-purpose model that can be used to perform hybrid retrieval. This approach leverages both dense embeddings and "learned" sparse embeddings, enabling a retrieval that considers both semantic-based similarity (dense) and lexical similarity (sparse). The resulting vectors of each definition, along with their metadata, are stored in a Milvus database [24], where two indexes are created: a FLAT index for dense embeddings and a *Sparse Inverted Index* for sparse embeddings.

5   System Architecture and Methods

The system is designed as a conversational AI agent built using the LangGraph framework[8]. When the user asks the system for the definition of a term, the agent identifies the relevant information in the natural language user query and uses it to activate the definition retrieval pipeline. This pipeline is responsible for retrieving relevant definitions, which are returned to the agent to process and generate an answer for the user.

5.1   Legislative Definition Retrieval Pipeline

The pipeline for the retrieval of relevant definitions is implemented in the form of an asynchronous function that takes as input the following parameters:

– the **user's question**, a string containing the text of the question asked by the user;
– the **definiendum**, a string specifying the term for which the user is requesting a definition;
– the **legislation filter**, a string indicating the legal framework to restrict the retrieved definitions to (allowed values are "EU" for the European Legislation an "IT" for the Italian legislation); the **date filter**, a string specifying a time range within which the retrieved definitions should have been in effect, which also supports open time intervals.

The two filters, legislation and date, are optional. If not provided, the pipeline will retrieve definitions without applying any filters. Once called by the agent, the function begins the process of retrieval by activating a pipeline composed by the following steps:

a) *Retrieval of Similar Definitions*: The most similar definitions to the input query are retrieved from the vector store. This is done using a hybrid

---

[8] https://github.com/langchain-ai/langgraph.

retrieval technique that leverages the two types of representations generated during the embedding phase (dense and sparse vectors) to rank definitions based on both their semantic similarity and lexical relevance to the query. The user's input question is first embedded into dense and sparse representations using the BGE-M3 model. Two simultaneous Approximate Nearest Neighbor (ANN) searches are then performed between each input embedding and the respective index of dense and sparse vectors, locating a subgroup of the k most similar definitions for each type. For dense retrieval, the metric used to calculate the similarity between the query and the definitions is the cosine similarity, while for sparse retrieval, the Inner Product (IP) is used. The scores of the two sets of results are normalized to a range between 0 and 1, and the final relevance score S of each definition is computed as the weighted average of the dense score S_d and sparse score S_s:

$$S = w_1 \cdot S_d + w_2 \cdot S_s \tag{1}$$

where w_1 and w_2 are the weights that balance the contribution of the dense and sparse score, respectively. k and the weights are hyperparameters that can be tuned. In the experimental settings of our system k was set to 10, and w_1, w_2 set to 1.0 and 0.7 respectively.

b) **Legislation Filtering**: The definitions retrieved in the previous step are filtered based on the legislation filter provided by the user. This is done by matching the dataset of provenance of each retrieved definition with the specified filter. Specifically, definitions from *EurLex* are classified as part of EU legislation, while definitions from *Normattiva* and *PDL* are mapped to the Italian legislation. If the filter is not specified, the pipeline proceeds to the next step without applying any filtering.

c) **Legislative Definition Timeline Construction**: To ensure that the system is able to take into consideration the most accurate and temporally relevant definitions, the pipeline constructs a timeline of the evolution of each definition using, based on the consolidated versions of the relevant documents. This is done by querying the eXist-db database to retrieve the consolidated versions of the documents containing the definitions using XQuery. For EU documents, the "Eurlex-Consolidated" supplementary dataset is queried, while for documents from Normattiva the original dataset is used. Documents from the PDL dataset do not have consolidated versions available. If a consolidated document is found, the definition from the earliest available version is retrieved, along with the corresponding FRBR expression date. Iterating through all the subsequent versions of the document, each version of the definition is compared with the previous oldest stored version. If a difference is detected, the definition is appended to the timeline along with the FRBR expression date of the version of the document from which it was extracted. This mechanism ensures that the timeline is populated with the date of the first appearance of each definition, along with the records of any modification made to it over time. If no consolidated version of the document is available, or if the definition cannot be found in the consolidated versions, the date and definition of the original document are added to the timeline.

c) *Date Filtering*: The timeline constructed in the previous step is used to filter the definitions based on the date filter provided by the user. This is done by matching the specified time range with the date of each entry in the timeline. Any timeline entry outside of the requested time range is removed, ensuring that only temporally valid definitions from the correct period are taken into account. If the filter is not specified, the pipeline proceeds to the next step without removing any entry.

d) *Keywords Retrieval*: For each remaining definition, keywords from the document from which the definition was extracted are retrieved from the eXist-db database using XQuery and stored in the metadata of the definition entry. Keywords are only available for the EurLex dataset, which uses terms from EuroVoc[9]. The Normattiva and PDL datasets do not have this information available.

e) *Definition Selection*: A list of the retrieved and filtered definitions are provided to the LLM, prompting it to select the most relevant ones in respect to the user's query. The prompt is constructed to give the LLM the persona of a legal expert specialized in legal drafting, and its objective is to return the ID of the most relevant definitions from the list provided. The model is also provided with the keywords retrieved in the previous step, and is instructed to rely on them as guide in case of ambiguity. Furthermore, shallow rules that help the model comply with the hierarchy of legal sources are provided, instructing it to prioritize definitions from the EU legislation in cases where multiple definitions from different legal frameworks might be relevant.

f) *Definition Generation*: If no relevant definition is found by the retrieval pipeline, the system resorts to generating a new definition for the requested term using the LLM. To ensure that the generated definition adheres to the legal standards and stylistic guidelines of the specific legal jurisdictions, two strategies are employed: first, the model's persona is set to that of a legal expert specialized in the relevant legal framework requested by the user (e.g. EU or Italian law). Second, we provide the model with the text of the 10 definitions retrieved from the initial step of the retrieval pipeline. These definitions serve as stylistic examples, guiding the model to mimic the structure, tone, and terminological choices appropriate to the chosen jurisdiction.

The output of the pipeline, either a set of retrieved definitions or a generated definition, is finally passed back to the agent, which can then provide it to the user as a response to their query in a structured and clear format. The agent is specifically instructed to, in case of a generated definition, provide the user with a disclaimer that the definition was generated by the system and may not be accurate or legally valid.

---

[9] https://eur-lex.europa.eu/browse/eurovoc.html.

5.2   Chatbot Application Architecture

The system is designed as a REST API service, and a browser-based chat interface built using the Streamlit framework[10] is also provided. The chat interface provides a comprehensive and transparent view of the system's internal process by displaying a widget that tracks inputs and outputs data of each component in the retrieval pipeline, allowing users to follow the filtering and selection steps applied to the retrieved definitions.

6   Experimental Settings

The LLM used to power the agent and the selection and generation steps in the evaluation phase of the system is Llama 3.3 70B Instruct, an open-weights, multilingual model from the LLama 3 family [1], which is capable of generating structured outputs and interacting with external tools. The evaluation was conducted using four datasets, tailored to assess the performance of the system's different components from both a quantitative and qualitative perspective.

6.1   Evaluation Datasets

LexDrafter Dataset: The dataset used to evaluate the LexDrafter framework [7]. It contains 1330 definitions covering 1007 terms that were extracted from a total of 108 legal acts from the Energy domain, crawled from the EUR-Lex portal. We split this dataset into two subsets, one containing the definitions of terms that are also in the system's own collection (696 terms), and the other containing definitions that the system would not be able to retrieve because not present in definitions dataset (634 terms). We use the first collection to test the reliability of the workflow, and the second to evaluate the quality of definition generation using automatic metrics;

Multi-legislation Dataset: We built this dataset to assess the system's ability to retrieve definitions that are present in multiple legislations. It consists of 20 definitions for 10 unique terms, each defined both in the EurLex dataset and in either Normattiva or PDL.

Point-in-Time Dataset: We built this dataset to evaluate the system's ability to retrieve definitions from a specific point in time. It includes definitions from the EurLex-Consolidated dataset that have undergone modifications over time.

Qualitative Dataset: This dataset was manually curated by legal experts. It contains 90 terms that are not explicitly defined in EU legislative documents, requiring the system to generate them. We use this dataset for qualitative evaluation of the definition generation component.

---

[10] https://streamlit.io/.

6.2 Quantitative Technical Evaluation

Table 1. Results of the system's workflow reliability assessment

(a) Failure rates for the definition retrieval pipeline

Failure source	Failure rate
Retrieval Failure Rate	2.01%
Generation Failure Rate	3.63%
Overall Failure Rate	2.78%

(b) Summary of the system's decision-making evaluation

Class	Acc	P	R	F1
Retrieval	–	90.53%	98.09%	94.16%
Generation	–	97.65%	88.54%	92.88%
Overall	90.98%	94,09%	93,31%	93,52%

(c) Summary of the automated generation metrics scores

Model	BLEU				ROUGE			BERTScore			BLEURT
	1	2	3	4	1	2	L	P	R	F1	
Ours	0.23	0.11	0.06	0.03	0.30	0.12	0.25	0.78	0.78	0.78	0.47
LD-LLaMa-2	0.25	0.13	0.07	0.04	–	–	–	0.83	0.81	0.82	0.47
LD-Vicuna	0.28	0.15	0.09	0.05	–	–	–	0.83	0.81	0.82	0.47

To assess the system's reliability, we conducted a series of technical evaluations using the LexDrafter dataset. Table 1a shows the failure rate reported by the system, calculated as the percentage of definitions for which the system failed to retrieve or generate a definition, instead returning an error. Table 1b shows the results of the evaluation of the accuracy of system's workflow, formulated as a classification task where the system is evaluated based on its decision to retrieve or generate a definition for a given term. We consider the system's decision to be correct if the system retrieves a definition when the term is present in the definitions dataset, or generates a definition when the term is not present. Table 1c shows the results of the evaluation of the generated definitions using automatic metrics, with LexDrafter's results for comparison. The metrics used are: BLEU [18], which measures the n-gram overlap between the generated and reference text to assess how closely the generated definitions follow the lexical choices of the references; ROUGE [12], which measures how many words or phrases from the reference appear in the generated definition; BERTScore [25], which computes the semantic similarity between the generated and reference definitions using contextual embeddings; and BLEURT [20], which provides a learned evaluation of the quality of the generated definitions by comparing them to the reference definitions using a fine-tuned BERT model.

6.3 Multi-legislation and Point-in-Time Evaluation

We use the Multi-legislation dataset to evaluate the system's ability to retrieve definitions of terms that are present in multiple legislations. Each of the 20 dataset entries is associated with a natural language query requesting the definition of a term within a specific legal framework. For entries from EurLex, the query follows the format: *"What is the definition of 'x' in the European Legislation?"*. For entries from the Italian datasets, the query is formulated as *"Quale è la definitione di 'x' nella legislazione Italiana?"*. We compute the coverage for this task as the proportion of queries for which the retrieved definition originates from the correct dataset. The results of this evaluation are reported in Table 2b.

The Point-in-Time dataset is used to evaluate the system's ability to retrieve definitions valid within a specified time range. The evaluation is conducted by querying the system with natural language questions derived from the dataset and comparing the retrieved definition's date with the reference date in the dataset entry. We compute the temporal coverage as the proportion of queries for which the system returned a definition whose date falls within the range specified in the query. The results of this evaluation are presented in Table 2a.

Table 2. Evaluation results for the temporal and multi-legislation filtering

(a) Point-in-time retrieval results		(b) Multi-legislation retrieval results	
Metric	Score	Metric	Score
Failure rate	2.43%	Failure rate	0%
Retrieval rate	87.80%	Retrieval rate	95%
Point-in-time coverage	87.80%	Multi-legislation coverage	95%

6.4 Qualitative Generation Evaluation

The automated metrics used in the previous section to assess the quality of the generated definitions are only able to provide a high-level evaluation of the system's performance in generating good definitions. BLEU and ROUGE can only provide an assessment of the lexical choices of the system, and while BERTScore and BLEURT enhance this measure by taking into account the semantic dimension of these choices, they still fail to capture elements such as legal validity, internal consistency, and alignment with established legal frameworks [14]. These aspects are crucial in the drafting of a correct legal definition, as even small deviations from standard practices can lead to significant misinterpretations of the legal content. For this reason, expert evaluation is essential. To address this, we conducted an expert-led evaluation using the Qualitative Dataset, in which experts were asked to evaluate the generated definitions by rating them on a scale from 1 to 5, from the perspective of 5 dimensions:

- **Accuracy**: Does the definition describe the correct legal content?
- **Contextual Appropriateness**: Is the definition appropriate for the specific legal domain and context?
- **Completeness**: Does the definition include all essential elements necessary to fully describe the legal concept?
- **Consistency**: Is the definition internally coherent and free from contradictions?
- **Timeliness**: Does the definition contain up-to-date information and references?

Additionally, two binary dimensions were evaluated:

- **Hallucination**: Does the definition contain any false or incorrect information, particularly in relation to the EU legislation?;
- **Irrelevance**: Does the definition include information that is irrelevant to the specific legal term being defined?

The average scores for each dimension across the 85 definitions in the dataset are presented in Table 3a. Table 3b shows the percentage of cases where each of the two binary evaluation criteria are present. Fig 1 shows the evaluation of each generated definition in a heatmap.

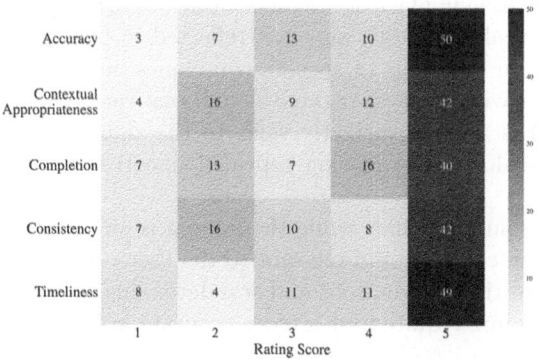

Fig. 1. Heatmap of the qualitative evaluation.

Table 3. Qualitative evaluation results for the generation of legal definitions

(a) Average scores for each dimension

Metric	Mean Score
Accuracy	4.16
Contextual Appropriateness	3.86
Completeness	3.83
Consistency	3.74
Timeliness	4.07

(b) Hallucination and irrelevance rates

Metric	Rate
Hallucination Rate	6.02%
Irrelevance Rate	1.20%

7 Discussion

7.1 Evaluation Results Analysis

The evaluation results indicate that the system's workflow is quite robust, with a low overall failure rate and a high accuracy in deciding whether to retrieve or generate a new definition.

The qualitative analysis by legal experts revealed some limitations in the system's ability to generate legally sound definitions. While the generated definitions are generally complete in their content, they frequently include examples to illustrate the concepts evoked by the definiendum, a practice generally discouraged in legal drafting, as it narrows the definition's scope and limits judicial interpretation. The general tone of the definitions tends to be more informal than typical legal texts, often using colloquial language and less formal legal terminology. This likely stems from the model's training data, which is not sufficiently grounded in legal sources. The narrow scope of the model's legal capabilities is further reflected in the way it handles specific legal concepts, struggling with more abstract terms (e.g. "Cooperation") and EU-specific terminology (e.g. "Country" is often used in place of "Member State"). Furthermore, legal principles such as technological neutrality were not reflected in the generated definitions, which often contain mentions of specific companies or products. The accuracy of legal references within the generated definitions varies significantly. In some cases, the model is able to correctly refer to the right legal sources, while in others, it fails to do so, referencing repealed, incorrect, or even non-existent sources.

These findings suggest that, while the system is able to generate structured definitions that are coherent and relevant to the user's query, it does not always adhere to legal drafting conventions and standards, highlighting the lack of necessary legal grounding required for a more accurate legal applicability.

7.2 Conclusions and Future Research

In this paper, we presented a system designed to assist in the retrieval and drafting of legislative definitions, potentially reducing the time and effort involved in drafting definition articles and promoting the reuse of existing legislative definitions. The system functions as a conversational agent, enabling natural language interactions with users. Its retrieval pipeline employs a hybrid search approach that combines dense and sparse embeddings to leverage semantic and lexical matching. Built upon a multilingual collection of documents, the system is capable of retrieving definitions in both Italian and English, and incorporates filtering by legislation and point-in-time retrieval. The evaluation of the generated definitions highlighted certain limitations in aligning general-purpose LLMs with best practices in legislative drafting, suggesting that the usage of fine-tuned models tailored to the legislative domain may be necessary for improved accuracy and consistency. The qualitative evaluation of the definitions generated by the system has shown that the model struggles with producing definitions that are legally sound, thus limiting the system's applicability to real-world legislative drafting processes. Future developments should focus on improving the quality of generated definitions by experimenting with legally grounded LLMs and integrating better solutions for handling normative references and compliance with the hierarchy of legal sources. Additionally, the evaluation has primarily focused on English-language EU legislation, and further assessment should be conducted to evaluate the system's capabilities in processing Italian legal documents. Our future goal is also to extend the research to better qualify the different types of definitions (e.g., technical, exceptions, membership) and to provide more precise instructions (using prompt) to the Agentic AI to cope with the specific pattern of definition expected by the end-user during the legal drafting. The ultimate scope of this research is to support legal drafting of legislative definitions while minimizing conflicts of norms, respecting the hierarchy of legal sources, and avoiding duplications.

Acknowledgment. This project is conducted with the support of the European Commission funds within ERC HyperModeLex. Grant agreement ID: 101055185.

References

1. AI@Meta: Llama 3 model card (2024). https://github.com/meta-llama/llama3/blob/main/MODEL_CARD.md
2. Alchourrón, C.E., Bulygin, E.: Normative Systems. Springer Verlag (1994)
3. Amato, F., Fonisto, M., Giacalone, M., Sansone, C.: An Intelligent Conversational Agent for the Legal Domain. Information **14**(6), 307 (2023). https://doi.org/10.3390/info14060307
4. Asif, M., Palmirani, M.: Legal definition annotation in EU legislation using symbolic AI. In: Kö, A., Kotsis, G., Tjoa, A.M., Khalil, I. (eds.) Electronic Government and the Information Systems Perspective, pp. 34–39. Springer, Cham (2024). https://doi.org/10.1007/978-3-031-68211-7_4
5. Bix, B.: Kelsen, Hart, and Legal Normativity. Revus. Journal for Constitutional Theory and Philosophy of Law / Revija Za Ustavno Teorijo in Filozofijo Prava **34**, 25–42 (2018)
6. Chen, J., Xiao, S., Zhang, P., Luo, K., Lian, D., Liu, Z.: BGE M3-Embedding: Multi-Lingual, Multi-Functionality, Multi-Granularity Text Embeddings Through Self-Knowledge Distillation, June 2024. https://doi.org/10.48550/arXiv.2402.03216
7. Chouhan, A., Gertz, M.: LexDrafter: terminology drafting for legislative documents using retrieval augmented generation. In: Calzolari, N., Kan, M.Y., Hoste, V., Lenci, A., Sakti, S., Xue, N. (eds.) Proceedings of the 2024 Joint International Conference on Computational Linguistics, Language Resources and Evaluation (LREC-COLING 2024), pp. 10448–10458. ELRA and ICCL, Torino, Italia, May 2024. https://aclanthology.org/2024.lrec-main.913/
8. European Commission: Joint Practical Guide of the European Parliament, the Council and the Commission for Persons Involved in the Drafting of European Union Legislation. Publications Office of the European Union (2015). https://doi.org/10.2880/5575
9. Greco, C.M., Tagarelli, A.: Bringing order into the realm of transformer-based language models for artificial intelligence and law. Artificial Intelligence and Law, pp. 1–148 (2023)
10. Katz, D.M., Hartung, D., Gerlach, L., Jana, A., II, M.J.B.: Natural Language Processing in the Legal Domain (2023). https://arxiv.org/abs/2302.12039
11. Lewis, P., et al.: Retrieval-augmented generation for knowledge-intensive NLP tasks. In: Proceedings of the 34th International Conference on Neural Information Processing Systems. NIPS '20. Curran Associates Inc., Red Hook (2020)

12. Lin, C.Y.: ROUGE: A Package for Automatic Evaluation of Summaries. In: Text Summarization Branches Out, pp. 74–81. Association for Computational Linguistics, Barcelona, Spain (Jul 2004)

13. Mamalis, M.E., Kalampokis, E., Fitsilis, F., Theodorakopoulos, G., Tarabanis, K.: A large language model agent based legal assistant for governance applications. In: Janssen, M., et al. (eds.) Electronic Government, pp. 286–301. Springer, Cham (2024). https://doi.org/10.1007/978-3-031-70274-7_18

14. Palmirani, M., Sapienza, S., Ashley, K.: A hybrid artificial intelligence methodology for legal analysis. BioLaw Journal-Rivista di BioDiritto **3**, 389–409 (2024)

15. Palmirani, M., Sovrano, F., Liga, D., Sapienza, S., Vitali, F.: Hybrid AI framework for legal analysis of the EU legislation corrigenda. In: Legal Knowledge and Information Systems, pp. 68–75. IOS Press (2021)

16. Palmirani, M., Sperberg, R., Vergottini, G., Vitali, F.: Akoma Ntoso Version 1.0 Part 1: XML Vocabulary. Tech. rep., OASIS Standard, August 2018. http://docs.oasis-open.org/legaldocml/akn-core/v1.0/akn-core-v1.0-part1-vocabulary.html

17. Palmirani, M., Vitali, F., Longo, G., Sante, E.D., Brega, A., D'Arpa, A., Corazza, M.: Legal drafting supported by AI: enhancing LEOS. In: Martino, S.D., Sansone, C., Masciari, E., Rossi, S., Gravina, M. (eds.) Proceedings of the Ital-IA Intelligenza Artificiale - Thematic Workshops. CEUR Workshop Proceedings, vol. 3762, pp. 482–487. CEUR, Naples, Italy, May 2024

18. Papineni, K., Roukos, S., Ward, T., Zhu, W.J.: Bleu: a method for automatic evaluation of machine translation. In: Isabelle, P., Charniak, E., Lin, D. (eds.) Proceedings of the 40th Annual Meeting of the Association for Computational Linguistics, pp. 311–318. Association for Computational Linguistics, Philadelphia, Pennsylvania, USA, July 2002. https://doi.org/10.3115/1073083.1073135

19. Queudot, M., Charton, E., Meurs, M.J.: Improving Access to Justice with Legal Chatbots **3**(3), 356–375. https://doi.org/10.3390/stats3030023, https://www.mdpi.com/2571-905X/3/3/23

20. Sellam, T., Das, D., Parikh, A.: BLEURT: learning robust metrics for text generation. In: Jurafsky, D., Chai, J., Schluter, N., Tetreault, J. (eds.) Proceedings of the 58th Annual Meeting of the Association for Computational Linguistics, pp. 7881–7892. Association for Computational Linguistics, Online, July 2020. https://doi.org/10.18653/v1/2020.acl-main.704

21. Tillett, B.: What is FRBR? a conceptual model for the bibliographic universe. Australian Library J. **54** (2005). https://doi.org/10.1080/00049670.2005.10721710

22. Vitali, F., Palmirani, M., Parisse, V.: Akoma Ntoso Naming Convention Version 1.0. Tech. rep., OASIS Standard, May 2016. https://docs.oasis-open.org/legaldocml/akn-nc/v1.0/csprd02/akn-nc-v1.0-csprd02.html

23. Vitali, F., Palmirani, M., Sperberg, R., Parisse, V.: Akoma Ntoso Version 1.0. Part 2: Specifications. Tech. rep., OASIS Standard, August 2018. http://docs.oasis-open.org/legaldocml/akn-core/v1.0/akn-core-v1.0-part2-specs.html

24. Wang, J., et al.: Milvus: a purpose-built vector data management system. In: Proceedings of the 2021 International Conference on Management of Data, pp. 2614–2627 (2021)

25. Zhang, T., Kishore, V., Wu, F., Weinberger, K.Q., Artzi, Y.: BERTScore: evaluating text generation with BERT, February 2020. https://doi.org/10.48550/arXiv.1904.09675

Decentralized Auction System for Tangible Assets and Its Application

Minh Tuan Le[1]([⊠])(iD), Do Thi Hong Hanh[2], Nguyen Trong Hung[2],
Do Phuong Nhung[1], Dang Khanh Hoa[1], Pham Thanh Cong[3],
Dang Hai Dang[1], and Nguyen Hoai Giang[1]

[1] Faculty of Electrical and Electronic Engineering, Hanoi Open University,
Hanoi, Vietnam
`lmtuan@hou.edu.vn`
[2] Lac Viet Auction Technology, Hanoi, Vietnam
[3] School of Electronics and Electrical, Hanoi University of Science and Technology,
Hanoi, Vietnam
`https://lacvietauction.vn`

Abstract. Most auction organizers currently rely on a centralized model for their online systems, acting as intermediaries and controlling the entire auction process. This results in human intervention in platform management, a lack of transparency and trust, high fees, and single points of failure. To address these issues, we propose a decentralized auction system by leveraging blockchain technology. Our solution builds auction functionalities on Binance Smart Chain, using ERC-721 NFTs for asset representation, IPFS for decentralized storage, and Chainlink oracles for external data verification. This paper presents the first blockchain-based auction solution fully compliant with Vietnam's legal framework for tangible state-owned assets. We applied this system to auction Vietnam's state-owned tangible assets, including vehicles and apartment units. Experiments demonstrated high participant satisfaction regarding fairness and legitimacy. Our findings suggest that blockchain-based decentralized auction systems enhance trust and transparency in real-world applications.

Keywords: decentralized · blockchain · auction · state-owned asset · NFT

1 Introduction

The evolution of auction services from traditional physical formats to digital platforms has transformed the way assets are bought and sold. The transformation has solved some limitations of the in-person auction service, but it has also introduced new challenges [1]. Most existing online auction systems are based on a client-server architecture, closed-source code and operate under a centralized governance model. This centralized model lacks transparency and fairness.

A. Kő et al. (Eds.): EGOVIS 2025, LNCS 16049, pp. 205–210, 2026.
https://doi.org/10.1007/978-3-032-02225-7_14

As a result, bidder trust and security are significantly compromised. Yet, trust, security, and fairness are critical elements in auction environments. One of the solutions is to leverage blockchain technology and smart contracts, which provide a decentralized and programmable environment that enhances security and trust in auction systems.

The first notable effort was the successful tokenization and auction of artwork on the Ethereum blockchain, which began in 2018 [2]. Since then, blockchain technology and smart contracts have emerged as a robust solution for reliable decentralized auction systems. Several decentralized systems have been developed for the auction of intangible assets, including energy trading [3], NFTs [4], sensing data [5], computing and spectrum resources [6,7]. The industry-leading auction houses, such as Sotheby's, Christie's and Millon, are actively engaged with blockchain technology through initiatives for secure and trustworthy auctions in digital art market use case [8–10]. However, these studies focus on digital and intangible assets while failing to consider statutory requirements, thereby leaving a research gap for tangible public asset auctions. To the best of our knowledge, no prior study has designed and implemented a decentralized auction system for state-owned tangible assets. To fill this gap, we develop a legally compliant blockchain-based auction system, specifically designed for tangible public assets within the context of Vietnam's statutory regulations.

The paper is structured as follows: Sect. 2 describes our decentralized auction system with a real-world application: auctioning Vietnam's state-owned assets. Section 3 summarizes conclusions and directions for future development.

2   Solution and System Architecture

2.1   Solution

The auction of state-owned assets in Vietnam is governed by a robust legal framework, primarily the Law on Property Auction 2016, supplemented by recent regulations such as Decree 50/2025/ND-CP and Decree 172/2024/ND-CP. The auction process must comply with these laws to ensure transparency, fair valuation, and efficient management of public assets, especially for online auctions. To overcome challenges in both the auction service industry and regulatory compliance, we propose a hybrid approach in which core auction functionalities (such as NFT minting, smart contract execution, bidding procedures, and auction logic) are implemented on a blockchain network (on-chain). This creates a secure and transparent environment for auction interactions (see Fig. 1). On-chain smart contracts are open-source and automatically self-execute to determine the winning bid, ensuring fair auction results. There are seven primary roles in the approach: (1) Auction Organizer (AO, also known as Auctioneer): The entity managing the auction. (2) State Agency (SA): State asset owner representative who delegates sales function to the AO. (3) Bidders (B): Participants submitting bids. (4) Winner (W): Successful bidder acquiring the asset. (5) Storage System (SS): Decentralized storage for asset metadata. (6) Oracle Network (OR): External data verifiers for real-world parameters and (7) Smart contracts: Code for auctions is automatically executed on-chain.

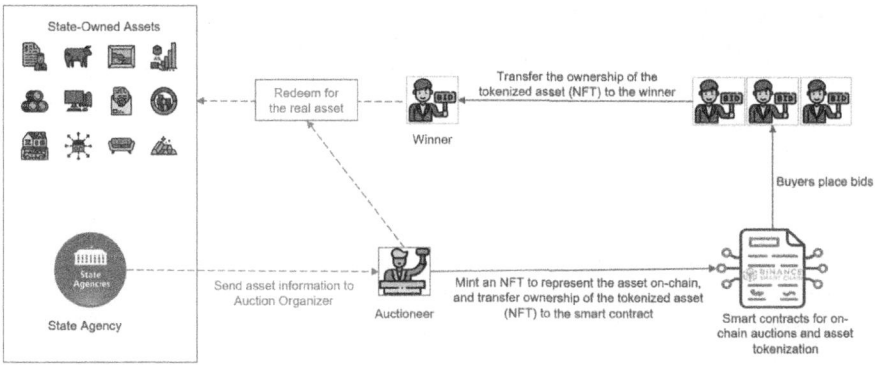

Fig. 1. Hybrid approach to state-owned auction service (Green: Off-Chain, Blue: On-Chain). (Color figure online)

2.2 System Architecture

We designed a multi-component system by integrating front ends, blockchain smart contracts, decentralized storage, and the oracle network (Fig. 2). It operates on Binance Smart Chain (BSC) for on-chain functionality, with IPFS for off-chain data storage [11], Chainlink oracles for external data verification [12]. The front-end, where the bidder and the auctioneer can view and interact with smart contracts, was developed using technologies such as HTML, CSS, and JavaScript. Smart contracts form the core of the system and were developed using Solidity 0.8.17 via Remix, an online IDE that supports the deployment, debugging, and testing of EVM-compatible smart contracts on BSC [13]. As most state-owned tangible assets (pre-owned vehicles and real estate units) are unique, they are digitized as non-fungible tokens (NFTs) using the ERC-721 standard. Figure 3 shows a detailed sequence diagram that illustrates how these components work together.

2.3 Results and Discussion

The proposed system was publicly deployed and successfully applied to the sale of two pre-owned vehicles and two apartment units [14]. A follow-up survey showed that, among the 313 qualified bidders, 204 participants reported a generally positive experience interacting with the system. All respondents agreed that the auction process was fair and legitimate. These findings suggest that blockchain-based auction systems can foster trust between participants. However, challenges related to user experience remain. Table 1 presents a summary of the experimental results, key issues identified, their implications, and proposed solutions for future development.

However, the scope of the current study is limited by the number of assets, participants and the duration of the testing period. Future research should include larger-scale deployments to comprehensively validate the system's performance.

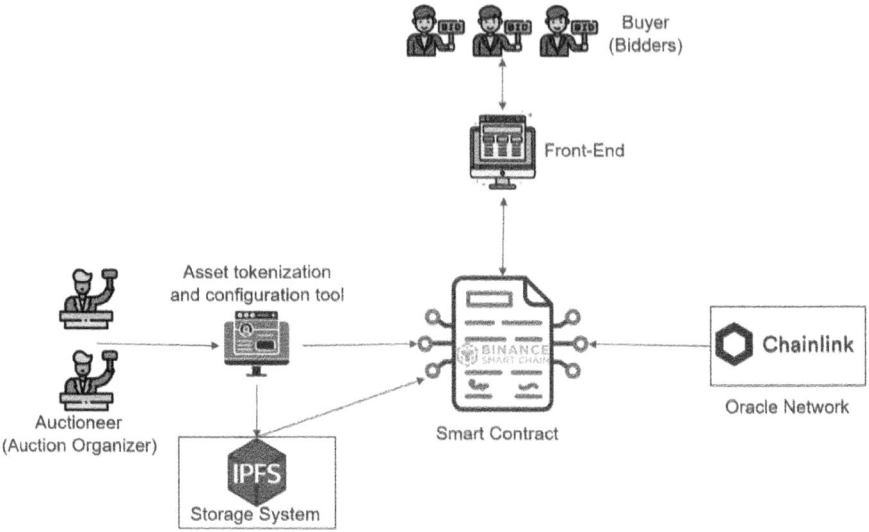

Fig. 2. Our System Architecture.

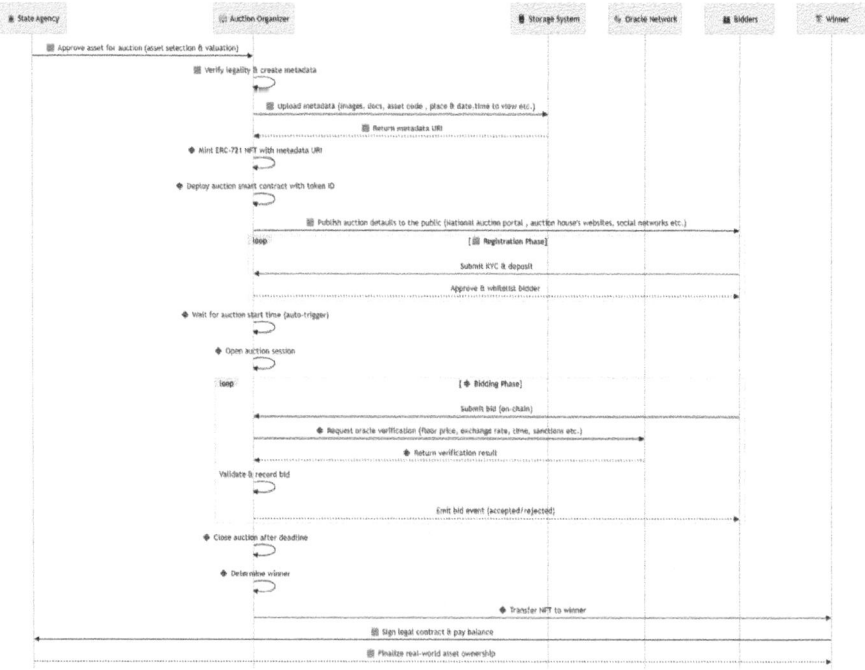

Fig. 3. Sequence diagram for state-owned asset auction.

Table 1. Key issues for future development.

Problem (User adoption)	Effect (on the auction platform and user experience)	Solution (Build on Layer-2 instead of Layer-1 networks like BSC or Ethereum)
Low transaction throughput may become a critical limitation for high-volume bidder interactions in future auction systems.	Frustrates users, disrupts bidding flow, and discourages participation in large-scale auctions.	Layer-2 offers higher throughput by processing transactions off-chain while maintaining Layer-1 security.
Transaction finality time is slow: 3 to 7.5 s in our experiment.	Slow transaction finality may disrupt the auction flow, potentially diminishing the overall bidder experience.	Layer-2 improves finality with near-instant confirmation, enabling real-time bidding.
Transaction costs in our experiment were approximately $0.30 per bid, indicating potential for further cost reduction.	High bidding fees adversely affect auction outcomes by reducing organizers' profits and raising entry barriers for bidders.	Layer-2 reduces transaction costs through off-chain processing, keeping fees low, even at high volumes.

3   Conclusion

In this paper, we present our approach to the digital transformation of auctions in Vietnam, including an overview of our decentralized auction system and its application to a real-world use case: auctioning tangible state-owned assets. By integrating blockchain technologies into the auction system, we enhance security and trust, making the auction service fundamentally fairer and more transparent. This approach redefines the mechanisms for buying and selling tangible assets via on-chain auctions while ensuring compliance with Vietnamese auction laws and regulations. To our best knowledge, this study represents the first blockchain-based implementation specifically designed to auction legally regulated tangible state-owned assets in Vietnam. Furthermore, we have identified novel challenges within this decentralized auction system, analyzed their impact on participants, and proposed potential solutions for future research and development.

Future Work. We aim to expand the system's capabilities by integrating zero-knowledge proof mechanisms to ensure bidder privacy. Additionally, integration with Vietnam's e-government platform, such as VNeID, could facilitate faster user onboarding. We also plan to improve the scalability by using Ethereum Layer-2 rollups or by migrating to alternative high-performance Layer-1 blockchains such as Solana, Aptos or Algorand. Another approach for achieving high-performance auctions is to build an application-specific chain on multi-chain Layer-1 platforms, such as Cosmos, Polkadot, or Avalanche.

Acknowledgments. This study was funded by the Lac Viet Auction Partnership Company and KOET Co., Ltd.

References

1. Shi, Z., de Laat, C., Grosso, P., Zhao, Z.: Integration of blockchain and auction models: a survey, some applications, and challenges. IEEE Commun. Surv. Tutor. **25**(1), 497–537 (2023)
2. Emem, M.: Andy Warhol's Multi-Million Dollar Painting Tokenized and Sold on Blockchain. https://finance.yahoo.com/news/andy-warhol-multi-million-dollar-162928721.html. Accessed 1 June 2025
3. Wang, N., Zhou, X., Lu, X., Guan, Z., Wu, L., Du, X., Guizani, M.: When energy trading meets blockchain in electrical power system: the state of the art. Appl. Sci. **9**(8) (2019)
4. Xiao, B.: NFT auction: implementing smart contracts for decentralized transactions. Appl. Comput. Eng. **53**, 9–18 (2024)
5. Steubs, R., Chen, Y., Tang, B.: A truthful and efficient auction mechanism for data preservation in base station-less sensor networks. In: Proc. IEEE Int. Conf. Commun. (ICC 2025) (2025)
6. Jain, V., Kumar, B.: Auction-based cost-efficient resource allocation by utilizing blockchain in fog computing. Trans. Emerg. Telecommun. Technol. **33**(7), e4430 (2022)
7. Zhang, H., Liu, M., Chen, Y., Zhao, N.: Blockchain and timely auction mechanism-based spectrum management. Future Gener. Comput, Syst (2025)
8. Christie's NFT Homepage. httpo://nft.christies.com/. Accessed 1 June 2025
9. Neuendorf, H.: Christie's Will Become the First Major Auction House to Use Blockchain in a Sale. https://news.artnet.com/market/christies-artory-blockchain-pilot-1370788. Accessed 1 June 2025
10. Leading Auction House Millon to Use Arteïa and Tezos Blockchain to Authenticate Art Sales (2023). https://xtz.news/authentication/leading-auction-house-millon-to-use-arteia-and-tezos-blockchain-to-authenticate-art-sales/
11. InterPlanetary File System Homepage. https://ipfs.tech. Last accessed 1 June 2025
12. Chainlink Homepage. https://chain.link. Accessed 1 June 2025
13. Remix IDE Homepage. https://remix.ethereum.org. Accessed 1 June 2025
14. Lac Viet Auction Homepage. https://lacvietauction.vn. Accessed 1 June 2025

A European Student eCard in the Context of the European Digital Identity Wallet

Tamas Molnar[1]($\boxtimes$) (iD) and Andrea Kő[2] (iD)

[1] Humboldt-Universität zu Berlin, 10099 Berlin, Germany
tamas.molnar@cms.hu-berlin.de
[2] Corvinus University Budapest, Budapest 1093, Hungary
andrea.ko@uni-corvinus.hu

Abstract. In recent years, multiple EU initiatives have been initiated to create an EU-wide compatibility for student IDs. We have been part of these projects since 2017 and created a best practice through these, which is based on our solution for the Campuscard Berlin. This includes the integration of components developed for the EDSSI L2 project, the internally developed Campuscard App, and the European Digital Wallet. We will demonstrate with this paper how large universities can adopt these emerging technologies effectively.

Keywords: Digital Identity · NFC · Smartcards

1 Introduction - The Road to a Common European Student eID

All stakeholders emphasize the importance of digital processes in students' mobility, especially in Erasmus. Digital processes simplify, speed up, and make mobility administration less costly and complex, while boosting the mobile student experience. They also improve traceability and support data exchange.

The European Student Card Initiative is a key initiative to enrich the European dimension in higher education and research. It has three main building blocks: Erasmus Without Paper, Erasmus+App, and the European Student Card. The Erasmus Without Paper (EWP) supports universities in implementing the digitalization roadmap and enables higher education institutions to exchange information on their students' mobility quickly and securely. Additional benefits are that it provides a digital workflow and a free public infrastructure for the participating Higher Education Institutes. The EWP journey started in 2013 and achieved several important milestones, like the EWP) launch conference in 2018, the technical testing of the Inter-Institutional Agreements (IIA) with the EWP Dashboard (Erasmus Dashboard) or the discussion on the future of digital Erasmus with key stakeholders in Spring 2025, which aims to collect needs, concerns, and ideas regarding the Erasmus+processes digitalization. [1] Erasmus+App offers a single point of entry for students into the Erasmus+program. The European Student Card provides a common European identity for higher education students. Students can get their student status verified easily across Europe with their European Student Card. [2] The Campuscard Alliance in Berlin was one of the pivotal partners in developing the European

© The Author(s), under exclusive license to Springer Nature Switzerland AG 2026
A. Kő et al. (Eds.): EGOVIS 2025, LNCS 16049, pp. 211–217, 2026.
https://doi.org/10.1007/978-3-032-02225-7_15

Student Card initiative in the last decade. With the development of a common ID system for universities in Berlin, at that time, which was the largest unified operating system in Europe, with a very high level of automation. The Campuscard Alliance in Berlin was founded by six universities in 2015 to create a standardised student ID system to supersede the obsolete paper-based IDs used by the institutions. [3] In this project, we created a self-service-based approach, where a large number of students could be handled based on a streamlined issuing process. As there were no solutions readily available on the market for the requirements issued by the universities, we developed all the components in-house, including the complete software stack, and even the composition and design of the hardware used in the card issuing and validation terminals. This enabled a 24/7 usable self-service approach, where over 140,000 student IDs could be issued with only a fraction of personnel required compared to competing traditional systems. As the transportation ticket on the ID makes it necessary to revalidate the cards each semester, we included a thermo-rewrite printer-based kiosk. These machines enable the 140,000 users to print their tickets onto the card each semester and allow the universities to have an automated process, which requires very little personnel. The development of the system was finished in 2018, and with the joining of four additional institutions, it became the largest unified student ID system in Europe. Since then, we have improved this service progressively and in 2019 started the development of the next generation of student IDs, a Campuscard App. One of the cornerstones of the development was the reuse of the existing infrastructure as much as possible, making the transition from physical cards to eCards in a cost-efficient fashion. In the case of Berlin, and as we later see, also for a large number of other HEIs (Higher Education Institution), this means that the NFC infrastructure has to be taken into account. Currently, a large number of HEIs in Europe build their student service infrastructure around NFC, mainly on the Mifare Desfire platform, which makes transitioning to an app a challenging task. The new Campuscard App was built in a way that it can fully replace the physical card and runs on both mobile platforms, iOS and Android. As with earlier systems, we had to make sure that the app works with the existing infrastructure without major modifications necessary. This means that for Berlin, the app must communicate with the Elatec TWN 4 NFC readers. In addition, data privacy has to be the highest priority, with no personal data transferred to third parties such as Apple or Google, not only to comply with the GDPR, but also to ensure good acceptance of the new app. Through these factors, it became clear relatively quickly that the existing technology on the market will not be sufficient to tick all boxes, and we will have to do several "firsts" during the project. In Berlin, the students use their cards for three main NFC-based services: transportation tickets, closed-loop payment at the canteens and identification for library access. Apart from the system behind the transportation ticket, where a smartphone solution was being developed by an umbrella organization of transportation providers in Germany [4], we had to create a completely new solution. This meant that we created a project where we built an app in multiple phases, where we could address the problems sequentially. First, the groundwork of the app was constructed, which included all basic features required by the app. These are the image of the card, the European Campuscard integration, and all support features. Then, in a second phase, the NFC component was integrated into the app. Our approach to addressing these issues was twofold. Our goal in Berlin is to create an app for our Berlin Campuscard Alliance, which can replace the current physical cards one-on-one, and we aspire to develop a system that can be reused throughout Europe and also by other HEIs who face similar problems as we did some years ago. We have therefore channeled our app development also into the EDSSI L2 (European Digital Student Service Infrastructure) project, where one of the main goals was the creation of a tech demo on TR Level [5], which has shown the feasibility of the approach for multiple HEIs throughout Europe. Additionally, from 2024 onwards a new goal has been set for all eGovernment systems in Europe, the integration of the European Digital Identity Wallet. This system is envisioned by the European Commission to be the common link and the ultimate digital identity to unify all identity documents in Europe. This also includes student cards and all their use cases. This paper aims to provide an overview of the European Student eCard journey, in the context of the European Digital Identity Wallet and focuses on a real-world approach applied by the Campuscard Alliance in Berlin. We highlight challenges, addressing the gaps in development while providing practical guidelines and examples for implementing this comprehensive framework in real-world practices. This paper is structured as follows. Section 1 provides an overview of the evolution of the European Student Card initiative implementation by the Campuscard Alliance in Berlin. Section 2 details the European Digital Identity Wallet, while Sect. 3 presents its challenges. Section 4 introduces the case based on the new European Digital Identity Wallet technology. The conclusion is summarized in Sect. 4.

2 The European Digital Identity Wallet

The European Digital Identity Wallet is a key initiative of the European Union aimed at providing EU citizens, residents, and businesses with a secure, standardized, and interoperable digital identity solution. It is part of the broader European Digital Identity Framework, proposed by the European Commission to enhance trust, security, and convenience in digital interactions across the EU. This wallet infrastructure is designed to allow individuals and businesses to securely store and share personal identification and credentials, such as passports, driver's licenses, diplomas, financial data and student credentials. It is expected to function as a mobile application, which allows users to store government-issued documents digitally, authenticate and sign documents electronically, verify their identity when accessing online and offline services and control which personal data is shared with third parties. In the case of universities, this will mean that most documents, which are currently issued either in a digital or paper form, can be integrated into a common EU-wide compatible system, which solves many issues on a theoretical level. The integration of the Digital Wallet into our existing card management system, which we developed for the card system, offers an opportunity to enhance security, interoperability, and efficiency within academic institutions. As the European Union moves towards a unified digital identity framework, universities must adapt their existing infrastructures to support digital credentials while ensuring compliance with privacy and security standards. Identity management (IdM) in higher education institutions typically relies on centralized identity providers (IdPs) and authentication protocols such as SAML (Security Assertion Markup Language) or OAuth 2.0. With the introduction of the Digital Wallet infrastructure, systems must support decentralized identity verification while maintaining compatibility with traditional card management architectures. The Digital Wallet is based on self-sovereign identity (SSI) principles, allowing students to retain control over their personal data and selectively disclose credentials as needed [6]. To facilitate integration, universities must establish interoperability between the Digital Wallet and their existing IdPs. This involves mapping wallet-based verifiable credentials (VCs) to existing student records in the card management. The Verifiable Credential Data Model [7] provides a standardized approach for representing identity attributes, which can be utilized to ensure seamless authentication across both digital and physical interfaces. However, integrating this model requires modifications to identity federation mechanisms and trust frameworks within academic institutions. The technical integration of the Digital Wallet into the card management system necessitates a hybrid architecture combining existing smart card infrastructures with digital identity frameworks. A layered approach can be employed, where the physical student ID card continues to function for legacy systems while the Digital Wallet enables advanced digital interactions, such as secure online authentication and digital signing of academic documents. [8] One key consideration is ensuring compatibility with authentication standards such as the European Digital Identity [9]regulation, which mandates the mutual recognition of digital identities across EU member states. The Digital Wallet must be integrated with the institution's identity provider using OpenID Connect or other federated identity protocols. Additionally, blockchain-based distributed ledgers can be leveraged for credential verification, ensuring immutability and trustworthiness of student identity claims. From a system design perspective, a modular approach is recommended, where APIs facilitate communication between the Digital Wallet, the card management, and external authentication services. Secure enclaves or hardware security modules (HSMs) can be deployed to manage cryptographic keys associated with digital credentials, ensuring compliance with the General Data Protection Regulation (GDPR) and other privacy frameworks. [10] Integrating the Digital Wallet into a student ID solution requires addressing several security and privacy concerns. One of the main challenges is ensuring data sovereignty while preventing unauthorized access to student information. Zero-knowledge proofs (ZKPs) offer a potential solution, allowing students to authenticate their identity without revealing unnecessary personal details. Another critical aspect is mitigating identity fraud and unauthorized credential issuance. A robust identity verification process must be established, incorporating biometric authentication or multi-factor authentication (MFA) to enhance security. Institutions should also implement continuous monitoring and anomaly detection mechanisms to identify and respond to potential threats in real time. Furthermore, adherence to the principle of minimal disclosure is essential to ensure compliance with GDPR. Students should have granular control over which attributes they share with third parties, utilizing attribute-based access control (ABAC) models to enforce privacy-preserving policies. Following these theoretical considerations, our approach is a phased implementation. This is advisable to ensure a smooth transition from the traditional card management system, in our case the KMS3 (trade name for our card management system), to a new Digital Wallet enabled solution, which will offer the full potential of this new technology. Initially, universities can conduct pilot projects in controlled environments to evaluate the feasibility and user experience of digital wallet-based authentication. These pilots should involve extensive user testing to identify potential usability and security concerns before full-scale deployment. We plan to start with a pilot implementation of the enhanced KMS3 card management solution later this year to show that the digital wallet can be integrated into existing systems of universities and offer a technology for other public institutions. As adoption grows, institutions should explore advanced use cases, such as integrating the Digital Wallet with learning management systems (LMS), library access, and digital payments. The long-term vision includes a fully interoperable digital ecosystem where students can seamlessly interact with both academic and non-academic services using their digital credentials. In conclusion, the integration of the European Digital Wallet into an existing student ID card management system represents a significant advancement in digital identity management. By leveraging standardized protocols, privacy-preserving technologies, and interoperability frameworks, academic institutions can enhance security, streamline administrative processes, and empower students with greater control over their digital identities. Future research should focus on refining implementation strategies, addressing scalability challenges, and exploring additional use cases for digital identity in higher education.

3   Challenges of the Wallet

Technological development is well-defined, with multiple organizations at both national and European levels planning to offer services using this technology starting in 2026. However, in our experience, which we gathered from the development and operation of a large-scale system for 10 years, there are several open questions regarding the future acceptance of the system by the actual users. We have the integration of the wallet in our roadmap and will give the students the possibility from 2026 to use this wallet technology for their student IDs. This will offer several benefits for them. The main block for EU-wide compatibility will be removed, and student IDs can be seamlessly used between different institutions, giving students unprecedented access to services. The main question remains, which we will have to solve for a successful operation, how to optimize the acceptance of the wallet so that students will transition from the physical cards to this new system. This is not only imperative so that technology can be used to its full potential, but also important, because the wallet system is a tremendous cost saver for universities. It seems to be a strange hypothesis that a cohort like students might have a low acceptance rate of new technologies, but in our experience, this is very much an issue, particularly when dealing with systems that might transfer personal data to third parties. In the case of the digital wallet, this is an issue by its design, where the personal data is either transferred to the government-issued app or Google or Apple Wallet. It is also clear that, because of legal limitations, higher education institutions cannot, as of now, make the use of this system compulsory and will have to offer a solution for students refusing it. This makes acceptance a major issue and can be show stopper if not solved at an early point of the system integration.

We will try to mitigate this by quantifying the user acceptance with the appropriate usability frameworks, like the Technology Acceptance Model (TAM) and the ISO-9241. There are also further questions which will have to be solved for a successful rollout of the system. As of now, it is unknown who will supply the digital wallet app, which can be used to display the student ID. Some providers are dashing forward and developing prototype apps, like the Lissi Consortium and other commercial enterprises, but most of these are, at this time, not certified and not fit for productive use. This is also evident from the large-scale pilot [11] we are involved in. A high acceptance of the system would only be possible with either an app from a public body or from an established commercial enterprise with high trust ratings. There are questions regarding students with no EU or EFTA citizenship. This problem is relatively unique to this case, as most digital services offered by the wallet are geared towards citizens. Higher education institutions might have up to 15–20% of students with non-EU citizenship, who will currently not be able to use the wallet. In Germany, the solution for this is being worked upon by the Federal Ministry of Interior, and will be available no earlier than 2027, but will require the student to integrate their electronic residence permit into the wallet to use the wallet for any other purpose. It is currently not clear who will be responsible for the certification of higher education institutions as a public body, so that certificates can be issued by the institution. This is also a major issue, as this determines the possibility for cross-border verification of the certificates and makes or breaks one of the main purposes of the wallet for higher education. All in all, there are several questions which have to be solved before the wallet can be integrated into the higher education landscape. In addition, a question is also how to motivate the users to use the wallet instead of the current systems and how to solve the multitude of issues to create a successful basis for EU-wide compatibility.

4   Conclusion

We have shown a way for the integration of the ESC and the future EU-Digital Wallet, and the technical challenges which emerge for large HEIs when dealing with these new technologies when trying to integrate these solutions into existing complex systems. We offer the best practice solution to these problems related to new services. As a next step, we have started to assess the possibility of channeling our highly advanced Berlin Campuscard App, the EDSSI L2 tech demo and the new European Digital Identity Wallet technology into a new project aiming to create a European eCard App. The goal is to create a fully functional and production-ready system, which can be adapted to the different requirements of different EU countries and also include the possibility to connect to any local NFC-based service. This would enable European HEIs to gather the technology for the app at a fraction of the costs involved in the development of a fully-fledged app, as the groundwork with all the high costs and time-consuming development and pitfalls was done either by the EDSSI L2 project or by the development of the Berlin Campuscard App. The app developed by the project consists of multiple layers. The common components are based on the Berlin Campuscard App, the EDSSI L2 components and the European Digital Identity Wallet technology. These include not only the backend and the frontend of the system, but also the NFC solutions and the possibility to export the student ID into either the national or any other wallet app, which is compliant with the appropriate EU standards. The national components include those required for national services in a member state. This can be a payment system or other nationwide services. Examples are the Izzly payment system in France and the VDV eTicket in Germany. The local components include those required for local services. An example is the German "Studentenwerk" payment system. The integration of the Digital Wallet makes it possible to overcome the technological barriers of smartphone-based solutions, which have until now made an EU-wide compatibility not feasible.

References

1. Leys, P., Mincer-Daszkiewicz, J.: Erasmus without paper: dream becoming reality. In: EPiCSeries in Computing (2022)
2. European Commission: European student card initiative (2025). https://erasmus-plus.ec.eur opa.eu/european-student-card-initiative/ewp.
3. Molnar, T.: The campuscard system: an innovative multifunctional smartcard solution for higher education institutions (2016)
4. VDV: e-Ticket Deutschland (2023). https://www.eticket-deutschland.de/motics
5. European Commission: Horizon 2020 – Work Programme 2018–2020 (2017)
6. de Castro Ribeiro, J.M.A.: SSI Technology in the Context of eIDAS 2.0, Porto: Universidade do Porto (2023)
7. Sedlmeir, J., Smethurst, R., Rieger, A., Fridgen, G.: Digital identities and verifiable credentials. In: Business & Information Systems Engineering, pp. 603–613 (2021)
8. Maliappis, M., Gerakos, K., Costopoulou, C., Ntaliani, M.: Authenticated academic services through eIDAS (2019)
9. Busch, C.: eIDAS 2.0: Digital identity services in the platform economy (2022)
10. Homburg, V., Lampoltshammer, T.J., Solvak, M.: From Electronic (2025)
11. DC4 EU Consortium: "DC4EU Consortium," (2025). https://www.dc4eu.eu/

Author Index

A. Kő et al. (Eds.): EGOVIS 2025, LNCS 16049, pp. 219–220, 2026.
https://doi.org/10.1007/978-3-032-02225-7

The manufacturer's authorised representative in the EU is Springer
Nature Customer Service Centre GmbH, Europaplatz 3, 69115 Heidelberg,
Germany. If you have any concerns regarding our products, please
contact ProductSafety@springernature.com

Printed and bound by CPI Group (UK) Ltd, Croydon, CR0 4YY
28/04/2026
02098521-0001